LONE WOLF

By the same author:

HOUSE OF PAIN

LONE WOLF

True Stories of Spree Killers

Pan Pantziarka

£110,918/

This edition first published in 2002 by
Virgin Books Ltd
Thames Wharf Studios
Rainville Road
London W6 9HA

First edition published 2000

ISBN 0 7535 0617 3

Design and typesetting by TW Typesetting, Plymouth, Devon

Printed and bound by Mackays of Chatham PLC

CONTENTS

ACKNOWLEDGEMENTS

I have used many sources for the research in this book: primary amongst them is the Internet. It would be true to say that without the Internet my research would have been more difficult and would have taken considerably longer.

Many of the events described in this book took place in relatively short periods of time. Inevitably, such traumatic experiences leave many victims and witnesses shaken and confused. In such circumstances, differing accounts of what happened are inevitable – it would be surprising if it were otherwise. For a researcher trying to piece together a number of disparate accounts and witness statements into cohesive narrative, these differing and occasionally contradictory stories have had to be resolved as best they could. In such a situation it is possible that the accounts of some of the events described in this book may differ from reports published elsewhere. This is to be expected, though I believe that for some events, such as the Hungerford massacre, Martin Bryant's Port Arthur slaughter and so on, no truly definitive account can ever be written.

Eyewitness quotes are from a variety of sources, including CNN, ABC News, the *Los Angeles Times*, the *Fort-Worth Star Telegram*, the *Chicago Times* and other similar sources.

I accept responsibility for any other errors or omissions.

I must also thank James Marriott, Irene Kappes, Despina Pantziarka, Barbara Panayi and Steven Kendrick for many interesting discussions and ideas. I would also like to thank David Brundle for making available the report into the Hungerford massacre, something that the Thames Valley Police singularly failed to do.

MICHAEL RYAN

Hungerford, England, 1987

On 19 August 1987 the early-afternoon peace and quiet of Savernake Forest, a few miles west of the quiet market town of Hungerford in Berkshire, was briefly shattered by a sudden burst of gunfire. The thirteen shots fired in the woods were to mark the start of one of the bloodiest chapters in the criminal history of the United Kingdom. Those shots were to shatter not just the dreamy quiet of a popular picnic spot but also, once and for all, the illusion that Britain was a safe haven from the gun madness that erupted so regularly in the United States.

The shots were fired by Michael Ryan, a 29-year-old resident of Hungerford and an avid gun enthusiast. A trip to the woods was something of a break for the unemployed loner: his usual destination of late had been a gun club that he had joined a few months previously. There he liked to do target practice. Not that he needed much practice: he was a good shot and he knew it. But shooting was something he enjoyed, so he took any and every opportunity to let off a few rounds – often more than a few. But for some unknown reason he had changed his routine that morning. Rather than heading for the Tunnel Rifle and Pistol Club in Devizes, he had gone to the forest instead.

Also in the forest that morning was Susan Godfrey, a 35-year-old mother who had brought her two small children out for a picnic lunch. Hannah and James, aged four and two respectively, had enjoyed their meal; the weather was good, and they knew that afterwards they were due to visit their grandmother, whose birthday it was. Their mother was just putting things away when a man who had been watching them from his car, parked nearby, came over to them. Dressed in black and holding a gun, the man ordered Ms Godfrey to put the children in her car.

Susan Godfrey complied with the order, managing to remain calm as she strapped the children into their seats, reassuring them that she would be back shortly. The children watched as the man grabbed hold of their mother – and the groundsheet they had been picnicking on – and marched her off, deeper into the woods. Moments later the children heard a volley of shots and then saw the man run back to his car and accelerate away sharply. The children sat quietly in the car and waited for their mother to return. They never saw her alive again.

The children dozed for a while, but eventually Hannah unstrapped herself and her younger brother. Then, holding hands, the children set off to search for their mother. They did not find her, nor could they find their way back to the car – they soon became lost. When they spotted a kindly looking old woman named Myra Rose, they told her what had happened. They described a man in black with a gun who had taken the car keys and their mother. Hannah described hearing the shots, but the child did not seem at all alarmed or in shock.

At first Myra Rose did not believe the children. The story was too fantastic, but clearly the children were lost and James, the younger child, would not let go of her hand. The only thing to do, she realised, was to find the children's mother, who was probably frantic with worry after losing her children.

A bit later, at around 2.00 p.m., a policeman, Sergeant Coppen, came across the abandoned car in the forest. The doors were open and a woman's handbag was lying on the front seat, along with a number of children's toys. He went in search of the driver and found her sprawled on her side, her blue print dress patterned with blood from a number of bullet wounds. She was dead, her body punctured by the thirteen shots the man in black had fired. Nearby, spread out on the long grass, was the picnic groundsheet.

The story the children had been telling was true, in every detail.

Having killed Susan Godfrey, the man in black, Michael Ryan, had driven at speed back towards his home town of Hungerford. On the way he turned off at the Golden Arrow Service Station on the A4. He was a regular customer there, though not an especially polite one as he never acknowledged the Asian staff or tried to engage in conversation. He filled the tank of his silver-grey Vauxhall Astra with petrol and then, rather than paying, he went to the back of the car to fiddle with something in the boot until the only other customer had driven off. When he was alone he stood up and pointed a semi-automatic rifle at Kakoub Dean, the wife of the owner of the petrol station.

The woman ducked as Ryan blasted at the pay kiosk. The shot punched a hole through the toughened safety glass but, amazingly, it missed her. Having missed once Ryan was not going to do so again. This time he walked into the shop and up to the counter. Kakoub was pleading for her life and trying to seek cover under the counter. Impervious to her sobbing Ryan calmly aimed the gun at her huddled body and pulled the trigger again. And again. And again.

It is difficult to imagine who was the more surprised, Ryan or Mrs Dean. The gun was out of ammunition. 'I know I am lucky to be alive,' she later recalled. 'He would have killed me. He didn't smile. He didn't blink. He didn't do anything. He just stared straight through me as if I wasn't there.'

Ryan turned, went back to his car and zoomed off towards Hungerford. It was about 12.40 p.m., and it would be another hour and twenty minutes before Sergeant Coppen would make the grisly discovery of Susan Godfrey's body. Five minutes after leaving the petrol station Ryan arrived home at 4 South View, Hungerford. The terraced council house just off Fairview Road, near to the High Street in the middle of the sleepy market town, was where he had spent most of his life and where he still lived with his widowed mother, Dorothy. According to a neighbour, Margery Jackson, Ryan looked 'as if he had been upset or angry' when he arrived home. He had good reason to be. He had just killed one person and had attempted to kill a second. He knew that it would not be long before the police were on to him: he needed to do something quickly if he was to get away.

Ryan's car already contained his 'survival kit'. As someone deeply interested in guns, war and survivalism, he knew exactly what to do. His kit included copious supplies of ammunition, a respirator, combat trousers, a balaclava, flak jacket, shoulder holster and a first-aid kit. He had been assiduously collecting army-surplus material for years, building up a stash of NATO cast-offs ready for an emergency. And the day had finally arrived when all his preparations were going to be put to the test.

With his kit Ryan had three firearms: the Beretta 9mm semi-automatic pistol that he'd used in the forest, an M1 carbine semi-automatic assault rifle and, last but by no means least, a Kalashnikov AK47, ready for the getaway that he needed to make. In fact, the Kalashnikov was loaded with armour-piercing bullets, military issue and imported from Hungary. But first Ryan needed to destroy as much evidence about himself as possible, and the quickest way to do that was to torch the house. He showed no hesitation in setting fire to the home in which he'd lived almost his entire life, dousing it with petrol before igniting the subsequent conflagration.

As the house started to go up, Ryan jumped into the car to make his escape only to find that the vehicle refused to start. The battered Astra had been severely neglected in the previous few months and now, just when he needed it most, the engine refused to turn over. Despite the testimony of many neighbours that, after his guns, his car was his pride and joy, Ryan now climbed out and raked it with gunfire. Without a means of escape he was sunk and he knew it. He had acquaintances in the police force and they had helped him out of minor scrapes before, but this time he knew that there'd be no way out for him.

He'd shot up his beloved car out of anger and frustration and these were probably still his major emotions when he turned the gun on his neighbours. With reckless abandon he took aim at Roland Mason who was working in his garden at 6 South View. Mr Mason didn't stand a chance as he was hit six times. His wife Sheila, who had been watching from the back door, was hit once and killed instantly by a massive head wound.

Margery Jackson, who had watched Ryan come home a few minutes earlier, witnessed the murders of her neighbours. She ducked down as she realised that she was probably next and telephoned her husband to warn him of what was happening. As she spoke, however, she saw that Ryan had spotted her. A hail of bullets smashed through the windows and door of the house, hitting her. 'I realised I'd been shot,' she later explained. 'There was a sort of burning pain in the back. In fact, quite a few bullets came into my home. He was jogging up and down, running up and down the lane outside. He must have run up and down the lane about ten times. I think he was determined to slaughter us up there. It was all very quick-fire.'

An elderly neighbour, Dorothy Smith, not realising what was happening, went outside to berate the person making all the noise. 'I said: "Is that you making that noise? You are frightening everybody to death. Stop it." He just turned his head to the right and looked at me. He had a terrible vacant look in his eyes and a funny sort of grin on his face. He looked to me as if he was brain-dead. I realised I was talking to Michael Ryan. I had, after all, known him for twenty years. But he looked so strange that day, I hardly recognised him. So I just yelled out to him that he was a stupid bugger.'

As Margery Jackson, injured but still walking, hustled Dorothy Smith inside, Ryan took off. He headed up a footpath that led to Hungerford Common. On the way he took aim at another couple of innocent victims. One was fourteen-year-old Lisa Mildenhall. She gives a vivid description of her wounding by the deranged gunman. 'I saw this man jogging along the road. He was carrying a great big rifle under his arm as if he was going to fire it. I stopped at the front door and the man stopped jogging as well. I immediately recognised him as Michael Ryan. I fixed my eyes at his eyes and he smiled at me. He then crouched down and aimed the rifle at me. I just froze by the front door. He fired the gun and I can't actually recall being hit. I thought he was playing about and that it wasn't a real gun, and that the blood was a capsule. I remember thinking, What a mess, and turned and ran inside. As I was running I could still hear shots being fired. I said: "Mummy, mummy, have I been shot?" She looked really shocked and then I realised I had been. There was a lot of blood. I felt weak and fell to the floor.'

As Ryan continued up the path he came face to face with another local resident, Ken Clements, accompanied by members of his family. Clements had apparently been warned that someone had 'gone berserk' with a gun and he was hurrying ahead of his family to investigate. Ryan simply raised his rifle, took aim and fired, hitting the old man and causing the rest of his family to take cover. Clements died shortly afterwards, the fourth murder victim of the day.

By this time a police helicopter had been called out and was circling overhead. Roadblocks had been set up along the routes that led to the High Street but few people had much idea of what was going on, other than knowing that a gunman was on the loose. The emergency services were overwhelmed with calls and the system was falling apart at the seams. Many of the policemen knew no more than that the gunman was suspected of having attempted an armed robbery at a petrol station. Susan Godfrey's body had yet to be discovered and linked to the other crimes. And, all the time, the house at 4 South View was billowing black smoke into the clear sky as the flames tore through it.

The chaos was such that one policeman, PC Roger Brereton, actually drove towards South View. He had been warned that the suspect was armed and dangerous and that he should proceed with caution but that was all. Ryan had returned to South View by this time and was firing at anything that moved, including his own dog. As Roger Brereton's car pulled into view it came under a hail of gunfire, with Ryan using both the Kalashnikov and the semi-automatic pistol. In all over twenty shots hit the police car and four of them hit the man inside. Barely conscious, Brereton made one last call to HQ: 'Ten-nine, ten-nine, ten-nine. I've been shot.'

PC Brereton died shortly afterwards. Ryan had not even bothered to walk over to check whether his victim was alive or dead. He didn't care. Not about anything. Nothing mattered any more.

Moving on down South View, Ryan saw another car driving towards him. Again he took aim and fired. This time he merely managed to injure his victims, a mother and daughter. Both described the half-smile, as though he were enjoying himself, on the gunman's face.

The next victim to die was 84-year-old Abdul Rahman Khan, shot twice with the Kalashnikov AK47 as he stood in his garden at the corner of South View and Fairview Road.

Ryan's next-door neighbour, Alan Lepetit, was shot next. He had heard that there was a gunman loose and, concerned about the safety of his wife and children, was walking home hurriedly when he was spotted by Ryan. The two men were well acquainted: Lepetit had even helped Ryan build a cabinet for his guns, not that it did him any good. Ryan shot him once, twice, hitting him in the arm and then, as the other man turned to escape, shot him once more in the back. Amazingly, Lepetit survived the attack.

The attack on Lepetit was witnessed by the crew of an ambulance that was reversing cautiously into South View. Ryan was not going to respect their mission of mercy. He fired several bursts at the ambulance, which changed direction and accelerated away after being hit repeatedly. Such was the chaos that the message that South View was a no-go area still not been properly understood. The experience of the ambulance crew was passed on to the fire service, though, and for the next four hours fire crews were held back while the fire at 4 South View spread to the neighbouring houses.

Neither had the message got through to the public. Despite the hundreds of police flooding into Hungerford, many roads were not sealed off and people were still able to get into the danger zone. One of these was Ivor Jackson, Margery Jackson's husband who had been warned by telephone earlier. A colleague, George White, had offered to drive Jackson home to his wife. As their car turned the corner into South View they saw the police car ahead of them. As Ivor Jackson later recalled: 'I saw that this police car ahead of us had hit a telegraph pole. The policeman was slumped inside. Suddenly our car was raked with machine-gun fire, with these bullets starting to come at us. I got three in the chest and I've still got one left in my head, which apparently went in through my ear. I realised that I had been shot and so I decided to play dead. But I still thought that I was going to die. Then, with Mr White no longer in control of his Toyota, we crashed into the police car ourselves.'

George White had been killed instantly as eleven bullets had hit his car.

While Ivor Jackson played dead another car drove into the war zone. Pulling up behind the Toyota, Dorothy Ryan,

Michael's mother, emerged from her car into a scene for which nothing in her worst nightmares could have prepared her. There were flames licking around the houses in her street, including her own home of twenty-seven years. The streets were littered with broken glass and splattered with blood. Dead bodies lay in crashed cars all around her. It looked as though sleepy Hungerford had been dropped into the middle of Beirut during the worst ravages of the Lebanese civil war.

Dorothy Ryan hurried down the road, clearly shocked. A man tried to stop her going any further but she insisted and pushed by him. She was Michael's sole surviving parent and, she felt, it was her responsibility to talk to her son and persuade him to stop the madness. Witnesses heard her cry, 'Stop, Michael. Why are you doing this?' as she rushed towards her burning house.

Suddenly Dorothy stopped. Her tone of voice changed. She was heard to plead 'Don't shoot me!' Two blasts of the gun followed and then silence. She fell and Ryan walked up to her. As she lay on her front he aimed the Kalashnikov and fired twice more, shooting her in the back at point-blank range. Her body lay just in front of George White's car, where Ivor Jackson, still playing dead, had heard the entire scene. For Ryan his mother was just another target to destroy, another body to add to the toll.

The police helicopter, circling overheard, was issuing warnings over its loudspeakers for people to remain in their houses. The cordon around the area was growing tighter, but people were still able to get through, and some were still trapped inside their own homes with little idea of what was happening.

Ron Tary, the mayor of Hungerford at that time, expressed a common feeling when he said: 'I still didn't know what to believe. I kept saying to myself that this can't be true. Chicago, yes. Liverpool or the East End of London, perhaps. But Hungerford? Surely not. Many people felt awful for a very long time that afternoon because they just were not able to find out what was going on. All the time we were trying to get information.'

By this time the police were preparing an armed response to the incident. It was a long time in coming, and the delay was to prove a source of bad feeling between the authorities and the ordinary population for a long time to come. The first armed officers had arrived in Hungerford a little after 1.00 p.m., but they seemed strangely reluctant to move forward to South View to confront the more heavily armed and dangerous individual causing the violence. These armed officers, members of the Diplomatic Protection Squad, trained to protect foreign diplomats, politicians and other VIPs, assembled on Hungerford Common as a team, but as they did so Ryan moved away from South View in the opposite direction.

Rather than head back to the common along the footpath he had used earlier, he made his way across the playing field that adjoined the school at the back of South View. He was still firing as he went, though amazingly his escape from South View was not witnessed by anybody and the police were to lose contact with him from then on. Unfortunately for 70-year-old Betty Tolladay, she did make contact with Ryan.

'I heard this banging. I thought it was children with fireworks or something,' she later recalled. 'A bit early, I know, but they do find all manner of things that make noises. So I went into the garden and said, "For God's sake, stop that noise – it's getting me down." '

Ryan's response was swift enough. He fired at the elderly woman, hitting her in the groin. The bullet smashed the top of her hip and part of her pelvis before exiting through her back. Ms Tolladay's description continues: 'I immediately fell to the ground. One leg was absolutely useless. But I sat up and dragged myself to my back door, got over the step somehow, don't ask me how, and along to the hall, and got the telephone off the table and dialled 999. I've only two words to describe what happened: "pure agony".'

When Betty Tolladay finally got through to the ambulance service – the phone system was creaking under the strain of the tens of thousands of calls flooding through it – she was promised help as soon as possible. That help did arrive, eventually – five hours later. The 70-year-old had managed to survive, despite the excruciating agony of her wounds.

From Betty Tolladay's house Ryan continued on his way, across the playing field towards the Memorial Gardens. There Francis Butler was out walking his dog. It was to be his last walk. As soon as Ryan spotted him he took aim and fired the Kalashnikov, with deadly results. The three armour-piercing bullets created gaping wounds in the young man's body. Leslie Bean, who worked in the area, reached the body soon afterwards. Butler was barely conscious and was losing blood rapidly. Bean tried to staunch the flow, knowing it was the only thing that might possibly save the injured man. However, as he struggled to stop the blood somebody shouted a warning that the gunman was on his way back. Reluctantly Bean made a run for it, knowing that if he had stayed there he too would have become a victim of the black-clad maniac with the guns. With him went Francis Butler's only hope. He was dead by the time help got to him a second time.

Ryan took more shots at people nearby, including two schoolboys who had witnessed his gunning down of Francis Butler. None of these shots hit their targets. At this point Ryan decided to abandon one of his weapons, leaving the M1 carbine close to his ninth murder victim. He was still armed with the Kalashnikov AK47 and the Beretta 9mm semi-automatic pistol, so he was by no means travelling light without the carbine.

The next victim to fall was Marcus Barnard, a taxi driver in the town who had only been a father for just five weeks. As he slowed near the Memorial Gardens, perhaps because of the burst of gunfire he had just heard, he saw Ryan emerging. A second later a shot rang out and Barnard was dead, a single round from the AK47 taking most of his head off.

At this point perhaps the full enormity of what Ryan was doing had started to sink in, for he was seen throwing his gun to the ground in disgust. A witness who had seen Barnard's execution described how: 'The man [Ryan] threw the gun to the floor in front of him as if in disgust. He looked down at the gun and shook his head from time to time. He looked bewildered, as if he could not believe what he had done. He moved away and then turned round. He still had a pistol. I stopped walking and he looked straight at me. I thought, he only has to take aim and that's me. As I walked away, he went to pick up the rifle.'

Ryan's moment of doubt proved to be short-lived. A few minutes later he shot and injured a woman driving along Priory Road, a short walk from the Memorial Gardens. Clearly the police operation to contain the violence was not working, as Ryan was moving around the town at will. The Tactical Firearms Unit, the specialist police squad trained to deal with such incidents, were still assembling and preparing to go into action. The police helicopter had lost sight of him. Hungerford was his, and he knew it.

John Storms, a washing-machine repair technician, was lost. Unable to find the address he was looking for, he had stopped in his van to peruse a map. He was a sitting target for Ryan, who crouched down to take careful aim. Storms assumed at first that the man with the gun and the commando gear was joking. As he told the press much later: 'I thought, that's a nice-looking gun. The man then dropped into a crouching position with both legs bent at the knee. He pointed the pistol at me with both hands holding it and at first I thought it was somebody messing about. Then there was a bang, there was broken glass, there was pain and then there was blood.'

Storms was hit and badly injured. He slumped down in his seat, but Ryan did not seem satisfied yet. As with a number of his other victims, including his mother, he had shot first to injure and immobilise so that he could then follow up with shots intended to kill. While Storms lay injured two more shots were fired. And then, in an act of pure heroism, Bob Barclay, a local man who had witnessed the shooting, ran out of his house, opened the van door and dragged the bleeding man from the driver's seat while Ryan, still armed, watched. Barclay dragged Storms into his garden, called an ambulance and tried to staunch the flow of blood. Storms had sustained serious injuries to his face and neck, and a bullet had missed his spinal cord by only a few millimetres. It is likely that if Bob Barclay hadn't risked his life Storms would have become another of Ryan's fatalities that day.

Ryan's next victims were Kathleen and Douglas Wainwright, who had driven all the way to Hungerford from

Strood in Kent. They were there to visit their son, a local policeman. They had almost reached their destination when they came face to face with Ryan, who had just been firing at John Storms. As Mrs Wainwright explained in her statement at the inquest: 'Automatically my husband put his foot on the brake. As we stopped there was this man right opposite my husband's window on the pavement. I heard about six or eight shots, one after the other, bang, bang, bang. The gun was pointed at my husband's window. I heard him groan twice, I looked at him and I knew he was dead. Blood trickled down his nose and out of his mouth and he fell to one side. I knew he was dead. I also knew that I had been hit. I only felt a sting on the breast and my finger and hand, though. This chap walked to the front of our car and started reloading his gun. I thought, "Oh my God, he's going to fire at me again" – but as he was loading he was walking forwards. You might say that self-preservation took over. I took off my seat belt and opened the passenger door as quietly as I could and ran.'

It later emerged that their son, PC Trevor Wainwright, was one of the policemen who had vetted Ryan's application to have his gun licence modified so that he could purchase more powerful firearms. 'It's bloody ironic,' he admitted. 'I would hate to think that I okayed a change in the licence for the gun that killed my father. But I really don't feel it's down to me because I didn't grant the licence – I merely did the checks. In fact, those checks were very thorough. I knew for a fact that Ryan hadn't been in any serious trouble with the police. I also knew that he was something of a loner, but you can't hold that against anyone.'

Meanwhile, there could be no better illustration of the hopeless confusion that was the police response to the massacre than the case of Eric Vardy. A carpenter, by trade, Vardy and another local man, Steven Ball, were on their way to a builder's merchant in a white Sherpa van, with Vardy at the wheel. They were aware that something was going on but like most people they had no real idea of what was involved. Driving up Tarrants Hill, which adjoins Fairview Road, they had seen a police car and a large crowd. There were no signs up, no police officers warning passing traffic of the danger.

Vardy and Ball assumed that there had been a fight or some other trivial incident and simply looked for an alternative route to take them to their destination.

As it rounded a corner the van suddenly came under fire. The windscreen shattered, Vardy's body was jolted and then the vehicle careened out of control until it smashed against a telegraph pole. Vardy had been hit twice, once in the face and once in the side. He was to die from the massive loss of blood that his injuries caused. His death was to be a source of long-lasting bitterness as many, including his wife and Steven Ball, blamed the police for not properly securing the area. Marlyne Vardy was widely quoted at the time: 'In my own heart,' she said, 'I blame the police for having let his vehicle go through and not attempting to stop the traffic, or to warn them that there was a gunman on the loose.'

Certainly, the police operation was taking time to coalesce. The Tactical Firearms Unit was finally kitted out, a command-and-control centre was becoming operational, lines of communication had been established, but on the ground it was still chaos. At times it seemed that the press and the media were ahead of the police.

Nothing like the Hungerford Massacre had ever happened in the UK before. Spree killing was something that happened in the United States or other countries where access to guns was free and easy. In Britain, which had some of the toughest gun-control laws in the Western world, the possibility that a heavily armed killer could go on a rampage and take a dozen or more lives seemed utterly remote and alien. Once news of Ryan's killing spree emerged the country's press and television descended on Hungerford *en masse*.

Sandra Hill was Ryan's next victim. She was another driver caught in the wrong place at the wrong time. She was killed by a single bullet wound to the chest. The twenty-year-old woman was Ryan's thirteenth victim.

The next two victims were gunned down in their own home. Having killed Sandra Hill, Ryan crossed the road and shot his way into the home of Victor and Myrtle Gibbs. The elderly couple stared in horror as the maniac with the guns blasted their front door and then strode towards them in the kitchen. Myrtle Gibbs, arthritic and wheelchair-bound, screamed as her husband threw himself across her. Ryan used the Beretta pistol to pump Victor Gibbs's body full of bullets before killing the sobbing, crippled old woman.

Ryan remained inside the Gibbs's house for a while, taking shots from it and injuring a number of people in the neighbouring houses, none of them fatally. He also took aim at a Ford Sierra containing a couple and their two small children. Ian Playle, Clerk to the Justices at Newbury Magistrates Court, was taking his family on a shopping trip to the market at Hungerford. They had been stopped at a police roadblock but, without being informed of the reason for the stoppage, they had decided to seek a back route into the centre of the town.

It was to be a fatal mistake, another for which the police were publicly blamed. Seconds after entering Priory Road the car came under fire. Before Elizabeth Playle had registered what was happening the car had crashed and her husband had slumped forward. Blood was pouring from her husband's neck and despite her best efforts to save him – she was a trained nurse – he died before an ambulance could get to him. As with Eric Vardy's widow, Elizabeth Playle castigated the police for their failures during that fateful afternoon.

Ryan decided at that point that it was no longer safe to remain in the Gibbs's house. He took off again, this time heading down Priory Road towards the John O'Gaunt comprehensive school. Along the way he shot and injured George Noon as he stood in the garden of one of the houses in Priory Road. He was hit in the eye and in the shoulder. A short while later the first police arrived on the scene. They grabbed Mr Noon's son and tried to handcuff him, convinced that he was the spree killer and not simply the injured man's son.

The police were now looking for Ryan and many calls flooded in reporting sightings of him. Many of these reports were false – people were understandably jumpy – but the calls still had to be checked out and eliminated. There were also shots still coming from South View, though it later turned out that these were caused by some of Ryan's ammunition exploding in the fire that consumed his home.

One team of policemen was assigned the front of the school, another the back. They proceeded with caution, aware that the killer was ranging through the area with firearms more powerful than police-issue Smith & Wesson .38 revolvers or pump-action shotguns. Eventually the teams were in place, though at that time they did not even know if Ryan had taken shelter in the school or not. Their task was simply containment. If he was in the building they were not to let him escape. If he was not there they were to stop him gaining access.

It would be another couple of hours before Ryan was spotted at a third-floor window, at which point the police declared that it was safe for ambulance and fire crews to arrive at the scene to attend the injured. Altogether Ryan had killed fifteen people, with Ian Playle the last of the fatalities. The rampage, from the moment Ryan had set fire to his house and turned the guns on his neighbours to the death of Ian Playle, had lasted no more than fifteen minutes.

Once Ryan had been spotted the police were able to begin the first stages of negotiation with him. These negotiations were carried out by Sergeant Paul Brightwell, who had headed the team around the school. By this stage Ryan had abandoned his beloved Kalashnikov AK47, throwing it out of the window.

Brightwell called up to Ryan and soon established that he was armed with the 9mm semi-automatic pistol and an Israeli fragmentation hand grenade. Ryan's concern seemed to be, belatedly, for his mother. The policeman refused to confirm that she was dead, though Ryan had little doubt that he had indeed murdered her. He also expressed concern for his dog, which, he claimed, he had shot with his eyes shut.

When Sergeant Brightwell stalled on supplying information about Ryan's mother, Ryan grew increasingly irate. He refused to give himself up until he knew for certain what had become of her. There is little doubt that he knew he had killed her, but he still wanted it confirmed. This was something that Brightwell steadfastly refused to do. Instead, he focused on getting Ryan to disarm and to surrender. Several times police marksmen had Ryan clearly within their sights, but they exercised a mercy that he had not.

'What are the casualty figures?' Ryan asked. Brightwell was probably being truthful when he replied that he did not know. At which point Ryan remarked: 'It's like a bad dream.' He then threw out the magazine of the 9mm pistol, informing the police that he had retained one last round. When asked what it was for, he simply replied: 'It's obvious, isn't it?'

At 6.24 p.m., after asking about his mother once more, Ryan got as close as he would to expressing something akin to regret. 'If only my car had started,' he told Sergeant Brightwell. He claimed that he hadn't meant to kill his mother, and then made the oft-quoted statement: 'I wish I had stayed in bed.'

There were many who would make that same wish, of course. Although Ryan clearly regretted getting up that morning, there was no expression of sorrow, remorse or pity for his numerous victims. His tone was one of self-pity and nothing more. The last few exchanges are worth quoting verbatim:

Ryan: Will I be treated OK?
Brightwell: Of course you will, Mr Ryan.
Ryan: Will I go to prison for a long time?
Brightwell: I don't know, Mr Ryan. It is not up to me.
Ryan: You must have an idea. I will get life, won't I?
Brightwell: I don't know, Mr Ryan. You will go to prison for a long time.
Ryan: It's funny. I killed all those people but I haven't got the guts to blow my own brains out.
Brightwell: Mr Ryan, just leave all your weapons in the room and do exactly as you are told. Don't do anything silly. Do you understand?
Ryan: What time is it?
Brightwell: Six-forty-five. What do you want to know the time for?
Ryan: I want to think about it. I am not coming out until I know about my mother.
Brightwell: Mr Ryan, I am still trying to find out. If you come down we will be able to find out together.

There followed a few minutes of silence and then the policemen heard a muffled shot from the classroom where Ryan had been holed up. The police could take no chances: Ryan might have finally found the courage to kill himself but, on the other hand, maybe he had fired at something in the room in frustration. He was, after all, still armed with a grenade, assuming that he had been telling Sergeant Brightwell the truth about the weapons he had retained.

A police dog was sent in first, and when there was no reaction from it the police assumed that Ryan had indeed killed himself. Explosives experts were sent in next, to ensure that Ryan hadn't booby-trapped himself. He hadn't. The single shot had been to his head. He was the sixteenth fatality that day.

With his death Michael Ryan took with him any hope of understanding what it was that had caused him to kill and maim so many. Clearly he had intended to rape Susan Godfrey in Savernake Forest. He was unmarried and had not been involved in any sexual relationship for a number of years. Had he gone out that day with the intention of finding a woman to rape? He was armed to the teeth, but that was nothing unusual: he took his guns with him everywhere. A more likely explanation is that Susan Godfrey had been in the wrong place at the wrong time. Sensing the opportunity, Ryan had gone for rape. It is not unreasonable to suggest that after years of sexual frustration he was desperate, and that the attempted rape was an act of desperation rather than an act of premeditation. However, it had all gone badly wrong. When Susan Godfrey had tried to escape his attentions he had snapped. The gun that was there to frighten her was suddenly turned into a murder weapon.

What followed was not inevitable. Having killed the mother of two small children Ryan could have come to his senses and given himself up. He was guilty of an horrific act, and with no mitigating circumstances he would have faced a life sentence and public vilification. But having killed once, he then attempted to kill again at the petrol station. Why? What drove him to compound one crime with another?

It is hard to believe that Ryan really thought that he could get away with his crimes. Yet clearly he returned home with the intention of making a quick escape. Dressed in army fatigues, heavily armed and totally psyched up, he imagined that his weapons skills and his knowledge of commando tactics would somehow allow him to evade capture. In the cold light of day the very idea of such an escape is ludicrous. Britain does not have the wide-open spaces of the United States or even of continental Europe. There is no wilderness to escape to, no jungle to hide in, no mountain retreat to disappear to. But Ryan was no longer thinking straight. Somehow, fact and fantasy had collided.

Once Ryan had started shooting in earnest, again because he was unable to cope with frustration, this time when his car failed to start, there seemed to be no way to stop. There was obviously something lacking in his character. We all develop coping mechanisms for those occasions when our plans go awry: it is a necessary skill that we develop first as children and adolescents and then as adults. In Ryan's case there seemed to be nothing in his psychological armoury but impotent rage and violence. An only child, there was evidence that he had always got 'his own way'. According to family friends and relatives, he was a spoilt child, and one who lashed out at his mother frequently.

At school he had been a small, lonely child, often bullied and always without friends. Scholastically he did badly, leaving school with few qualifications. Predictably, he drifted from one unskilled dead-end job to another. Not that he ever wanted for things financially. His hard-working, indulgent parents ensured that he had the money to buy the weapons he coveted and the cars that he neglected.

But not all spoilt children go on to become mass murderers. Not all bullied children become spree killers. In the days and weeks that followed the Hungerford Massacre there was a good deal of speculation in the press. Ryan's life was examined in intimate detail as people sought clues to understand the inexplicable. For a British public unused to American-style spree killings, the massacre was a rude awakening. Many people could not understand how a man like Ryan could gain access to an AK47 or an M1 carbine. What possible reason could a person have to possess guns such as those? In the wake of the massacre British gun-control laws were tightened still further, and certain types of weapon – such as those that Ryan had used – were outlawed completely.

The picture of Ryan that emerged was of a lonely, isolated man with a dreary home life, living in a fantasy world that revolved around guns and ammunition. An avid reader of survivalist literature and a viewer of Rambo-style adventure videos, Ryan was not the kind of character to inspire probing psychological analysis. Isolated in life, he became even more isolated in death. Having himself shown no mercy, no compassion, it was only to be expected that he would elicit little sympathy or understanding from a public appalled by his crimes. *L110, 9181*

A depressed loner who had become increasingly isolated following the death of his father, it seemed, with hindsight, that an explosion of violence was bound to happen. The ferocity of the explosion when it happened was unprecedented in the United Kingdom, and there were few people who would have imagined it possible. Many hoped then that he was a one-off, a freak of nature or a monster, and as such that others like him would not follow.

Sadly, that has been shown not to be the case.

And, time and again, after the blood is cleaned away and the body count totted up by a press eager to feast on the gory details of pain, suffering and death, the questions outweigh the answers by far. Is there a spree-killer profile? Can we predict and contain the violence? What can we do to reduce the incidence of mass murder?

In many respects there is a good deal more understanding of the motivations and behaviour of serial killers than of spree killers. In part this is simply because most serial killers are eventually apprehended and imprisoned. During the subsequent court cases and after sentencing, extensive psychiatric assessments become possible. In a sense, the fact that 'live' serial killers are available for examination means that they can be studied and much can be learned from their individual life histories. Also, the *modus operandi* of serial killers, many of whom kill in a ritualised, totemic manner, means that by unravelling their rituals and exposing them to scrutiny, we can glean an understanding of their warped psyches at work. It is also a fact that most serial killers are driven by strong psychosexual urges: they kill for sexual gratification. No matter how warped and inhuman the crimes, we all understand the strength of sexual desire. This central pivot of the serial-killing impulse makes some form of identification possible between the serial killer and members of the general public.

For all these reasons it is no surprise that serial killers have become familiar characters in films, music and literature. Serial killers are evil incarnate, secular demons who embody the darkness that lies hidden in the human psyche. They are outside everyday experience, yet clearly linked to it. Like supernatural demons of old, they exist to frighten us, and by doing so they serve to remind us of the limits from which we cannot stray. We are frightened by them and thus our own 'normality' is confirmed.

Spree killers, on the other hand, generally do not survive the killing spree. Michael Ryan was typical of this type of mass murderer. Spree killers tend to kill themselves or to be killed by the police; very few are arrested or incarcerated. With few 'live' subjects, any studies of spree killers can only be based on retrospective data. Trying to piece together a person's mental state from second-hand life histories does not make for good psychiatric or psychological source data. That does not mean, however, that we cannot learn from examining such life histories. There is a difference between investigating to make informed social observations and analysing to create scientific hypotheses. The fact that few academic studies have looked at spree killers as a group does not mean that we should regard the issue as uninteresting. From a sociological point of view, there is much that we can learn about the subject: it is, in fact, extremely instructive to examine in detail a number of case histories so that common elements can be discerned. Are there personality traits that are shared by many spree killers? Do they come from similar backgrounds? What triggers the explosions of violence? Can we learn from previous cases?

Without the central psychosexual motivation of the serial killer, we have to ask what is it that drives a man – and it is never a woman – to kill and maim on such an enormous scale in such a compressed time-frame? Where a serial killer may rack up half a dozen victims before capture, the victims are likely to have been murdered over a two- or three-year period, if not longer. A spree killer like Michael Ryan may kill the same number of victims, but the violence will take place in a matter of minutes.

If sexual desire is the axis of identification between the motivation of serial killers and the 'ordinary' public, it is rage that may serve as the means to link ourselves to the violence of spree killers. We have all suffered extreme anger and rage, we have all reached breaking point, but few of us snap in such a spectacular fashion. In the same way, we have all felt desire but few are driven to rape and murder because of it.

This book looks at a number of cases of spree killing, examining both the personal histories of the killers and the acts of violence that these men commit. At times the violence is harrowing, and one cannot fail to be moved by the suffering of the victims and their families. However, the aim is to understand, not to demonise, and as such the life stories of the killers are presented in the hope that common elements can be drawn out. Only by doing so can we take the first steps to a fuller understanding of the spree killer, both as victim and as executioner.

THOMAS HAMILTON

Dunblane, Scotland, 1996

On 13 March 1996, Dunblane was to join Hungerford in Britain's national consciousness as a place forever associated with violence and death. The small town, with a population of around seven thousand, is about seven miles north of Stirling, in the Central Region of Scotland. It is an area steeped in history that has sometimes been violent and turbulent, but never as horrifying as what was about to happen.

The morning started normally enough. It was a clear, crisp day, with frost on the ground and ice on cars and windows. The pupils of Dunblane Primary School, one of the largest in Scotland with around 650 pupils aged from five to eleven, started school at 9.00 a.m. Registration, which usually took around ten minutes, was followed by assembly, though with so many pupils the school assembly hall, which could not accommodate them all, was used in rotation by different groups of classes. On this Wednesday it was the turn of years one, two and three to finish registration at 9.10 and then to file through the school in class groups to the hall. As always, the classes were accompanied by their teachers, keeping the noisier children in line as they excitedly marched into the hall. Years one, two and three, 250 children in all, were the youngest in the school and their excited chatter would take a minute or two to dampen down so that the assembly could commence.

Class thirteen of the year one cohort, 25 five-year-olds and three six-year-olds, had already changed into their PE kits during registration so that they could go directly to the school gym once assembly had finished. Kitted out in shorts and plimsolls, the children would sit impatiently through prayers, led by the school chaplain, waiting for the chance to let off steam in the gym.

As the assembly was coming to a close a white van entered the lower car park of the school. The innocuous-looking driver, Thomas Hamilton, a bespectacled middle-aged man, parked the vehicle next to the telegraph pole by the fence. He emerged a second later and calmly used a pair of pliers that he'd brought with him to cut the telephone lines. It was highly unlikely that he knew he was cutting off the lines to the surrounding houses rather than the school. Having cut the wires, he possibly felt more confident about what he was doing – in any case, he remained cautious as he unloaded his equipment from the van. He crossed the car park and, skirting the main entrance, he entered the school through a door on the north-west side of the school, next to the toilets beside the school gym.

By this time the assembly had finished and the pupils had returned to their classrooms, except for class thirteen who had gone directly to the gym. They had only just passed the door through which the harmless-looking man had entered a moment earlier. The 28 children were accompanied by their teacher, Mrs Gwen Mayor, PE Teacher Mrs Eileen Harrild and teaching assistant Mrs Mary Blake. The children were told to wait in the centre of the gym, away from the equipment, while the adults discussed the arrangements so that Mrs Mayor could leave to attend a meeting elsewhere in the school. This delay probably cost Mrs Mayor her life.

Thomas Hamilton, wearing a dark jacket, black cord trousers and a woolly hat, carefully donned a pair of ear defenders, unpacked his weapons, took a deep breath and then moved into action. He kicked open the door of the girls' toilets and fired a shot into it before moving quickly to the assembly hall where he fired a further two shots. It is possible that he paused at this point. He had been expecting to find the assembly hall filled with children: it was intended to be the central scene of the slaughter he meant to unleash on the innocent children of Dunblane. Instead of a hall teeming with children and adults he found a cavernous, empty room where the noise of his shots echoed uselessly around him. Whatever doubts passed through his mind at this point, he knew there was no turning back. The gym was just a few steps from the assembly hall and it was to be his next port of call.

The teachers in the gym were startled by the shots and they turned to the door as Thomas Hamilton came in, an automatic pistol in his hand. He advanced a few steps and then started firing rapidly, indiscriminately. Mrs Harrild was hit four times, on both forearms, the right hand and the left breast. Amazingly, she did not die. She managed to stumble to the stores area of the gym, followed by some of the children. Her colleague, Mrs Mayor, was not so fortunate: she was killed instantly, shot several times in a volley of automatic gunfire. Mrs Blake tried to usher more of the children into the stores area but she was hit, though she too managed to get away from Hamilton.

One child lay dead and many others were seriously injured. Hamilton had so far discharged a total of 29 shots in rapid succession. Four injured children had also made it into the stores along with the two injured teachers. The teachers tried to calm the children as they listened to the screams and cries of their wounded friends. They lay helplessly on the floor, in pools of blood, terrified beyond measure as they waited for the inevitable. From the gym they could hear more shots and more anguished shrieks from their friends.

Hamilton made his way along the east side of the gym, firing another six shots. He stopped halfway, turned and fired another eight shots before walking to the centre of the gym. He then moved through the room methodically, in a semicircle, firing another sixteen shots. Point-blank. One after the other. Killing the children already injured or those cowering and weeping on the floor. He did not pause. He did not turn away.

A child from another class passed the gym and, hearing the shots and the screaming children, looked into the room. He saw Hamilton standing over the children, methodically finishing them off. Hamilton turned and fired at the horror-stricken boy. He missed but the child was hit by splintering glass as he ran off. Shaken by this intrusion, Hamilton moved to the south of the gym and started firing through the window in all directions. He opened the fire-escape door and let off another volley of shots, possibly aiming at an adult passing through the playground. Stepping outside, he fired more shots, this time towards the school library. A bullet struck a member of staff, Mrs Grace Tweddle, dealing a glancing blow to her head.

Class seven, housed in a classroom in a hut near the fire escape, were the next targets of Hamilton's rage. Alarmed by the shooting, and by the sight of Thomas Hamilton firing wildly from the fire escape, the teacher, Mrs Catherine Gordon, screamed at the children to duck down. The frightened youngsters hit the floor just as Hamilton raked the classroom with gunfire. Nine shots entered the room, the bullets embedding themselves in books and other class equipment, one shot striking a chair that was still warm from the child who'd been sitting there a moment earlier. Astonishingly, nobody in the class was hit.

Hamilton turned back and re-entered the gym. He still had hundreds of rounds of ammunition with him but, surrounded by the bleeding bodies of the dead and injured children and their teachers, he walked to the centre of the room. He dropped the automatic pistol and took out a revolver. He placed the muzzle in his mouth, pointed it upwards and took his own life.

From start to finish Hamilton's murderous rampage had lasted no more than five minutes. In that time he'd taken the lives of fifteen children – Victoria Elizabeth Clydesdale, Emma Elizabeth Crozier, Melissa Helen Currie, Charlotte Louise Dunn, Kevin Allan Hasell, Ross William Irvine, David Charles Kerr, Brett McKinnon, Abigail Joanne McLennan, Emily Morton, Sophie Jane Lockwood North, John Petrie, Joanna Caroline Ross, Hannah Louise Scott, Megan Turner – and one adult – Gwen Mayor – before ending it all. A sixteenth child – Mhairi Isabel MacBeath – died later at Stirling Royal Infirmary. He had also injured seventeen children and adults, some seriously.

Thomas Hamilton was born in Glasgow on 10 May 1952, the son of Thomas and Agnes Watt, née Hamilton. He was called Thomas Watt, like his father. The marriage proved to be a rocky one, and not long after Thomas was born his parents separated, eventually divorcing in 1955. Being a single mother in the Scotland of the middle 1950s was not an easy option, and divorce then carried with it a certain stigma that made things even more difficult. Almost inevitably, Agnes soon moved back in with her parents in the Cranhill district of Glasgow, taking her young son with her.

A year after the divorce of his parents, four-year-old Thomas was formally adopted by his grandparents and his name was changed to Thomas Watt Hamilton. His grandmother became his mother and his grandfather became his father. The change in roles was completed when he was told that his real mother was his sister. We cannot know how young Tommy reacted to these changes, but children are accepting creatures; they adapt to change because they do not always recognise it as such. When Thomas's adoptive parents moved from Glasgow to Stirling in 1963, he and his 'sister' moved with them. They remained together until 1985 when Agnes moved into a house of her own, leaving Thomas with his 'parents'. Even after his adoptive mother died, in August 1987, and his adoptive father moved into old people's accommodation in 1992, Thomas remained alone in the family home, visiting Agnes once or twice a week.

We carry our childhood with us always: it is constantly there, forming us, moulding us, a thread that runs through our adult attitudes, behaviour, personalities. As children, we form identities based as much on our relationships to others as on any other external factors. We become who we are in reaction and in relation to the complex web of emotional and social interactions around us. For these relationships to change suddenly, to twist and turn and become something different, makes our own identity seem fluid and subject to change. And in this sea of shifting, unstable relationships the instinctive reaction, especially that of a child, is to seek stability, to seek certainty, to demand some form of control.

Clearly the pressures on Hamilton were not so great that they produced *visible* signs of emotional trauma. He did not show any obvious and outward indications of behavioural problems as a child. He remained with his adoptive parents until the end, safely ensconced in the home that they had created for him. He did not grow up to hate and despise his real mother: he kept in touch with her, visiting her often, staying with her frequently. Like many children he internalised the trauma. It became a part of him, helping to form the Thomas Hamilton who could gun down crying children as they wept at his feet.

After attending Riverside School in Stirling and Falkirk Technical College, Hamilton gained a number of O levels in 1968. He was taken on as an apprentice draughtsman in the County Architect's Office. Later, in 1972, he became self-employed when he opened a hardware store in Stirling that specialised in DIY goods, ironmongery and, eventually, the sale of fitted kitchens. We know that at this time Hamilton was an active Venture Scout and perhaps we can see a link, however tenuous, between the Scout ideals of self-reliance and independence and his choice of business. It suggests that not only was he looking for a degree of self-determination in his working life, but that it extended much further. So much so that he chose to trade in tools and supplies, surrounding himself with physical implements which actively enabled that self-sufficiency.

In July 1973 Hamilton applied for the post of Assistant Scout Leader of the 4th/6th Stirling Troop. At this point vetting procedures were brought into play to assess his suitability for a role that gave him a degree of access to – and authority over – groups of young boys. The Scout Association takes this background checking extremely seriously and will as a matter of routine liaise with the police and local authorities to ensure that known sex offenders are excluded. Additionally, other members of the Scout Association are sounded out to confirm or dispute an applicant's suitability. Thomas Hamilton, still only just into his twenties and with ample enthusiasm, duly passed through these checking procedures without adverse comment.

A few months later he was seconded to nearby Bannock-burn, to act as leader of the newly revived 24th Stirlingshire Troop.

However, his rise through the ranks of the Scout Association was halted almost immediately. A number of complaints about his behaviour were raised at around this time, particularly regarding his behaviour during overnight trips with the young boys in his charge. On one occasion the children had had to spend the night with Hamilton in his van, during extremely cold weather, on a trip to Aviemore. The accommodation he had organised had been double-booked, according to his explanation to the Scout Association's Commissioners. He was instructed on the occasion of this first complaint to double-check all bookings in the future.

No accusations of improper conduct were made at this point. It was merely seen as inappropriate behaviour by Hamilton. But the warnings from his superiors were ignored and the incident was repeated, with a group of boys again forced to spend the night in the van with him. On this occasion the repercussions were stronger and both incidents were investigated. Alarm bells rang instantly when it was discovered that on neither occasion had *any* bookings been made for accommodation. Hamilton had deliberately engineered situations where groups of children had been forced to spend the night with him in the cramped confines of a van.

The County Commissioner for the Scout Association, Brian Fairgrieve, met with his superiors and it was decided that the two incidents, along with a number of more minor complaints, were sufficient to warrant Hamilton's compulsory resignation from the Association. This news was relayed to Hamilton directly by Fairgrieve, who formed the opinion that Hamilton was clearly not a fit and proper person to leave in charge of young boys.

'I formed the impression that he had a persecution complex, that he had delusions of grandeur and I felt his actions were almost paranoia', Fairgrieve is quoted in evidence presented to the Cullen Enquiry following the massacre. He also expressed doubts about Hamilton's intentions towards the boys.

Following this meeting, Hamilton was informed that his warrant was being withdrawn. Every adult with a position of responsibility within the Scout movement, whether as Scout Leader, Commissioner or other senior rank, requires a warrant to certify that he or she has been granted that authority and responsibility. Withdrawal of a warrant, therefore, was to all intents and purposes expulsion from the ranks of the Scout Association. In May 1973 the District Commissioner, Mr R. Deuchars, wrote to Hamilton requesting that the warrant should be returned. It was the first of many such letters and it was to take a number of months before Hamilton was finally forced to comply with this request.

The suspicions of paranoia expressed by Brian Fairgrieve are important, as they pre-date the massacre of 13 March 1996 by more than twenty years. It was an element of Hamilton's personality even in his early twenties and therefore, presumably, something he had carried over from his childhood rather than a facet of his personality formed through many years of adult setbacks and struggle. We can speculate about the source of this paranoia and the suspiciousness that Hamilton so clearly displayed even as a young man. Was it a consequence of the rearrangement of his closest relationships in his childhood?

Hamilton's expulsion from the Stirlingshire Scouts did nothing to deter him from his ambitions. He attempted instead to become a Scout Leader in Clackmannanshire, only to find that his name had been added to the Scout Association's blacklist. He was, from then on, an undesirable as far as the Scout Association was concerned, and in no circumstances was he to be involved in *any* Scout activities. Mr Deuchars had added Hamilton's name to the register that is consulted not only by the Scout Association but also by outside bodies who wish to request references from the Scout Association for job applicants and so forth. The reasons cited were Hamilton's immaturity and irresponsibility.

Furthermore, Mr Fairgrieve had written to the Scottish Scout Headquarters in June 1974 warning them that Hamilton was not fit to be a member of the Scout movement. He wrote: 'While unable to give concrete evidence against this man I feel that too many "incidents" relate to him such that I am far from happy about his having any association with Scouts. He has displayed irresponsible acts on outdoor activities by taking young "favourite" Scouts for weekends during the winter and sleeping in his van, the excuse for these outings being hill-walking expeditions. The lack of precautions for such outdoor activities displays either irresponsibility or an ulterior motive for sleeping with the boys . . . His personality displays evidence of a persecution complex coupled with rather grandiose delusions of his own abilities. As a doctor, and with my clinical acumen only, I am suspicious of his moral intentions towards boys'.

Hamilton responded to these activities against him by starting a protracted campaign of letter-writing and complaints. He had, he contended, been victimised unfairly. This campaign continued on and off for many years, and his complaints grew more and more acrimonious as time went on. He also became quite devious as he attempted to inveigle his way back into the Scout movement. For example, he sent the Central Regional Council a copy of a letter dated 28 April 1974 and addressed to Mr Deuchars tendering his resignation, criticising Mr Deuchars and stating that he intended to transfer to another district within the Scout movement. Of course, no such letter had been received by Mr Deuchars: it was merely a ploy designed to give the impression that Hamilton had resigned of his own accord rather than been expelled.

In April 1977 Hamilton stated, in correspondence, that he was no longer interested in holding a warrant. '. . . I do not want my good name to be part of this so-called organisation in this district'. It was not, however, the end of his efforts to rejoin, nor did it mark the end of his campaign of increasingly paranoid letters and protests.

As late as 1978, four years after the withdrawal of his warrant, Hamilton was attempting to regain a position in the Scout movement. He wrote to a Scout official in the Trossachs region offering his services as Scout Leader. As with all other such attempts this too ended in failure. His demand for a Committee of Inquiry in February 1977 was also refused. By this point Hamilton was complaining that not only had the Scouts ruined his reputation but that they were working with the police against him.

Expulsion from the Scouts was a bitter blow and it added fuel to the fire of Hamilton's paranoia. He came to believe that forces were conspiring against him, and that these forces included the Scout Association, the police and various local authorities. At no point does it appear that he questioned his own activities. He felt a sense of injustice that aggravated his developing persecution complex and, concomitantly, a barely suppressed anger and rage towards those he felt had wronged him.

Without a place in the Scout movement Hamilton had no means to gain access to young children. He was interested in young boys, particularly pre-teen boys between the ages of eight and twelve. Many predatory paedophiles adopt a variety of personas and strategies to get close to children. Such men are drawn to organisations that grant them positions of power and authority over children. They become adept at winning their trust and, just as importantly, the trust of their parents. It is not uncommon for such men to move from place to place, often changing identity, and to become serial offenders – abusing children as they work their way from locality to locality. The Scouts, the Church, play-groups, charities . . . the list of organisations that such men infiltrate is endless.

Thomas Hamilton, however, seems not to have conformed to this particular type of offender profile. His desires, it would appear, were more specific. It was not just young boys *per se* in whom he was interested. He seems to have been attracted to young boys in particular situations and dressed in particular ways. The Scouts offered him most of these elements: young boys in uniform; young boys in a semi-military situation; young boys under his direct control. So his response to exclusion from the official Scout movement was not to move to a different area, nor to adopt a different identity, nor to shift his focus to the Church or some other type of established organisation. Instead Hamilton decided to form his own scouting organisation.

The first of these organisations on record was formed by the late 1970s and was called the 'Dunblane Rovers'. The Public Enquiry into the Dunblane massacre listed fifteen different boys' clubs that Hamilton is known to have organised. It is feasible that there were more, especially in the middle 1970s before he came to the attention of the police and other authorities.

Hamilton's methods of operation were simple. First he would canvass an area with leaflets advertising the formation of a boys' club. It was important to garner as much public support as possible from parents and teachers. Frequently, although not always successfully, he would also approach schools to try to get them either to endorse or advertise his clubs. The club would have a sporting theme, typically offering training in football and gymnastics, and the age group that would be targeted would be from around seven to eleven. None of the clubs was open to girls since Hamilton was simply not interested in them.

Hamilton would sometimes pretend that there was a club committee consisting of parents and helpers, but this was simply a ruse to obscure the fact that he ran the clubs largely by himself. Occasionally he would have help from parents and volunteers, recruited through advertisements, but often he was on his own. Hamilton had obtained at some point a Grade Five certificate from the British Amateur Gymnastics Board, which qualified him to offer coaching in gymnastics if supervised by someone with a higher qualification. There were few such people associated with him, but the fact that he was qualified to some extent was enough to allay the fears that some parents might have had.

As Hamilton's confidence grew he formed an imaginary 'Boys' Club Sports Group Committee' that was supposedly organising the clubs. The grand title was both a figment of his imagination intended to give the impression that he was not acting alone and also a testament to his delusions of grandeur. Whether the fictitious title ever fooled anybody for long is open to question, but initially at least his clubs proved to be extremely popular. Some of them are on record as attracting up to seventy boys, though the high opening numbers would often dwindle as time went on.

Hamilton frequently managed to obtain permission to use school premises after hours, hiring halls and gymnasia from local authorities, again adding a veneer of respectability to his activities.

Once enrolled, the children would soon find themselves forced into the uniform that Hamilton provided for them. He liked 'his boys', as he referred to them, to wear loose-fitting black swimming trunks. No other sports kit was allowed: it had to be black, loose and provided by him. Parents who complained were simply told that this was to eliminate any problems caused by clashing colours and styles. Furthermore, Hamilton insisted that the children should put on the black trunks in the gym itself rather than in the changing room. He liked to watch: in the changing room they would be out of his sight.

Once they had donned Hamilton's kit, the boys would then begin his idiosyncratic gymnastic exercises. Derived from army-style PE of a previous era, these were often over-strenuous for such young children and seem to have been based on a style of 'physical jerks' that was by then no longer in use in modern gymnastics. The children were often hectored, shouted at and forced to exhaust themselves while Hamilton watched and, frequently, photographed.

Hamilton had a long-standing interest in photography. Indeed, after the failure of his hardware business in 1985, he took up buying and selling cameras in order to augment the state benefits that supported him. He also worked on occasion as a freelance photographer. In 1989 he bought himself a video camera to add to his 35mm cameras. Of course, this interest in film and photography tied in with his interest in the children. He liked to photograph and video them clad in their ill-fitting black trunks while they performed his exercise routines. Often the films and photos focused on the boys' bodies, particularly on their bare chests and the areas between their knees and waists. There is good evidence that Hamilton kept the photographs in large bound albums and displayed on the walls of the home he inhabited alone.

Hamilton took the video films and photographs without parental permission, indeed without the parents even knowing about them. When quizzed, he would respond that he did not need permission and that the materials were for advertising purposes. The focus on the children's bodies was explained as being necessary for training purposes: he said that he needed to see which groups of muscles were being used. He sought to allay parental concerns by offering copies of the videos and pictures to those parents who wanted them. Rather than allaying such fears, the films and pictures of half-naked, frightened children only confirmed that there was something deeply suspect about Thomas Hamilton. In the words of the Cullen Report into the massacre: 'Their overriding impression was that there was something unnatural'.

Many parents who witnessed this style of training and saw at first hand Hamilton's domineering and aggressive manner were often horrified. The fact that he often ran the clubs single-handed only added to their feelings of disquiet. Many felt uneasy when they saw him shouting at the children and forcing them to adopt uncomfortable positions. It was felt by some that he was 'getting something' out of dominating the boys. Inevitably many parents would withdraw their children and would warn other parents that there was something 'not quite right' about Hamilton. Indeed, George Robertson MP, whose son attended one of Hamilton's clubs in Dunblane, withdrew his son permanently after he and another parent visited the club in April 1983. He reported seeing 'a large number of small boys in shorts, stripped to the waist, being bossed around by two or three middle-aged men, swaggering around in a very military-type way'. It was, concluded Mr Robertson, '. . . like the Hitler Youth'.

This inevitable withdrawal of children from the clubs only added to Hamilton's feelings of paranoia. Parents did not stop their children joining because of anything that he had done; it was because people in the Scout movement were spreading malicious rumours about him. He merely wanted to keep the children off the streets, to provide some focus for them, to combat the junk food that parents gave their children. The Scouts were afraid of the competition . . .

Of the children who did remain in the clubs, and it must be stressed that at no point did Hamilton ever alienate *every* parent or child he was involved with, he clearly had his favourites. Sometimes a child would only have to attend a club once for Hamilton to take a fancy. In such cases he applied pressure on the parents to let the child attend more regularly. He would often pick the child up directly and drive him to the club, making sure that he found out as much as possible about the child's home and family life. This again is a classic tactic adopted by child abusers, and one that caused concern among some parents.

It was not just the parents who were wary of Hamilton. Some of the boys reported feeling uncomfortable around him: he frightened them or made them nervous in some way. Again and again children repeated that he was weird. When a parent did withdraw a child from one of his clubs Hamilton would respond by writing long, paranoid letters complaining that his life was being ruined by rumour and innuendo. He would become aggressive and angry, suggesting that it was up to the parents to dispel the ugly rumours about him. At times his behaviour was seen as threatening or intimidating.

Similarly, anyone who expressed concern about the way Hamilton ran things soon found that his polite façade would fall away. He would become angry and defensive, thus adding to the impression that he was doing something wrong. Why would he act so shiftily, why would he become so aggressive? It did little to create a good image and served merely to reinforce the unease that more and more parents were beginning to feel. In Hamilton's mind, however, things were different: parents withdrew their children because of rumour and innuendo. He could not perceive the vicious circle whereby his behaviour pushed people further away from him, adding to the rumours and his poor reputation.

No matter how successful the clubs, it is clear that Hamilton saw them merely as a means to an end. The club itself was a vehicle to grant him access to the children in order to select those boys that he wanted to take with him on 'summer camps'. And it was through one of these camps that Hamilton first came to the attention of the police.

At one point Hamilton claimed to have organised well over fifty summer camps, though his figure has never been officially verified and may be no more than another example of his delusional character. Typically, he liked to select the younger boys in his clubs to attend the summer camps for one or two weeks. One such camp was organised in the summer of 1988 on the island of Inchmoan, in Loch Lomond. The camp was run single-handedly by Hamilton, who thus had free reign to impose his will on the children in his care.

Several of the boys complained to their parents on their return home and these complaints in turn were passed on to the police. The camp came under the jurisdiction of the Strathclyde police, who dispatched two officers to the island on 20 July. PC George Gunn and PC Donna Duncan arrived to find that the campsite was in chaos, with mess everywhere and food and dirty dishes strewn on the tables, and that the children's sleeping bags were damp to the touch. There was no sign of fresh food at all: everything was tinned or powdered and, in the police officers' words, 'not very wholesome'. The same thing could be said for the campsite as a whole.

The thirteen children attending the camp were inadequately dressed and appeared to be cold and wet. Some of them were dressed only in swimming trunks and were playing, unsupervised, around the water about thirty metres from the camp. Thomas Hamilton was the only adult in attendance. Several of the boys had scratches all over their legs, the result of hiking through the thick bracken that covers the island. Long trousers were banned, Hamilton explaining that such trousers took longer to dry than bare legs. When questioned, very few of the boys said they were actively enjoying themselves: many were homesick and complained that they had not been allowed to contact their parents. It was alleged that Hamilton had smacked a number of the boys, an allegation he did not deny and which he justified by saying that some of the boys were bullies and had been disruptive.

The only method of transport to and from the island was a small rowing boat on which there was an inadequate number of lifejackets.

The police officers did not like what they saw. They felt uneasy about Hamilton (who was courteous throughout) and, like many other adults who had come into contact with him before and after this particular camp, they felt he was 'not quite right'. PC Gunn offered to take the children home but none of them wished to go, not even those who had complained. Although the officers were unhappy with what they saw, there was nothing else they could do. They returned to base where they duly submitted a report and contacted the parents. Later, Hamilton and the boys were taken to the Dunbarton Police Office where six of the parents came to collect their children. At this point none of the children or their parents complained about Hamilton. In fact, as stated at the Public Enquiry after the massacre, some of the parents even praised him.

The police, however, were not so happy with the situation. Statements were taken from the children and an official report passed to the Procurator Fiscal (the Scottish equivalent of the Crown Prosecution Service, whose task it is to assess whether there is a case to be answered and, if so, whether it is in the public interest for it to go ahead). The children's statements, however, were inconsistent and contradictory. There seemed to be no case for Hamilton to answer. When the boys were interviewed again the evidence was even more confusing: their differing accounts flatly contradicted each other on several occasions. The conclusion was that there was no case to answer and Thomas Hamilton was not charged with any offence. This is not to say that the authorities had no misgivings. The Procurator Fiscal, Mr James Cardle, recommended that the police should take up the matter with the social services and other local authorities.

For Hamilton this brush with the law only served to inflame his paranoia. As with the Scouts he responded with a vigorous campaign of counter-complaint. He alleged that PC Gunn had been incompetent and untruthful. He circulated letters to PC Gunn's superior officers and indeed throughout the Central Scotland Police Service. At one point he even turned up at a police station and demanded to discuss PC Gunn's report with him. When PC Gunn denied the request Hamilton refused to leave and it was only the threat of arrest that forced him out. His complaints were not dismissed as the work of a crank, however, and an investigation was duly launched. This concluded, in October 1988, that PC Gunn had acted properly.

For a while Hamilton seemed to accept this, but a short while later he wrote to the Chief Constable alleging that PC Gunn was a Scout leader and should therefore never have been appointed to investigate his camp. There was, he claimed, 'a long resentment shown to our group by many adult members of the Dunblane Scouts'. By now the police investigation had been conflated in Hamilton's mind into part of an organised conspiracy against him. The police and the Scouts together were part of a 'brotherhood'. This idea became fixed and obsessional, a central pivot of his paranoid persecution complex. And, like many paranoids, he publicised this idea to all and sundry in an effort to expose what he saw as the malicious forces at work against him. He wrote letters to newspapers, to the police, to his MP and councillors, to the heads of local schools. He prepared leaflets and circulars to send to parents and other local residents.

Hamilton made a more formal complaint against PC Gunn in November 1988, claiming that the officer had lied and that he had carried out an 'unlawful and unnecessary exercise of his authority' in investigating the summer camp. The formal complaint was again fully investigated, and the officer in charge, Inspector James Keenan, took Hamilton's statement. It took three hours to deliver and, in addition to the direct complaints about PC Gunn, it included criticisms of the police in general, comments about their lack of professionalism, allegations of incompetence and so on. Inspector Keenan also re-interviewed the children who had been at the camp, as well as other people who had been camping on the island at around the same time. These witnesses spoke highly of Hamilton's abilities as an organiser and a leader, in contrast to the view formed by the police officers.

The results of the inquiry were delivered on 22 May 1989. The report exonerated PC Gunn and PC Duncan. It also showed that they had performed their duties in a fit and proper manner. Predictably enough, this did not satisfy Hamilton. The report was a cover-up, he claimed, another part of the conspiracy against him. By now his paranoia was in full swing, and every problem, every set-back, would be attributable to the invisible conspiracy around him.

Concern about Hamilton's activities was growing and, although no concrete allegations of sexual abuse had ever been put forward, more and more people were becoming concerned about his activities. He was by now finding it harder and harder to hire council premises and school buildings to run his clubs. Also a number of parents were taking active steps to oppose him.

One such parent was Mrs Doreen Hagger, whose son had attended one of the summer camps at Inchmoan Island. When her son complained, she and another parent, Mrs Janet Reilly, had gone out to the island to help Hamilton run things. Mrs Hagger claimed that Hamilton had rubbed suntan lotion on the boys and that he had also asked some of the boys to rub suntan lotion all over him, on some occasions even when he was not wearing any underwear. Although she did not witness this, it was enough to convince her that Hamilton was out to abuse the children. Accordingly, she did her best to persuade other parents to join her in trying to stop Hamilton's activities.

In May 1989 Doreen Hagger and Janet Reilly assaulted Hamilton as he emerged from one of his clubs in Linlithgow. She poured various substances, including suntan lotion, over his head so that she could be arrested for assault. A press photographer and a reporter were on hand to witness the event. She hoped that a court case would give her the opportunity to expose Hamilton and his activities to the full glare of the police and media. Unfortunately for her he reacted calmly. He even smiled for the cameras, and politely refused to press charges.

In July 1991, Hamilton organised another summer camp. This time it was held at Mullarochy Bay, Loch Lomond, with around twenty boys between the ages of six and eleven present. Again, parental complaints led to a police investigation. Hamilton had informed parents that the camp would be supervised by at least four adults but, as usual, he was in sole charge for much of the time. Children complained about being smacked and of being videotaped. This time DC Grant Kirk, accompanied by a social worker, was assigned to investigate.

Hamilton was cautioned and interviewed at the camp on 23 July. He admitted to slapping one boy, whom he claimed was a troublemaker and a bully. The video, he explained, was made because they were creating a film along the lines of *Lord of the Flies*. As before, the police officers were extremely concerned by what they saw but there was no direct evidence of sexual abuse. Hamilton denied that he had taken any still photographs and he handed over the video camera and the film he had taken to date.

Two days later, DC Grant returned with his superior officer, DS Hughes, ostensibly to return the video camera but actually so that the senior officer could see for himself what was going on. Once again, the children were cold and wet, clad only in black swimming trunks and forbidden to dress even when it was raining. The boys were not being properly supervised and were often out of any adult's line of sight, playing at a jetty or around the water and none of them wearing any form of life jacket.

One of the boys told the police that he had been taken by Hamilton into an individual tent and photographed wearing red swimming trunks. The police feared that this boy was being singled out for future abuse, a charge that Hamilton vehemently denied. Again he stated that he had not taken any still pictures. Five days later, on 30 July, he handed over six boxes of slides and more than 150 photographs. This was not, however, the complete haul. A film processor in Stirling had contacted the police after becoming alarmed by the photographs that Hamilton was having developed. The police were informed that there had in fact been nine boxes of slides, not six. A seventh was taken by the police when Hamilton arrived to pick it up, but two boxes were never recovered. The slides included a large number of the boy in red trunks, though in the photos he was not wearing these. The child was clearly a favourite and had been given special jobs in the camp by Hamilton.

Hamilton responded by making an official complaint against DS Hughes, forcing Hughes to hand over his investigation to another officer. Again children were interviewed, as was Hamilton, but eventually the Procurator Fiscal could find no hard evidence of criminality. There was much unease but without anything concrete there was no criminal charge that could be brought against Hamilton.

However, during the course of his investigations DS Hughes had discovered that Thomas Hamilton possessed a valid firearms certificate. On 11 November 1991 DS Hughes wrote to CID headquarters to request that serious consideration should be given to withdrawing the certificate. DS Hughes stated: 'I am firmly of the opinion that Hamilton is an unsavoury character and unstable personality ... I firmly believe that he has an extremely unhealthy interest in young boys which to a degree appears to have been controlled to date. It was his ploy, whenever challenged, to engage in "smoke screen" tactics which divert attention from the focal issue and this is the purpose for the profusion of correspondence to MPs, Procurators Fiscal, the Chief Constable and the like. I would contend that Mr Hamilton will be a risk to children whenever he has access to them and that he appears to me to be an unsuitable person to possess a firearm certificate in view of the number of occasions he has come to the adverse attention of the police and his apparent instability.'

In addition to detailing the accusations against Hamilton, including the details of the missing photographs, DS Hughes concluded: 'The Procurator Fiscal at Stirling has not yet decided on whether or not he will proceed with the case against Hamilton but at the moment it appears in all likelihood that he will not. I respectfully request that serious consideration is given to withdrawing this man's firearm certificate as a precautionary measure as it is my opinion that he is a scheming, devious and deceitful individual who is not to be trusted.'

Discussion took place between various officers of the Central Scotland Police Force, who eventually decided that no action should be taken. Having reached this conclusion, nothing was marked in Hamilton's firearms file held by the police, nor were details included on his criminal intelligence file. These omissions proved costly for the people of Dunblane. It is abundantly clear that if the police had acted on DS Hughes's recommendation, or indeed on the misgivings of other officers, then Hamilton's firearms licence would have been revoked. Instead it was renewed and extended in February 1992 and again in 1995.

While continuing his increasingly heated and irrational correspondence with the police, press, MPs and other figures of authority, Hamilton carried on with his activities. Because of the complaints and the other trouble that the summer camps had caused, he decided on a change of tack. In June 1992 he organised a 'Residential Sports Training Course' at Dunblane High School. The local authority felt that this would be preferable to a summer camp as it would allow for a greater level of supervision and provide better facilities for the children.

The facilities may have been better but, predictably, the supervision was not. On 29 June 1992 a police officer found three young boys dressed in their pyjamas wandering through the town. They explained that they had been at the sports training course but that they were fed up with the discipline that Hamilton was imposing and wanted to go home. The police officer was already aware of Hamilton's reputation and decided not to get directly involved with him. Instead, he contacted the parents who came to collect their children.

The next day, Hamilton explained to the police that the boys had escaped via the fire exit. The police accepted his explanation and the matter was closed. However, on 2 July one of the parents complained to the police about the lack of supervision, the high levels of discipline and Hamilton's active discouragement of any form of contact between the children and their homes. The police interviewed the three boys and reports were passed to the Child Protection Unit. More warning bells were sounded. Mr A. Kelly of the Child Protection Unit wrote to the Senior Assistant Director of Education at Fife Regional Council: 'I feel that the events of 29 June 1992 in Dunblane in a sense serve as a warning. If the kind of circumstances as described are allowed to continue without some kind of intervention, I consider that other children may be placed at risk. In like situations arising unchecked, I fear that a tragedy to a child or children is almost waiting to happen.'

Again a report was filed with the Procurator Fiscal at Stirling. Again no action was taken: no criminal act had taken place.

In June 1993, following further complaints about Hamilton's clubs held at Denny High School and Dunblane High School, the police were issued with a warrant to search his house for photographs, photographic equipment, documentation and other items that might be relevant to ongoing investigations. The police were aware that Hamilton had been taking photographs of children, especially his favourites, on their own. While he had been more than willing to provide parents with photographs, these did not include the pictures of the boys posing only in his uniform of ill-fitting trunks. In the opinion of a number of officers these particular pictures were semi-pornographic. However, none of them could be considered indecent: the boys were not naked and there was nothing overtly sexual about the poses. No action arose from this investigation.

Similar investigations were conducted and reports made during the next few years. In each case a parent or other adult would make a complaint. The police or local authority would investigate. Hamilton, paranoia rampant, would hit back with counter-accusations. And in the end nothing would happen. In every case Hamilton was found to be acting within the bounds of the law. No matter how distasteful his activities, no matter how irrational or obsessional he became, he never strayed from within the strict confines of the law.

The net effect of this string of complaints and investigations was to confirm Hamilton in his paranoid world-view, and, just as importantly, to peel kids away from his boys' clubs and training courses. And, as all this was going on, he was adding to his collection of handguns.

Hamilton had been granted a firearms licence in February 1977 when he was still in his early twenties. This was initially for small-bore firearms but was extended five years later to include full-bore arms. He was a member of various gun clubs in the Central Region, though he was never very active. Hamilton was simply not the clubbable type: he rarely joined in with the social side of these clubs. It is clear that he preferred the company of young boys. He found it difficult to mix with other adults and tended to avoid doing so unnecessarily. According to the Secretary of the Stirling Rifle and Pistol Club, 'Hamilton was a loner, he wouldn't engage in social conversation with anybody; it is known also that women members didn't particularly like being around him. He was a bit of a creep in their eyes.'

Although Hamilton did not often take part in the frequent competitions that are a feature of gun clubs, occasionally he liked to take part in an event called a 'police pistol'. This involves taking six shots at a target from a given distance and in a given time period. In Hamilton's case he preferred to rapid-fire a dozen shots, blasting again and again. It disturbed the other competitors, and despite clear requests he would not be persuaded to adhere to the rules.

Hamilton was not averse to showing off his guns to the children at his clubs and to their parents. In all cases he was scrupulously safety-conscious, observing all the rules when it came to handling the weapons. Even so, some parents felt uncomfortable when he came round to their homes carrying guns, despite the fact that they were unloaded. Some saw it as threatening, and at least one incident was reported to the police. At the Public Enquiry, Doreen Hagger, who had previously complained about Hamilton after the Inchmoan summer camp, claimed that he had threatened her with a gun in the street. However, Lord Cullen, who presided over the Public Enquiry, dismissed this report as a fabrication.

What is not in dispute is Hamilton's attachment to his guns. If the children attending his clubs were his 'boys', then his guns were definitely his 'babies'. In March 1977 he bought a .22 Smith & Wesson revolver; in September 1977 a .22 Anschutz rifle; in August 1978 a .22 Browning pistol; in December 1979 a .357 Smith and Wesson revolver (with which he was to take his own life in March 1996) and a .270 Sako rifle. Hamilton traded guns, actively buying and selling and always making sure that he had adequate supplies of ammunition. By December 1984 he had also purchased a 9mm Browning pistol and a .223 Browning rifle. In February 1986 he acquired a 9mm Beretta pistol. In September 1995 he obtained a second 9mm Browning pistol and in January 1996 another .357 Smith & Wesson revolver.

Hamilton had acquired legally all four guns that he carried with him on the day of the massacre: two 9mm Browning pistols and two .357 Smith & Wesson revolvers. Had the police taken action to remove his firearms certificate it is unlikely that Hamilton would have had the means to carry out his slaughter.

By late 1995 the boys' clubs were in decline. Numbers were dropping away and Hamilton was having to go further and further from home in order to start up new clubs in areas that did not yet know him. His methods of attracting parental support and, just as importantly, local-authority permission to hire school premises, were as devious and underhand as ever. He made claims about mysterious club committees, used other adults as covers for himself and so on. The Dunblane Boys' Club was still in existence, but few of the children attending it were actually from Dunblane: many were being bused in from other areas to make up the numbers.

All the time it was getting harder to continue, and this served to increase Hamilton's bitterness and frustration. He was becoming more outspoken in his views, pinning the entire blame for his difficulties on a 'brotherhood of Masons' that included the police and the Scouts. He took to leafleting parents, explaining that he was the victim of a smear campaign, claiming again that his life was being ruined by rumour and innuendo. This behaviour only served to accelerate the decline in club activity.

With more time on his hands Hamilton turned from his boys' clubs to his other favourite activity: shooting. After shooting in a competition in 1995 he was given a lift home by a club member, during which he is remembered as sitting in the back of the car beside a young female club member, quietly stroking his guns. 'That is a right weirdo, that one,' she is reported to have said at the time. 'He talks about guns as though they were babies.'

In February 1996 Hamilton took a marksmanship test, which he passed, with the Callander Rifle and Pistol Club and applied for membership. At the end of the month he took part in a police-pistol event during which he fired a 'fusillade of shots' at 25 metres (the requirement is twelve shots in two minutes) and at ten metres from the target he fired off four shots before he could be stopped, instead of the regulation two shots in two seconds. It was how Hamilton always liked to shoot: rapid-fire volleys as though once started he found it difficult to stop. One probationary member of the club stated that Hamilton fired more rounds than anyone he'd ever seen before.

In conversation, too, guns were increasingly centre stage. Hamilton had recruited a young sports undergraduate, Ian Boal, to help him run a boys' club in Bishopsbriggs. The young undergraduate, studying sport in the community, was keen for the experience, though he had been recruited with the promise that he was going to be running the club largely on his own and was quite upset to find that Hamilton was so closely involved. Of course, the younger man's more modern methods were at odds with Hamilton's dated and militaristic techniques and the two soon fell out when Boal wrote a letter criticising Hamilton's system.

Previously Hamilton's non-club conversations with Boal had been dominated largely by cameras, but by the second half of 1995 and on into 1996 guns had become the main topic. Hamilton would talk about his love of weapons, his active shooting at ranges and so on. In February 1996 he was talking in detail about ammunition, explaining what different types of bullets could and couldn't do. He spoke about the 'spray' of a bullet that disintegrates inside its target rather than passing through it. Hamilton even spoke of doing 'experiments' where he would fire into books so that he could see how the ammunition sprayed through the pages.

Even the films Hamilton watched reflected this renewed interest in guns. He was enjoying films like *Alien* and *The Terminator* because of the guns, getting off on the spectacular violence of shots and explosions. He even offered to let some of the children watch *Alien*, a film with an 18 certificate due to its violent content.

Hamilton's resurgent interest in guns provided an escape not only from the problems he was having with his boys' clubs but also from his growing financial difficulties. His finances had been precarious for a long time, and any money that had come in (such as the payment he had received for the sale of his business) had been spent paying off existing debts and overdrafts. Although he charged fees for attendance at the boys' clubs, these were generally quite low and did little to cover his costs. Making money was not the real motive for these clubs and it is clear that he ran at a loss. Hamilton made some profit from dealing in cameras but this was offset by the withdrawal of his unemployment benefit in November 1993. The magazine *Amateur Photographer* refused to take his advertisements, thus reducing Hamilton's business dealings even further.

Hamilton was in arrears with his council tax, had a bank overdraft of £3,511, had reached the limits of his credit-card transactions and still had £2,350 to pay off on a loan he'd taken out to fund his camera business. An application for a further loan was refused. Hamilton was broke and there was nothing on the horizon financially. It is little wonder, then, that he increasingly sought refuge in violent films like *Terminator* and such fantasy-fuelled activities as shooting. With gun in hand, advancing squarely towards the target and firing shot after shot, his feelings of powerlessness and impotence would have been temporarily dispelled.

At the beginning of March 1996 Hamilton had fixed on another boy as a favourite. The eleven-year-old boy was an attendee of the Bishopsbrigg Boys' Club, and his parents soon became aware of Hamilton's distinctly unsettling interest in their child. Hamilton would offer to pick the boy up and take him to a different club, in Stirling. When Hamilton collected the boys for the club in Bishopsbrigg he would take an increasing amount of time between picking up this particular boy and collecting the rest of the children. He also showed the boy some of his guns and offered him a copy of *Alien* on video.

The parents complained to the boy's head teacher, who duly contacted social workers. After a delay of a couple of weeks, the head teacher was informed that a social worker would be visiting the parents shortly. That was on 12 March. The visit never took place.

On 6 March, Hamilton made a phone call to the Scout Association to find out who its patron was. On being informed that it was the Queen he also asked for details of other high-ranking officials within the organisation. He wanted, he explained, to let them know about maladministration within the Scouts. He claimed that they had 'put it about' that he was a pervert, and that this information was being passed around schools in a bid to stop him starting up new boys' clubs. They were ruining his life – he could no longer walk down the street without being harassed, his reputation was in tatters, he was nearly bankrupt. In short, all the ills of his life, all of the problems that Hamilton was suffering were because of a vicious and organised campaign against him.

On 7 March Hamilton wrote to the Queen, detailing his familiar litany of complaint. The letter ended: 'I turn to you as a last resort and am appealing for some kind of intervention in the hope that I may be able to regain my self-esteem in society.'

Later that week at the Dunblane Boys' Club Hamilton called out one of the children who attended Dunblane Primary School. The boy, only nine years old, was seated on a bench while the other boys carried on playing football. Hamilton then started asking detailed questions about the layout of the school. The boy explained: 'He asked me the way to the gym and the way to the hall. He asked what time certain classes went to the gym and the main way into the school. He asked directions about once he was in the main hall, how to get to the gym and where the stage was. He asked how to get to the assembly hall, and I told him to turn right after the main entrance. He said what day do all people go on the stage to do the play. I didn't know and he said to ask the P7s to find out. He asked if the younger children, like the primary ones to fours go to the assembly at a different time to the primary fives to sevens. I told him that the assembly was on a Wednesday morning and that the younger ones went after us. He asked me what time did assembly start and gym, I said 9.30 for assembly. I didn't tell him the time for gym . . . The other question was something to do with the gym fire exit. I think it was how many fire exits there were to get out of the gym. Mr Hamilton asked me these questions every single week. He had been asking me these questions for a long time, about two years. He didn't ask me any more questions and said I could go back to playing football.'

It is reported that on hearing of the massacre the boy's reaction was: 'It can't be Mr Hamilton, he was a nice guy.'

At around the same time, 7 or 8 March, Hamilton got into a conversation with a retired police officer in which he rehearsed his familiar paranoid complaints about the Scouts and the police. He also asked whether the police kept guns at all police stations. On being informed that this was only the case at offices that were manned 24 hours a day, he responded by saying that there was a need for a permanent armed-response unit in the area. It was clear to the retired policeman that Hamilton had a good level of knowledge about these matters, possibly derived from reading books and magazines.

Hamilton saw his mother on 11 and 12 March. He bathed at her house on the twelfth, had something to eat and spoke to her for around four hours. She noticed no change in his behaviour or in his mood. This was certainly not the case as far as other people were concerned. Later that day he went into Stirling to hire a van for the next day. The receptionist at the hire company was quoted as saying: 'He unnerved me quite a bit . . . the way he spoke, mainly. He spoke very slowly, very clearly, precisely, but with no emotion or expression . . . there was just nothing, nothing in there. You couldn't have held a conversation with him.'

That evening an acquaintance phoned Hamilton to discuss the sale of some cameras. The conversation was subdued and Hamilton sounded unhappy and depressed. He said that he felt lonely. The conversation fizzled out quickly.

Besides, there were preparations to be made. There were the extended box-type ammunition magazines for the Browning pistols to prepare. These could hold twenty rounds of 9mm ammunition rather than the usual thirteen rounds. There were 25 such magazines, and each was carefully labelled with an orange sticker at the front and a yellow sticker at the back so that there would be no fumbling around trying to replace them as each one was spent. Ammunition needed to be loaded into these magazines in strict sequence, with metal jacket soft-nosed hollow-point bullets at the bottom of the magazine; full metal jacket semi-wadcutter bullets in the middle; and full metal jacket round-nosed bullets at the top. The purpose of this was to reduce the chance of the firing mechanisms jamming. Nothing could be left to chance.

In all, 501 rounds of 9mm ammunition were loaded. Hamilton also packed away 230 rounds of ammunition for the two .357 revolvers.

Hamilton also took time to prepare the canvas bags to carry all of this ammunition. These were tied in such a manner that they could not accidentally close, and had been padded with cardboard to stop them collapsing in on themselves.

And then, on the morning of 13 March, with his preparations complete, Hamilton went into action.

The shock of the Dunblane Massacre reverberated around the world. Even in the United States, inured to gun violence and mass murder, the carnage created a wave of sympathy for the victims and their families. It is no exaggeration to say that people the world over felt grief-stricken. This 'slaughter of the innocents', the cold-blooded gunning-down of weeping children, ranks as a particularly callous, vicious crime.

If it had been Thomas Hamilton's intention to punish the people of Dunblane for his perceived problems, then he had succeeded beyond measure.

BENJAMIN NATHANIEL SMITH

Chicago, USA, 1999

Although the police at first refused to accept that a string of drive-by shootings was racially motivated, by the end of Friday, 2 July 1999, it was clear that there was a racist spree killer loose on the streets of Chicago. The first reported attacks occurred early that evening, and it was apparent immediately that somebody was out to attack members of the city's sizeable Jewish community.

At around 8.20 p.m. a car pulled up near the junction of Estes and Francisco Avenues. The timing was perfect as members of the Orthodox Jewish community walked to and from synagogue for the evening's services. The driver of the car climbed out and started walking towards a group of Jews. When he was around five metres away he pulled out his guns and started blasting. There were screams and people dived to take cover as the unidentified gunman fired repeatedly with a .22-calibre handgun and a .38 pistol. High-school teacher Hillel Goldstein, 34, on his way home after attending services at a nearby synagogue, fell to the ground as he was hit in the stomach.

Michael Messing and his teenage son Ephraim also came under fire. The sixteen-year-old boy was rooted to the spot as the gunman fired shot after shot. 'He got out of the car and started shooting at us. We were easy targets,' his father reported. The father pulled his son to the ground as three or four shots were fired at them. 'Luckily he missed us,' Messing continued.

The driver calmly returned to his car and moved off slowly. He seemed in no hurry to make his escape. 'He was driving slow. I think he was still looking to shoot people. He wasn't looking to get away,' Messing added.

The gunman took the corner slowly and, finding more targets along North Francisco Avenue, he started firing from his vehicle. He loosed off several more shots, this time hitting

Eric Yatos in the upper leg. It was 8.22 p.m., and, having hit his first two victims, the driver finally sped off down Francisco Avenue. More shots were fired as he steered with one hand while shooting with the other. There were two more casualties of this random violence, Dean Bell and Gidon Sapir, both wounded, neither of them seriously.

A few minutes later the car was moving up North Whipple Street. More shots were fired but luckily these missed the intended targets. Ian Huper was not so lucky. He was driving north along North Sacramento Avenue – a one-way street – when a car sped towards him, going in the wrong direction. The driver of the oncoming vehicle opened fire suddenly, hitting Huper in the right side and right forearm.

There were more shots reported in the district as the driver scoured the streets looking for victims. He found another at around 8.35 p.m. Ephraim Wolfe, a fifteen-year-old boy, was on his way to synagogue with a friend when they came under fire. Wolfe was the unlucky one of the two: he was hit in the right leg. His friend was luckier: the gunman missed him.

In the space of no more than fifteen minutes six people had been injured and a shudder of fear swept through the Jewish community. Instinctively they knew they were the targets and, whether the police accepted that there was a racist motive or not, it was clear to the community that it had been singled out for attack. Although the individual victims had been selected at random, the common factor was that they were all Jewish.

'He said nothing to anybody. He just fired on them,' said Chicago Police Lieutenant Nick Nickeas.

Ten minutes later the gunman was at the corner of Foster Street and Hamlin Avenue in Skokie. He spied a black man out jogging with his young son and daughter and they became his next targets. A hail of shots blasted out and the man, Ricky Byrdsong, a former basketball coach at the Northwestern University, was hit in the lower back. Other shots strafed nearby buildings, shattering windows and causing people to dive for cover. Again the gunman drove off, leaving Ricky Byrdsong seriously injured.

Finally, more than twenty minutes later, at approximately 9.20 p.m., an Asian couple on their way to a supermarket overtook a car on Willow Road in Northbrook, over ten miles from Skokie. The car was driving slowly, almost kerb-crawling, and as they overtook it they honked their horn at the driver. He responded with a terrifying volley of shots before zooming off. The couple, too frightened to reveal their names, were badly shaken but otherwise unharmed. Donna Reissman, who lives just off Willow Road, said she heard the shots being fired. 'It was two or three bangs,' she said. 'We just assumed from the time of year that it was fireworks.'

All the shootings were linked, that much was clear. The drive-by shootings were carried out by a lone individual driving a light blue vehicle, all the witnesses agreed on that point. It was also clear to people on the street that the assailant had deliberately targeted minority ethnic groups: Jews, blacks and Asians. Despite police reticence on the matter there was obviously a racist gunman on the loose in the streets of Chicago.

Warnings were issued in the synagogues almost immediately. One young Jew, nineteen-year-old Zachary Engler, was quoted as saying: 'In the synagogue they are giving a warning that something bad has happened and telling us to be careful, but to not let things get out of control. It's not the first time this has happened. It's not the first time this has happened to Jews or to blacks or to Asians. It's the way of the world. It's sad, but it is.'

As Friday night gave way to Saturday morning the toll became clear. Of the first six victims two, including fifteen-year-old Ephraim Wolfe, had serious injuries, two had lighter wounds and two were able to leave hospital and return home that same evening. Ricky Byrdsong was not so lucky: the 42-year-old underwent major surgery but the surgeons were unable to save him. In the early hours of Saturday morning he became the first fatality of the racist spree killer. For his family the Fourth of July holiday had turned into the worst of nightmares.

Initially the police had little to go on. The gunman was white, in his early to late twenties, of medium build and around six feet tall. He was driving a light blue Ford Taurus or Mercury Sable with the passenger-side window shot out.

The police adopted a cautious approach, refusing to categorically state that the shootings were hate crimes. Pat Camden,
a spokesman for the Chicago police, stated: 'Preliminary
indications seem to indicate that the shootings are the work
of one person. We have shell casings from three locations that
will be analysed and will tell us if the offender is one and the
same.'

While drive-by shootings may be fairly common occurren-
ces in some of America's gang-ridden inner city areas, these
shootings had occurred in relatively crime-free suburbs. The
streets around Ricky Byrdsong's home are lined with trees,
and residents feel safe walking or jogging through the
neighbourhood even late at night. A long-time resident of the
area, Leslie Schwartz said: 'It feels surreal because this has
been an oasis of peace.'

The Mayor of Chicago, Richard Daley, made a statement
condemning the shootings and attacking racism. 'There is no
place in Chicago for that kind of behaviour,' he stated. He was
joined by the Reverend Jesse Jackson who criticised the
shootings as 'race-based hatred' and called on America to
reassess its culture of violence. US Representative Jan
Schakowsky, representing much of the North Side and North
Shore area, made a statement that was explicit about the
motivation for the attacks and also pointed out the significance of the date – 4 July. 'To me it seemed like someone with
a perverse sense of Americanism has somehow taken this
weekend to target ethnic minorities.'

During Saturday the sealed-off scene of Ricky Byrdsong's
murder became a makeshift shrine, with well-wishers arriving
from all over the city to share the family's grief and to make
public their outrage at what had happened. 'There is no
rational explanation,' Byrdsong's wife Sheryalyn said. 'He was
such a good guy. All you can do at a time like this is turn to
the source of your faith.'

While people tried to come to terms with what had
happened, the gunman was still on the loose. At approximately 1.15 p.m. in Springfield, a 31-year-old black man became
the first target of the day. Firing from a light blue car, the
assailant managed to hit his victim in the lower back. Fifteen

minutes later the gunman fired at two other black men, neither of whom he hit.

From Springfield the gunman drove to nearby Decatur. He fired three shots at a black minister, Pastor Stephen Anderson, hitting him twice, in the shoulder and hip. A third bullet struck the minister's mobile phone, which saved him from almost certain death. After the shooting, the Pastor described what had happened as he returned home from a 4 July holiday party. He had just parked his car and was getting some stuff off the back seat when he spotted the light blue car cruising slowly towards him. 'I paused to wait to have it pass,' he explained. 'As he passed, he shot me three times. I had about eight or nine nieces and nephews in front of the house. My brother chased him, but he got away.'

The minister also gave a vivid description of meeting the gunman head on. 'It was like he just had a deadness in his face, like, you know, "I'm going to kill you,"' he remembered. 'When I looked at him, he looked at me, and it was, like, this is it. Pow, pow, pow.'

The deadness in the gunman's face was matched by his grim silence as he carried out his shootings. There were no shouted threats, no obscenities: nothing but a stony silence as he fired again and again at his intended victims. It was as though he had steeled himself for violence and had deliberately adopted a soldier's impassive demeanour.

Police efforts began to focus on a likely suspect. Benjamin Nathaniel Smith, a 21-year-old student with a history of racist activity. Eyewitnesses had linked him to the car via the number plate. It seems too that some of his fellow racist activists checked out by the police had pointed the finger of suspicion his way. While police followed up on these leads another drive-by attack took place late that Saturday night.

Just before midnight a group of Asian-Americans were walking home near the University of Illinois in Urbana when a light blue car pulled up. Without warning, four shots rang out into the silence of the night. One of the men, Steven Kuo, went down instantly, hit in the thigh. The bullet severed his femoral artery, leading to a heavy loss of blood. He was rushed to Carle Hospital in Urbana for emergency surgery. In the early hours of Sunday morning his condition was pronounced 'serious but stable'. Again, the gunman had disappeared by the time police arrived on the scene.

The actual death toll after two days of random violence was, miraculously, still only one. Despite the killer being armed with at least two guns and carrying ample supplies of ammunition, it seems that he was nonetheless a bad shot. Although some of the injuries were serious, few of them were really life-threatening. Of course, this was no consolation to the family of Ricky Byrdsong, struggling to come to terms with life without him. It also did nothing to dispel the sense of paranoia that the shootings had engendered in Chicago's various ethnic minority communities.

Mark Steinberg, a member of the Jewish community, linked the attacks to a history of anti-Semitic violence, including the Holocaust. 'It feels like living through the past again. These things still happen again today. I can't tell you that I feel safe to go outside right now. I can't tell you I feel safe letting my children play outside,' he said. 'This is pure, absolute, one hundred per cent hatred.'

By Sunday morning police throughout the state of Illinois were on alert for Smith. An ex-girlfriend of his, Elizabeth Sahr, told reporters: 'He is not going to stop until he's shot dead. He's not going to surrender. He's not going to give up until he leaves this world.'

At 11.00 a.m. a blue Taurus pulled up outside the Korean Methodist Church in Bloomington, Indianapolis. Churchgoers were gathering for the Sunday-morning service, among them a doctoral student, Won-Joon Yoon. A friend, Pyungho Kim, describes what happened after the short drive from his house to the church. 'Won-Joon and I got out of the car and started to walk on the grass. The distance between the kerb and the church is no more than 25 yards, I believe. We walked side by side, but Won-Joon was about half a step behind me. I do not remember what we were talking about, perhaps we were laughing about something. At the mid-point, near a short bush in front of the church, I suddenly heard firecracking sounds.'

Won-Joon fell forward onto his friend, knocking them both onto the ground. At first Pyungho assumed that Won-Joon had simply stepped on a pile of fireworks carelessly left in the churchyard. As he says in his account: 'I sat up saying, "It was a firecracker, Won-Joon." But I saw a couple of bloodstains about the size of a ping-pong ball on the back of his T-shirt. I looked at his back and there was a deep wound just beneath his right shoulder. It looked like something gouged a piece of flesh in the back that I later realised was a bullet hole. It was as big as my mid-finger's nail. Not much blood, not many wounds except that particular one. Up to that point, I still thought that he was overreacting to something that wasn't serious at all.

' "After all, it was a firecracker, Won-Joon." I talked to myself since Won-Joon seemed to me just fainted. Nonetheless, his wound looked so deep and he simply was lying on his face and did not move at all.'

By this point people were crowding out of the church to see what had happened. In the ensuing chaos someone dialled for an ambulance, and police squad cars were arriving at the scene. Someone noted the fleeing car's number plate. It matched Smith's.

Won-Joon was dead.

A warrant was issued for Smith's arrest, and a charge of murder filed in connection with the student's death. The local police were already familiar with Smith; he had previously come to their attention in Bloomington after he had been seen littering residents' drives with racist and anti-Semitic leaflets the previous year.

Later that evening at the Lakeview BP petrol station, just off Interstate Highway 57, a van pulled in for some fuel. The driver, a local man, Mr Miller, was paying for this when the blue Taurus cruised in. While Mr Miller paid for the petrol, his wife Penelope and their daughter remained in the van. The driver of the Taurus had started to fill his car up when suddenly he grabbed his backpack from the rear seat and slid into the driver's seat of the van.

The young man demanded that Mrs Miller and her daughter get out. When they hesitated he pulled a gun. 'Get out. Get the fuck out of the car right now if you want to live to see tomorrow,' he threatened. The woman and her daughter fled and the van sped out onto the street with its side door still open.

Petrol station employee Bryan Prusz watched as the woman came running through the door, screaming hysterically. She was screaming 'Call the cops, call the cops,' he said. He dialled the number and handed the phone over to her. She relayed to the police precisely what had happened and told them that the van was speeding north on Interstate 57. The information about the carjacking was broadcast on the Illinois State Police emergency radio network.

One of the officers responding to the call was Marion County deputy David Hiltibidal. Like most of his colleagues he had no idea who he was chasing other than that he was wanted for murder. He began driving south from Salem on Highway 37. Marion County Sheriff's Detective Todd Garden moved south on Interstate 57. Soon Hiltibidal had spotted the van driving north on Highway 37. He took up pursuit at a distance and radioed his colleagues. Garden headed off Interstate 57 and joined Highway 37.

The small town of Salem, with a population of under 8,000, was hosting a 4 July firework display for around 2,000 people and Smith was heading directly for it. Marion County Sheriff G.L. Benjamin was in his squad car at the display and ordered an unmarked squad car to go and verify at close quarters that the van really was the suspect vehicle.

Soon all three cars were following the van as it neared the south of the small town. The police knew that Smith had to be stopped: there was no way they could risk him getting close to the large crowd at the display. As Detective Garden relates, 'We pretty well made the decision we were going to have to force him off the road before he got up there. Fortunately, he did that for us.'

Smith crashed the van off the road, exploding both the air bags and momentarily stunning himself. Officer Hiltibidal ran to the back of the van while another officer took the passenger side. 'We were basically yelling "Show us your hands. Put your hands up. Show us your hands." We knew there were weapons in the vehicle and we didn't know where they were,' Hiltibidal explained afterwards.

There was no response from Smith, so the officer opened the passenger-side door, at which point Smith reached over to grab his green rucksack. As he moved, the officer saw that Smith was covered in blood. It was wet, glistening all over his body. Fearing that Smith was reaching for a weapon, the officer started grappling with him. 'I pulled the door open on the van and I grabbed his arm. I pinned his hand and I fought with him and I ended up in the back seat,' Hiltibidal continued in his account.

Despite his injuries Smith was still struggling and screaming as the police tried to subdue him. He was spun round between the front seats of the van and pushed into the rear of the vehicle, kicking and screaming all the time. Another Sheriff's officer, Detective Mount, smashed the driver's side window as Smith and Hiltibidal continued to struggle. At that point two muffled shots sounded and it became clear that Smith had a .22 in his right hand.

In the ensuing chaos Todd Garden ran round to the passenger door and, flashing his light into the interior of the car, saw Smith holding the gun. 'What I got in my mind was his face,' he recalled afterwards, 'because I could see his face as he was struggling with Hiltibidal. I could see we had a troubled situation because I could tell we didn't have him yet.' Acting quickly, Garden reached into the van and prised the gun from Smith's hand.

Once he was disarmed, Smith, now bleeding heavily, was cuffed and pulled from the van. The two shots he'd fired had resulted in self-inflicted wounds. Although he was badly injured Smith was still struggling, though he was saying nothing to the officers who'd finally captured him after this three-day spree. Smith was bundled into an ambulance and Garden rode with him, recalling that 'he was still somewhat combative' on the way to the hospital.

Smith died at 10.40 p.m. on Sunday night. The preliminary verdict was that his death was suicide. The van had crashed after Smith had fired a single shot into his mouth, just below the chin. His aim was as good then as it had been for most of his rampage. Rather than blowing his brains out and ending it all, the bullet had missed his brain and lodged in the front of his skull. In the end he'd died of massive blood loss after shooting himself in the chest. It was hardly the blaze of glory that he'd obviously anticipated for himself. Rather than a clean, heroic exit it had taken a number of shots and several emergency resuscitations at the hospital before he finally gave in to the loss of blood.

Smith's one-man race war was over for good.

Even before his botched suicide investigators were discovering who Benjamin Nathaniel Smith really was, and, just as importantly, what it was that had driven him to such desperate action.

Smith's name had come up a number of times in the course of the initial investigation into the attacks on the previous Friday and Saturday. He was known as an active white supremacist, a neo-Nazi activist with a long history of political activity directed against Jews, blacks and other ethnic minorities. A number of his associates had passed his name to the police after being questioned in connection with the attacks. On the other side of the ideological fence, he had been suggested to the police as a potential suspect by 'The Centre for New Community', an anti-racist group. The group's director, the Reverend Dan Ostendorf, had met with the Chicago police on the Friday evening and suggested that Smith might be a strong suspect in the shootings. The group, which monitors extreme right-wing hate groups, was already familiar with Smith's history of far-right activity.

Smith, a 21-year-old student, was a member and supporter of the extremist group known as the 'World Church of the Creator', based in Peoria, Illinois. This group believes in 'Racial Holy War', a battle cry that is taken up by the group's largely skinhead supporters. Smith too had cropped his hair and adopted the skinhead uniform as his own. However, despite the almost caricature proletarian uniform, Smith himself was from a comfortable suburban background. It is commonly believed that neo-Nazism, particularly its distinctively skinhead variant, draws support primarily from disillusioned white working-class youth. However, Smith clearly did not conform to this stereotype.

Smith's father, Kenneth, is a doctor, and his mother, Beverly, a lawyer who deals in real estate. The family, along with Smith's two younger brothers, had moved to Northfield in 1997 from nearby Wilmette, another leafy suburb north of Chicago. The new family home, a comfortable old house in one of the area's wealthier districts, included a swimming pool and a private tennis court. The family home is only three blocks away from the Indian Hill Country Club, one of the most elite and prestigious clubs in the state of Illinois, a place for the upper classes to relax in lush, sumptuous surroundings. It is a world of privilege far removed from the poverty-stricken ghettos and housing projects a few miles away in the city. As Smith later wrote, he came from 'a well-to-do mostly white area.'

And yet this comfortable, luxurious life nevertheless managed to nurture the hatred that festered so violently inside Benjamin Smith.

At high school Smith appears to have been a reasonably bookish student, with an interest in philosophy and Islam. He attended New Trier High School and showed no outward signs of racism. Indeed, he had several Jewish friends at school, including one, Scott Dubin, who described Smith as his best friend after first meeting him when they were both thirteen years old. After Smith's death, Dubin seemed at a loss to explain the change in his former friend. 'I myself am Jewish,' he is quoted as saying. 'He must have really, really changed. He's not the same person.'

This perplexing change was no doubt a gradual one, and an early clue to the anger that was burning inside Smith can be seen in his entry to the school yearbook in 1996. His entry was simply the slogan 'Sic Semper Tyrannis' – 'Thus always to tyrants'. These are said to have been the words declaimed by John Wilkes Booth after assassinating President Abraham Lincoln in 1865. Booth, an actor sympathetic to the Southern cause during the American Civil War, murdered the president before being killed in turn a short while later. His words have become something of a rallying cry for a certain type of American extremist. Timothy McVeigh, the man who killed 168 people when he committed America's worst terrorist outrage – the bombing of the federal building in Oklahoma City in 1995 – is said to have worn a T-shirt bearing the same slogan on the day of the bombing.

Smith himself claimed that his 'racial awakening' started in eighth grade (when he was thirteen or fourteen years old) when his class was studying the Holocaust. Writing a few months before the 4 July spree, he claimed that 'The entire course was made to instil a strong and lasting sense of white guilt.'

After graduation Smith enrolled as a student at the University of Illinois at Urbana-Champaign in the autumn of 1996. By then the sense of anger that he harboured was already evident. Far from being the promising student that everybody expected him to be, he was soon in trouble with the authorities. In the four semesters that he attended at the university he came into contact with the police at least five times. On one of these occasions, in September 1996, soon after Smith started at the university, the police responded to a call about a Peeping Tom at the women's halls of residence. As they arrived to investigate they saw Smith running away. He was stopped and asked for identification, to which he supplied a fake driver's licence in the name of Erwin Rommel, Hitler's famous field marshal.

It is not known whether Smith was guilty or not of peeping, but the possession of the fake ID in the name of a famous Nazi is more than a little indicative that he was already moving steadily towards the extreme right. And if it is true that he was peeping into the female dorm, then it becomes highly significant. A confused or deviant sexuality is a factor that is common among serial killers and many spree killers.

There is more indirect evidence that Smith may have been having problems with his sexuality from his then girlfriend Elizabeth Sahr, also a student at the university. She met Smith during her first year and their relationship continued throughout most of 1997. At first everything seemed fine, and Smith appeared both interesting and charming. However, it did not take long for Sahr to note a change in him. He began to be verbally abusive, and this soon became more physical. 'He was pretty much a textbook abuser,' Sahr explained the day after Smith killed himself. 'At first they're charming as hell and get you to believe that they love you and care for you. Then they turn.'

Eventually Sahr was forced to take out a protection order against Smith for domestic violence. She had had enough of being attacked and beaten up. 'Something clicked and I realised that I had to get away or I would be dead,' she declared later.

It is possible to conjecture that Smith was having some kind of sexual problem, though there is little direct evidence to tell us what form this problem may have taken. However, sexual dysfunction appears to be a trait common to many spree killers, as we have already seen in the case of Thomas Hamilton. Certainly there is no evidence that Smith became involved in any other relationship after he and Elizabeth Sahr split up. If anything, without an emotional relationship his political activities became more important to him and occupied increasing amounts of his time. As Sahr has stated, she was not even aware of the depth of his racist views until towards the end of their relationship. 'He was completely anti-Semitic, completely racist, especially towards Asians, Jews and African-Americans.'

It was at university that Smith began to become more active as a racist. As he explained himself in the newsletter of a racist group: 'What set me into action was when I was forced to live in the dorms. I was from a well-to-do, mostly white area (with significant Jewish infestation). I discovered that the vast majority of black, brown and yellow students were here because the government was paying their way. That bothered me. I felt as if what was once our government had begun to turn against white people.'

Smith began to hand out leaflets and put up posters in the dorm. Inevitably this brought him into conflict with fellow students and with the university authorities. With his relationship with Elizabeth Sahr also in tatters by January 1998, it was almost inevitable that he was going to drop out from university. By the middle of February Smith was informed that disciplinary charges were being drawn up against him and that the university planned to conduct a tribunal to discuss whether to expel him or not. He had been in trouble for fighting, for possession of marijuana, he had come into contact with the police after attacking Elizabeth Sahr, he had been found to be keeping offensive weapons (knives) in his dorm room and the police had linked him to the alleged peeping incident.

The day after being informed of the threat of disciplinary charges Smith's parents telephoned the university to say that their son would not be returning. By now Smith's behaviour was becoming increasingly fanatical and predictably paranoid. His appearance had changed, reflecting the growing extremism of his views. He had shaved his head, adopted the skinhead uniform and had his body tattooed, with the words 'Sabbath Breaker' inscribed permanently across his chest.

When Smith returned home few of his former friends could recognise him. The one-time serious student was now a neo-Nazi intent on recruiting others to his cause. He made contact with Patrick Langballe, a former New Trier High School student a couple of years older than Smith. Langballe was accused in 1997 of spray-painting swastikas on a Northfield synagogue. 'Ben looked Patrick up when Patrick's story hit the news,' recalled Geri Langballe, Patrick's mother.

In the spring of 1998 Smith moved to Indiana, enrolling at the University of Indiana at Bloomington. Soon after starting at the university he came into conflict with the authorities there too. He was caught putting racist leaflets on car windscreens at the university campus. He was called in to talk to Richard McKaig, the university's Dean of Students. Smith was on his best behaviour, however: he remained polite during the discussion in which he defended his right to express his views on campus. McKaig reminded Smith that he had to remain within the rules and regulations governing the university, but agreed that Smith had every right to express his views no matter how abhorrent they were to many others.

At this point there is evidence to suggest that the racist literature that Smith was distributing was from the American White Nationalist Party. This group was formed in the early 1970s and never achieved much in the way of membership: it is now part of the much larger National Alliance. This group is led by William Pierce, author of the notorious *Turner Diaries* which prefigured many of the most violent activities of America's white supremacists, including the Oklahoma City bombing.

Smith had also started calling himself 'August Smith', deciding that his first name – Benjamin – sounded too Jewish. He continued to campaign within the university, but he made sure that he did not stray outside its rules. There is no doubt that the paranoid world-view that extreme beliefs such as his foster only added to his already inflamed sense of grievance. His near-expulsion from the University of Illinois had nothing to do with his trouble with the police, his violence against his girlfriend and fellow students, nothing to do with allegations of drug use or of peeping at female students and, in his own mind at least, had everything to do with a conspiracy against the white race.

Smith stepped up his activities, leafleting away from the university in the town of Bloomington. He took to writing letters to University newspapers and local papers in the town, always signing himself 'August Smith'. He liked to pretend that he was part of a larger group of white supremacists active in the area but there is little evidence to support this, and it is clear that for much of the time Smith worked alone. He was an isolated, lonely figure, but that seemed to make no difference to him. As far as he was concerned he was engaged in a battle for the survival of the white race.

'I think it is pretty clear that our government has turned against white people,' Smith wrote in July 1998 in the university's student newspaper. 'Our people,' he concluded, 'the Great White Race, are slaves to a deceitful, alien government, a controlled media, and a suicidal religion.'

At the time Smith was living in an apartment complex called Touchdown Terrace, where most of the resident students were either black or Asian. Most of his neighbours were from ethnic minorities but he kept a low profile and few of them knew that he was an avowed white supremacist. One neighbour, black student Tyrese Alexander, described Smith as being unfriendly but not threatening. On a few occasions Alexander had tried to start conversations with Smith but was ignored. 'He wasn't an intimidating guy,' Alexander said. 'He didn't give off a demeanour that he was prone to violence. He just seemed to dislike people.'

Smith's activities in Bloomington inevitably caused a reaction among anti-racists. Before Smith arrived there was little overt racist activity in the town, so his arrival and the sudden upsurge in racist propaganda caused groups to form to oppose him. In November 1998 anti-racists organised a march through the town to show their opposition to racism and racist propaganda. Many hundreds of residents took to the streets and, as they neared the town's main street, they were faced with a lone protester. Benjamin Nathaniel Smith, flanked by police, cut a pathetically isolated little figure as he held up a placard that read 'No hate speech means no free speech'.

One of the organisers of the march, Jeffrey Willsey, recalls: 'Here we are as a community coming together, and here's this poor guy standing out there all by himself, entirely alone.' Willsey said, 'I thought, this is a really pathetic human being.'

While most of the anti-racist activity was peaceful there were incidents where Smith was physically confronted and on a number of occasions his apartment was attacked and vandalised. Far from making him stop and think, these actions only spurred him on. Opposition fuelled Smith's sense of destiny and fed his rampant paranoia. To stand alone against five hundred people, to represent, in his own eyes, the last hope of the white race in the face of an anti-white conspiracy, would have evoked a delicious feeling of martyrdom to complement his paranoia.

Eventually Smith was asked to leave Touchdown Terrace, not because of complaints by his black, Asian and Hispanic neighbours but because of the vandalism that his presence encouraged. For the most part it was clear that his neighbours saw him not as a threat but as weird, socially inadequate but essentially harmless. 'He really didn't have an intimidating presence,' one of his neighbours was later quoted as saying. 'We just thought he was weird and left it at that.'

However, the fact that Smith was asked to leave would have added to the growing sense of grievance that he felt. Like many spree killers, he seemed not to have been able to accept responsibility for his actions. Expulsion from Illinois University, marches to oppose him, smashed windows in his apartment, all of this would have been seen as injustices wreaked upon him by a malevolent society out to destroy him and the white race.

By this time Smith was also clearly involved with one particular extremist sect, the Illinois-based World Church of the Creator. This group, which preaches Racial Holy War (RaHoWa), had long been considered one of the most rabid and extreme groups on the American far right. Formed by neo-Nazi Ben Klassen in the early 1970s, the group combines Hitler-worship and National Socialist ideology with a virulent anti-Christianity. 'Creativity' is a pseudo-religion in which the 'white race' has been elevated to an abstract object of worship.

Like many groups on the far right, the sect has delusions of grandeur and awards its supporters and members grandiose titles in an effort to build esteem and bind the group together. Members are called 'Creators', the Christian calendar is rejected and years are no longer reckoned as AD but as AC (After Creativity), and the group is led by a Pontifus Maximus (Supreme Leader). Matt Hale, a would-be lawyer, is the current Pontifus Maximus of 'Creativity', though as Creativity is a religion rather than a political party Hale also styles himself a Reverend. It should be noted that in the United States religious organisations enjoy certain tax advantages compared to political organisations. The WCOTC even has charitable status, though how any organisation that preaches racial war and declares that non-whites are 'mud people' can be described as charitable is open to question.

Smith was a member of the WCOTC by May or June 1998, and was heavily involved in distributing fliers, plastering swastika-laden stickers and posters on walls and so on. He liked to pretend that he was working as part of a group and used various aliases and phoney names to this end. In any event he was tireless in the cause and he distributed many thousands of the WCOTC's leaflets and newspapers. In July 1998, a year before he went on the rampage, he was confronted by two of the residents of Bloomington who dialled one of the false names attached to the posters.

On being contacted by Russ Bridenbaugh and Mike Leonard, Smith denied putting up the posters. 'I haven't put out anything in Bloomington since I received a letter from the city's legal department, threatening me with a $100-a-day fine for every day I distribute materials,' Smith told them. On being questioned about the swastikas Smith moved onto the defensive. 'There's been too much propaganda associated with the swastika,' Smith had said. 'We're not a National Socialism organisation, we believe in racial socialism.'

Smith remained calm during the discussion. He did not become aggressive nor did he give any indication of impulsive or violent behaviour. However, despite his temperate tone of voice there was nothing temperate about his views. Echoing Creativity propaganda he dismissed non-white races as 'mud people' and took exception when compared to the Ku Klux Klan. The Klan, he explained, was a Christian organisation while Creativity was determinedly anti-Christian. 'We believe that Christianity is a suicidal religion,' Smith said, quoting Creativity dogma word for word. 'We reject Christ's Sermon on the Mount. If someone tries to take your cloak you should give them your hat and your cloak too?

'We really think the final struggle is coming and we have to reject those ideas that have no place in the real world,' Smith had concluded.

It took another year before these words were put into action.

Smith's ceaseless activism earned him a degree of notoriety in the media. It also earned him the thanks of Matt Hale and his so-called Church. In January 1999 Hale awarded Smith the grand title of 'Creator of the Year' for all of his propaganda efforts. This award only served to spur Smith on. It is clear that the two men had built up a good relationship, with Smith a faithful follower of his 'Supreme Leader'.

In April 1999 Hale was up before the Illinois Board of Admissions to the Bar in an attempt to get a licence to practice law. Hale, who had studied law at the University of Illinois, decided to call on Smith to act as a character witness at the hearing. Smith, who under Hale's influence had switched from English to Law as his major subject at the University of

Indiana, came to the hearing well prepared. He had let his hair grow and had covered up his tattoos with a sober blue suit and tie. During the meeting Smith described Hale as the 'most principled man I have ever met'. Although they had only met face to face a handful of times he said that they spoke at least once a week. As an example of the good counsel of the 'Reverend', Smith is quoted as admitting that he had 'considered violent acts to achieve racial goals, but Hale counselled me to act peacefully'.

Again, however, this temperate tone was at odds with his words. 'We're in a life-and-death struggle for our people,' he stated.

That same month Smith was arrested in the Chicago suburb of Wilmette, where he had been born and brought up. This time the police charged him with littering after he and another racist left hundreds of leaflets on lawns and driveways.

In June Smith appeared at the Cook County Circuit Courthouse, where he argued that his activities were protected by the First Amendment. 'They're saying we can't put out this literature,' he was quoted in the press. 'Well, the Constitution says we can.' The case was adjourned and was still pending in July.

In early June Smith applied for and received an Illinois State Firearms ID card, a prerequisite for anybody in that state wanting to purchase a gun. The fact that Elizabeth Sahr had filed a protection order against him should have disqualified him, but the order had been issued against Benjamin *August* Smith and in his application for the ID he had reverted to his real name. So he slipped through and the ID was duly issued to him on 18 June.

Smith followed up a week later, on 23 June, by attempting to buy three weapons from a gun shop in Peoria Heights. He tried to buy two Smith & Wesson 9mm handguns and a twelve-gauge shotgun from Tony Schneider of the Heights Gun and Hunter Supply store. A computer background check on would-be gun purchasers is carried out in the state of Illinois as a matter of routine and in this case it picked up the protection order against Smith for domestic violence. When he returned to the store on 24 June he was told that his application had been turned down.

Smith's reaction was extremely controlled. Yet again he showed no signs of anger or agitation. 'He seemed perfectly normal,' Schneider said. 'He said he was going to check it out and see why he was denied.'

It also meant that the state authorities were informed that Smith had attempted to purchase guns, and it would lead to the withdrawal of the firearms ID by 30 June. By then Smith had already taken an alternative course of action; his calm demeanour masked a clear determination to succeed.

Two days after his application was turned down Smith approached an unlicensed gun dealer in the town of Pekin in central Illinois. Donald R. Fiessinger advertised in the classified sections of local newspapers, selling guns that he had purchased legally to those without permits and thus securing himself a high level of profit. On 26 June Smith arrived at Fiessinger's apartment where he examined the weapons in the man's huge arsenal of handguns and rifles. Smith decided to go for a Bryco .380-calibre semi-automatic handgun. He returned to Fiessinger's apartment again on 29 June, this time to purchase a .22-calibre Ruger semi-automatic pistol. These were the weapons with which he murdered two and injured many others later that same week.

On 1 July agents from the Bureau of Alcohol, Tobacco and Firearms (ATF) raided Fiessinger's apartment. They had instigated an investigation into his gun dealing on 21 June and had dispatched undercover operatives to buy guns from him. In the 1 July raid that followed the agents recovered 27 assorted firearms, $330 in cash and receipts of numerous small-arms sales, including a record of the sale of the two guns to Smith. The paperwork was still being processed at the end of that week.

The next day, Friday, 2 July 1999, was also decision day for the Illinois Board of Admissions in considering Matt Hale's application to the Bar. The Pontifus Maximus of Creativity clearly wanted to gain admission to the Bar so that he could use his position to defend white supremacists and neo-Nazis. The Board decided against granting him a licence to practise law in the state of Illinois. They had decided that Hale's extreme views meant that he failed the Bar's 'character and fitness' requirements. Clearly Smith's character witness had not been enough to sway the Board.

Smith moved from violence in rhetoric to violence in action on the day that Matt Hale was refused a licence. The timing could not have been more appropriate in the view of Smith and those like him. In their opinion Hale had been turned down by the Jewish establishment out to destroy the white race in general and Matt Hale and his followers in particular. That Hale had been turned down on the eve of the 4 July weekend was, to them, deeply symbolic.

The Fourth of July, Independence Day, has an almost mythical status in the eyes of many patriotic Americans and in the minds of Smith's comrades on the far right it resonated with as much power and symbolism as Christmas and Easter do for many committed Christians. For those on the far right, from the Ku Klux Klan to the militia movement to neo-Nazi sects like the WCOTC, it marks the founding of a racially segregated, slave-owning federation of states with little or no central government and a constitutional right to bear arms. For them the current Unites States is an abomination, a betrayal of everything that the founding fathers fought for. In Smith's own words: 'America has become increasingly non-white and the constitutional rights of racial activists have increasingly been infringed upon.'

As Elizabeth Sahr told reporters at the time: 'This is his Independence Day from the government, from everything . . . He is not going to stop until he's shot dead. He's not going to surrender. He's not going to give up until he leaves this world.'

Sahr was right, of course. The day after Smith killed himself the FBI raided his last known address, an apartment in Morton, Illinois, only six miles east of Peoria, the head-quarters of Matt Hale and the World Church of the Creator. The apartment was almost bare, with no bed and no furniture, and was stacked high with WCOTC literature, flags and office equipment. At first the police were not even sure that Smith had been living in the place: it looked more like an office or a warehouse for hate literature. Matt Hale later confirmed that Smith had indeed been living in the apartment. A search also unearthed receipts for the ammunition that he had used in his rampage.

Even before Smith had killed himself the police and press were onto Matt Hale and his cultish 'Church'. Conveniently, Hale claimed that Smith had in fact stopped paying his membership dues in April or May and was therefore technically no longer a member. This did not mean that Hale condemned Smith's actions. Smith was a 'martyr for free speech', he declared. 'He is a pleasant person who believes in his people, the white people, I can't say anything bad about him,' he added.

Hale was also quick to link the attacks to the decision not to grant him a licence to practise law. 'I think it was more of a spontaneous act of rage at what he believed was persecution of me, of our church, and of our ideas . . . Why? Because of the timing involved and because I know he was very passionate about me getting my law licence.'

Did Hale accept any responsibility for Smith's actions? 'Just as the pope in Rome isn't responsible for some wacko who plants a bomb at an abortion clinic,' he stated to the press, 'our church and myself can't be responsible for what anyone does with our policy. We state we're completely legal, non-violent and peaceful.'

His choice of words was deliberately careful. He did not condemn Smith but was careful not to explicitly condone his actions. He did not claim that 'we are non-violent and peaceful'. He said, '*we state* that we are non-violent'. His training as a lawyer was evident in all of his activities, and he was careful never to stray from the confines of the law.

Did Hale have any inkling of what Smith was going to do? He and Smith had last met a few days before the weekend of violence. 'When I spoke to him he never gave any inkling of being able to do this,' Hale said. 'If I had had any inkling of this, I would have, of course, taken him aside and said, "Ben, brother, this isn't the way. We need you free, we need you alive, we need you amongst the public to pass the word, to spread the message of truly the greatest idea the world has ever known, and that is our religion, Creativity." '

Conveniently, it emerged later that Smith had also written a letter, on the day on which he had embarked on his violence, in which he distanced himself from Hale and the WCOTC. The letter, addressed to Hale, arrived the day after Smith's death. The letter was sent by registered mail which meant that the dates on which it was sent and received were fully logged, proving that it was sent prior to Smith's acts of violence. That Smith was so considerate as to send such a letter in such a fashion made matters doubly convenient for Matt Hale when it came to absolving himself of responsibility for Smith's actions. 'Although I have not been a member of the World Church of the Creator since April 1999,' Smith wrote, 'due to my past public support of that legal religious organisation run by Matt Hale, I find it necessary to formerly [sic] break with the World Church of the Creator because I'm unable and unwilling to follow a legal revolution of values.'

Did Hale feel any sympathy for Smith's victims and their families? There were no expressions of sympathy, only denials of direct responsibility, denial of foreknowledge and praise for Smith as a martyr and as a loyal and effective 'brother Creator'. In the eyes of Hale and his followers the victims are 'mud people', members of inferior races not worthy of respect. When Smith's parents released a statement condemning racism, Hale's reaction was swift and to the point: 'If they don't believe it's worthwhile to keep the white race white, then I do believe that their views are as misguided or wrong as perhaps they thought Ben's were.'

The police conclusion at an early stage was that Smith had acted alone. There was no evidence that he worked with an accomplice. There was no direct evidence that he had worked on the orders of Hale or anyone else. The supplier of the guns, Donald Fiessinger, was investigated and it was shown that he had no links with any political organisations. He traded guns for money, not for ideology.

The controversy over the activities of Matt Hale and his fellow neo-Nazis continues. There were many who blamed the Internet or American gun culture for the sudden explosion of violence. But although the far right makes effective use of the Internet, it did not turn Smith into a killer. While the easy availability of guns is a problem in America, countries such as

Great Britain where the control of firearms is extremely strict are not immune from similar explosions of rage and violence.

Why did Smith turn into a racist in the first place? What was it that turned a privileged young man, an able student with an interest in philosophy and history, into a neo-Nazi skinhead and follower of an almost laughably extreme movement like the WCOTC?

In Smith's case it appears that there was a conjunction of racist feeling, clearly allied to some unknown grievance, with a personality prone to paranoia and feelings of persecution. It is possible to link this in some way with feelings of sexual confusion or inadequacy. In the words of Mark Hamm, professor of criminology at Indiana University and an acknowledged expert on the phenomenon of right-wing extremism: 'It begins with a grievance. They see themselves as being the victim of some sort of social injustice perpetuated by minorities or by a government who supports the advancement of minorities to the exclusion of whites. As wrong-headed as it may sound, within their separate reality, that makes sense.'

However, Smith came from a wealthy background and so if there was some kind of grievance it is unlikely to have been grounded in the harsh economics that make some working-class people receptive to fascist propaganda. Whatever the grievance, and we shall never know for sure what it was, there were other factors at work as well.

'The more you get to know these people, you begin to detect a pattern,' Hamm continues. 'There's something psychologically amiss. They have deep-seated conflicts going on over their identity, over their sexuality.'

Was this the case with Smith? The evidence is slender but not missing altogether. The violence against Sahr and the accusations of peeping through windows are both indications that sexual confusion may have been a factor.

Susan Sontag has written about 'fascinating fascism', and there is little doubt that for some people fascism and sexuality are inextricably linked. For some this is kept purely at the level of theatre: the uniforms of fascism, whether it be the black boots and leather of the SS or the functional uniform of the male skinhead, become fetishised. They are used as a turn-on, and the peaked cap of the SS or the Doc Marten boots of the skinhead become emblematic, signifying sexual power roles in sadomasochistic sex play. In most such cases there is a clear separation between sexuality and politics – adoption of a fascist uniform for sexual purposes does not mean an identification with or support of fascist or racist ideas and policies. The homoerotic aspects of skinhead culture, for example, are well attested and there is a significant gay skinhead subculture.

For others, however, the sexual aspect becomes entwined with the political. On the gay skinhead scene there are some real fascists and racists present. Some of them, like the members and supporters of the Gay Nazi Front, are 'out' about their sexuality and their politics. They see no contradiction between supporting Nazism, which killed thousands of gays in concentration camps, and their sexuality. It should also be noted that there have been numerous cases where leading Nazi activists have been gay. Just as importantly, there are numerous 'closet' gays in the Nazi skinhead scene. They either refuse to acknowledge their sexuality to others for fear of attack, or else they refuse to acknowledge their own feelings to themselves. In time some gay Nazi skinheads, like the leading British Nazi Nicky Crane who was active during the 1980s, eventually accept their sexuality, but not before taking part in anti-gay activities and propagating viciously anti-gay (and anti-Semitic and racist) ideas.

Once Smith was involved in the Nazi scene there was a hardening of his attitudes and beliefs. His devotion to Matt Hale, a relatively young man only a dozen or so years older than Smith, was undoubted. His fanaticism was well established. Former members of the WCOTC spoke of Smith's wish for 'martyrdom'. To die in the cause of the white race was an ideal that was not abhorrent, not to Smith, not to Hale, not to many on the extreme right. Smith's acts were essentially suicidal, though in his case having missed so many other targets during his spree he almost fumbled his own death too. His hatred of 'niggers', Jews and 'mud people' was deeply ingrained. In his eyes non-whites were subhuman, and shooting them was equivalent to shooting vermin.

Still the question remains: what drove Smith to commit his crimes? Was it purely a spontaneous reaction to Hale's failure to get a law licence? Was it a pre-planned act carried out at the behest of the WCOTC? Or was it an acknowledgement that for all of his propaganda efforts he was getting nowhere? For all the months of leafleting in Bloomington there is no evidence that he managed to recruit a single other person to his group. Elizabeth Sahr points out: 'The things he was doing were not working – distributing pamphlets and things . . . He wanted to make a name for himself, to show people that this could be done if you wanted to do it.'

With Smith dead we shall never know for sure what finally triggered his killing spree. However, the fact that he found the time and the head-space to write to Matt Hale formally distancing himself from the WCOTC before going into action suggests that it was not a sudden, random, spontaneous act. It was a calculated act of war and aggression. An expression of racial hatred. The logical outcome of Smith's neo-Nazi beliefs.

MARK ORRIS BARTON

Atlanta, USA, 1999

Electronic day trading is part of the brave new world of Internet e-commerce, allowing amateur investors to tap into the same stocks-and-shares trading systems as the large finance houses and stockbrokers. It cuts out the middleman and allows individuals to deal direct, to move money from fund to fund, stock to stock, buying and selling at will. It's the promise of instantaneous communications writ large and applied directly to the lifeblood of the world's financial community. It is the way of the future but, in the case of Mark Barton and his victims, that future is stopped dead in its tracks.

Electronic day trading is closer to gambling than to anything else. The day traders depend on minute shifts in share prices to grab a profit when they can. This is not about long-term investment. It isn't even about medium-term investment. It is purely about the here and now, the instant buck, grabbed in the split second when a share price shifts up or down a notch. Electronic day traders depend on small gaps in the market. They buy big at one price and then wait for the share to go up by a fraction of a percentage point and then sell fast. The profits on an individual deal might be small, but spread over an intensive eight- or nine-hour day in front of the monitor the profits could, conceivably, be massive.

To say it is a risky business is an understatement: not only are the markets extremely volatile, it only takes one or two bad deals for a day trader to lose all of his or her capital. And with no capital the game is over. Like gambling, day trading is dangerous and addictive, the promise of large rewards attracting new converts all the time. Where large investment houses have the capital to sit it out and to ride the fluctuations of the market, day trading has attracted a core of small investors who have no such cushion. For them day trading is like doing the high wire without a safety net to save them should they stumble. Day traders include students gambling their loans, pensioners betting their homes and their pensions and, in the case of Mark Barton, professionals giving up their jobs in order to risk everything on the ebb and flow of the stock market.

Mark Orris Barton was born in 1955, in Sumter, South Carolina, a small town east of the state capital of Columbia and known primarily as the home of the massive Shaw Air Force Base. Barton attended Sumter High School from which he graduated in 1977, though he seemed to have left no lasting impression among his fellow students. Even his name was spelled incorrectly in the graduation yearbook in which his photograph was missing and there were few school achievements listed. This quiet, rather nondescript student then attended the University of South Carolina in Columbia. He studied chemistry and gained a degree in the subject on graduating in 1979, though again he seems to have made no impression on fellow students or even with his professors, none of whom claimed to remember him.

He was also an active churchgoer: he is remembered by a fellow Methodist, Cindy Haley, as 'highly intelligent, much, much more intelligent than most people'. Despite this intelligence he seems to have been a rather isolated, lonely figure. 'He was very quiet, kind of a loner,' Haley added. 'I don't remember him having many friends.'

The Church and his family were central to Barton's life, and by the early 1990s he was married to Debra Spivey. They had two children, Matthew, the eldest, and his younger sister Elizabeth Mychelle. From the outside they were a happy Christian family, normal in every way. From the inside things were very different. Mark Barton was already having an affair with Leigh Ann Vandiver, almost ten years younger than his 36-year-old wife, and, like Barton, married and an active churchgoer.

In July or August 1993 Barton took out an insurance policy on his wife's life with Investors Life Insurance Co. of Nebraska. This policy, worth several hundred thousand dollars, was in addition to a $100,000 policy that he had taken on her life in 1986.

A few weeks later, Debra and her mother, Eloise Spivey, went out to spend the Labour Day weekend (the first weekend in September) at Lake Weiss, Alabama, while Barton stayed at home to look after the two children. When the bodies of the two women were found hacked to death, suspicion immediately fell on Barton. When investigators discovered that not only was he having an affair but that he had been boasting to work colleagues that he and his girlfriend Leigh Ann would be together by October those suspicions were confirmed. However, the investigation into the murder of Barton's wife and mother-in-law were beset by jurisdictional difficulties due to the interstate nature of the crime. The murders occurred in Alabama while Barton was living in Georgia.

There was no evidence of forced entry into the camper van where the women's bodies were found, and nor was there much evidence of robbery: the place had been trashed and purses scattered around but cash and jewellery had not been taken. It was clear to investigators that the victims had let the murderer into the van, so it was obviously somebody that they knew and trusted. The scene had been left looking like a botched robbery, but clearly robbery had not been the motive. It was murder, pure and simple. Furthermore, Debra Barton's injuries were much more severe than her mother's. She had been hacked to pieces with a hatchet. In the words of one of the investigators, 'all the anger was directed towards the wife'.

From the beginning all those involved in the murder investigation were convinced that Barton was the killer: there was no other real suspect. When somebody did attempt to confess to the horrific crime the confession was easily shown to be false, the work of a crank who liked to admit to murders he hadn't committed. Barton, however, strenuously protested his innocence. He had been at home looking after his children. How could he have travelled across the state from Georgia into Alabama, murdered the women and then made it back home without disturbing the children? Under repeated and strenuous questioning Barton stuck to his story.

Richard Igou, District Attorney for Cherokee County, Alabama remembered the case well. 'I was in the room when

Mr Mark Barton was questioned,' he said. 'They worked for quite a while investigating and never could prove it was him, but they always felt like it was.' As far as the homicide team in Alabama was concerned there was simply not enough evidence even to attempt a prosecution. All they had was motive and circumstantial evidence.

This view was strongly disputed by Captain Jerry Wynn who headed the Georgia side of the investigation. He claimed that one witness had spotted someone who matched Barton's description at the camp. This witness was never called upon to pick Barton out of a police line-up. The Alabama police, in contrast, contend that there were over five hundred people at the camp and that such precise identification was not possible: it would have been easy for the murderer to slip in and out unnoticed.

The Alabama police seized Barton's car in a quest for evidence. Amazingly, they decided to retain only the floor mats and allowed Barton to keep the car so long as he promised not to clean it. Wynn was furious. 'I thought that was outrageous,' he said.

Wynn insisted on bringing in a Georgia State Police crime-scene expert who tested Barton's car and house for blood. He found that the gas and brake pedals had recently been thoroughly cleaned with an industrial solvent. Still the car was tested with Luminol, the same substance that the LA police had used to test O.J. Simpson's car for blood after the murder of Nicole Simpson.

As Sam House, a retired Georgia Bureau of Investigation agent, told CNN, several spots tested positive for blood: the steering wheel, the console, the gearshift lever knob and the top corner of the driver's door. Further tests found blood on the floor of Barton's garage where the car had been parked, on the kitchen wall and in a sink near the kitchen. 'All that suggested he had blood on his hands,' House said. However, the minute quantities meant that there were not enough of the samples to undertake DNA testing, nor were further samples taken.

On being questioned about the blood, Barton claimed that his wife had cut herself with a kitchen knife at home, and that the blood in the car was his, the result of picking spots on his leg until they bled. Later it transpired that Barton had also put in a call to the manufacturers of Luminol to discover the chemical properties of it. Given his training as a chemist this kind of information would have been more useful to him than to a layperson.

Despite Barton's assertion to the contrary, police were convinced that he *could* have slipped out of the house, driven the hundred miles to the camp site, committed the murders and still got back home in time for when the children would wake up. Without further blood or DNA analysis the investigation was stymied. With no hard physical evidence, the case rested purely on circumstantial details. The Alabama authorities decided they could not successfully prosecute the case.

Cherokee County District Attorney Danny Smith was quoted by the Associated Press as saying: 'We knew morally that he had done it, but we could not prove it legally.'

Jerry Wynn was furious with this attitude. He was – and remains – convinced that Barton was guilty and that the case should have gone to trial. On several occasions, Wynn, who coincidentally had gone to school with Debra Barton, confronted Barton directly. 'I looked him in the eye and told him at least six times that Mark, you killed your wife, you killed your mother-in-law and just, you know, if you say that to someone that's not guilty, you get a response of anger. He didn't react. He listened. He was listening when he should have been angry at me. If I accuse you of doing something like that and you haven't done it you should be mourning. You should be upset. He wasn't upset at all.'

This icy calm was not about to be put to the test, however. Barton repeatedly refused to undergo a polygraph lie-detector test. In desperation the Alabama police called in the FBI and assigned a psychological profiler to the case. Peter Smerick viewed the crime scene, went through the case notes and built up a composite picture of a type of man who would commit murder in order to profit financially. Barton fitted the profile completely. 'I was convinced that he was responsible for the death of his wife and mother-in-law,' Smerick recalls. But matching a psychological profile did not constitute proof: it merely confirmed what everybody already suspected but could not prove.

The insurance companies were also convinced that Barton had committed premeditated murder. They refused to pay up for almost two years, but in the end they came to a settlement and Barton received over $450,000, part of it paid into a trust fund for the children. Eventually the first insurance company, Primerica, also paid out on the $100,000 policy on Debra Barton's life.

To many people at the time it seemed that Barton had got away with not one but two murders. For Bill Spivey, Eloise's husband and Debra's father, the grief of losing his wife and his daughter simultaneously was compounded when Barton refused to let him see the children.

Leigh Ann Vandiver lost no time in moving in with Barton and, much to Bill Spivey's disgust, even attended Debra's funeral with Barton. Wynn tried to warn Vandiver's parents that Barton was dangerous. 'Get your daughter away from him,' he told her mother, 'he'll hurt her.' It did no good. Leigh Ann was so deeply involved with Barton that nothing could shake her faith in him – not even the allegations of sexual abuse that came out of the blue several months after the murder.

Barton's daughter, Mychelle, only two and a half years old at the time, complained to a day-care worker that she had been fondled or molested by her father. An investigation was launched immediately and father and children were extensively interviewed by a psychologist. When dealing with such a small child gaining any kind of actionable evidence is difficult unless there is direct physical trauma. In Mychelle's case there was no such evidence, and so the conclusion, yet again, was that there was not enough proof to instigate a successful prosecution or, in this instance, to remove the child from the family.

In carrying out these interviews the psychologist formed a very clear picture of Barton. As reported to District Attorney David McDade, the impression was that Barton was 'certainly capable of having committed the murders and certainly capable of homicidal thoughts and acts.'

The pressure was coming down on Barton, and at the time he felt certain that he was going to be arrested at any time. He even told relatives that he expected to die soon. Investigators hoped that he was making veiled threats of suicide, and certainly some of them are on record as saying that they wished they'd piled on the pressure even more so that he would have felt forced to turn a gun on himself.

Despite Leigh Ann's attachment to Barton, there were doubts in her family about the wisdom of what she was doing. Barton was rightly viewed with suspicion and the relationship with his new wife's family was never a very warm one. This can only have added to the pressures he was under, and it would have exacerbated the feelings of paranoia that he was by now experiencing.

By October 1998 the five-year-old marriage was already under strain. Barton was jobless and had started day trading, though it is unclear whether or not the trading preceded the loss of his job. In October Leigh Ann, fearing for her own safety, left him and the children. According to Leigh Ann's sister, Dana Reeves, Leigh Ann had become frustrated at having had to support the family for more than a year and after frequent arguments with Barton she had moved out.

Why would Leigh Ann fear for her life? If she was as convinced of Barton's innocence as she pretended to be then there should have been no fear at all. Leigh Ann's ex-husband, David Lang, was convinced that she knew more than she would admit. 'I always believed that Leigh Ann had some suspicions or that she had known about it or she knew something about it, but just never said for fear of whatever would happen to her,' Lang has said. Perhaps it is no coincidence that at the time of the original investigation into the murders Barton had done his best to block all police access to Leigh Ann.

Dana Reeves, on the other hand, is convinced that Leigh Ann knew nothing of the murders of Debra and her mother. It is possible that Leigh Ann only became aware of the truth as she saw other sides of Barton's personality. He was capable of presenting himself in an extremely positive light. To the outside world he was the very picture of suburban normality.

In fact one neighbour, Sabrina Stowers, went so far as to describe Barton as 'a great guy. He was a great father. He was the kind of man that I would want for a role model for my son.' The picture of the contented, happy family man was a façade, a cover for the real Mark Barton: capable of murder, accused of sexually abusing his daughter and clearly an extremely manipulative personality. In the words of Captain Wynn again: 'He's a very controlling, very smart person.'

Whatever the reason, Leigh Ann was definitely afraid of Barton by the time she left him. She moved into her own apartment, complete with a security system that made her feel safer. When her sister asked directly whether Barton had been physically abusive Leigh Ann's answers were always evasive.

By this time Barton was trading full time. He had hired a terminal and high-speed link from one of the day-trading firms, who also took a commission on every deal. Many of these firms, according to a report published by the North American Securities Administrators' Association in August 1999, seriously overstate the success of their day-trading clients. In fact, their report showed that only around 11.5% of these clients actually deal at a profit. Like the vast majority of day traders, Mark Barton was losing money heavily.

By Christmas 1998 Barton had lost around $300,000 on trades that had gone wrong. It was money that had come not just from his own accounts but also from the trust funds set up in the names of his children. This was the money that their mother had died for. Leigh Ann was furious at these massive losses and her anger added to the strain on the already shaky marriage. Barton was often in tears or hysterical, but he could not stop his day-trading activities. The hours spent in front of the computer screen, the tension and the excitement of watching the market move one way or the other had become addictive. Barton was locked in and his only hope was to recoup the losses by gambling again and again.

With his own sources of capital dwindling, Barton started to borrow money from fellow traders and from the dealing firms. His losses continued to mount and All-Tech Investment Group, through whom he dealt, suspended his trading rights in April 1999. By that time his losses amounted to more than

$400,000. This did not deter him, and he switched to trading through Momentum Securities Inc., a firm across the street from All-Tech in the fashionable Buckhead financial district of Atlanta. He opened an account with Momentum on 13 May, stating that he had assets of $750,000, including $250,000 in cash. Doubt has to be cast over these figures, and it is probable that Barton was exaggerating his net worth in order to open the account so he could continue to trade. What is not in doubt is the scale of his gambling: his initial transaction with Momentum was for $100,000.

By early July Barton had persuaded Leigh Ann to take him back. According to her sister, Leigh Ann had become deeply attached to Barton's children. She missed them and felt that she wanted to stay with them, to be part of their lives. Besides, Barton's financial problems meant that he was going to be evicted from his house and Leigh Ann could not bear to see the family without a home. Despite her earlier fears and misgivings Barton and the children were allowed to move into her apartment in Stockbridge.

It was possible that Barton had also convinced Leigh Ann that he would cease day trading, but if this was so then he was definitely not true to his word. He continued to play the markets and play them badly. His losses were growing and without the capital to cover them his debts were growing too. According to James Lee, president of Momentum, 'From our very preliminary review of our records, it appears that he traded at our Atlanta office on a total of 15 days in the period June 9, 1999 through July 27, 1999. His trading resulted in an approximate $105,000 loss.'

The strain of such losses would be hard for anyone to take but in the case of Mark Barton the strain was simply too much. After losing $20,000 in the last few days of July Barton crossed the line.

On 26 July 1999 Barton visited his attorney's office and changed his will. He had decided to leave everything to his two children rather than to his estranged wife.

The next day, Tuesday 27 July, while Leigh Ann slept beside him, Barton smashed her head in with a hammer. Then, to make sure she was dead, he placed her body in the bath to drown out any signs of life. While the children still slept soundly in their beds he then wrapped the body in a blanket and carefully concealed it in a cupboard.

The next morning Barton made excuses for Leigh Ann's absence and sent the children to school. When they returned he made still more excuses. He then killed his children in the same way that he had murdered his wife: he beat them to death with a hammer, then placed them face down in the bath to make sure they were not breathing.

Matthew, aged eleven, was laid out carefully on his bed, his body wrapped in blankets and towels so that just the face was visible. A Gameboy was placed on the body, like a final parting gift. Next to the strangely serene body Barton left a hand-written note: 'I give you Matthew David Barton, my son, my buddy, my life. Please take care of him.'

Mychelle, aged seven, was laid out on her bed in the same manner, ritualistically surrounded by her toys, in the way that serial killers sometimes leave totems with the bodies of their victims. Again a handwritten note was left beside the body: 'I give you Mychelle Elizabeth Barton. My daughter, my sweetheart, my life. Please take care of her.'

Finally, Barton tidied up Leigh Ann's body in the master closet of the bedroom. Her note simply read: 'I give you my wife Leigh Ann Vandiver Barton, my honey, my precious love. Please take care of her. I will love her forever.'

With all the bodies arranged, the mess cleaned up and the signs of trauma obscured with blankets and towels, Barton switched on his computer in order to compose a note to explain his actions to the rest of the world. The note, printed out on clean white paper, was left in the living room ready to be discovered by the police.

The letter was later read out to the press by an officer from the Atlanta police, the text published the world over:

July 29, 1999, 6.38 a.m.
To Whom It May Concern:
Leigh Ann is in the master bedroom closet under a blanket.
I killed her on Tuesday night. I killed Matthew and Mychelle
Wednesday night.

There may be similarities between these deaths and the death of my first wife, Debra Spivey. However, I deny killing her and her mother. There's no reason for me to lie now. It just seemed like a quiet way to kill and a relatively painless way to die.

There was little pain. All of them were dead in less than five minutes. I hit them with a hammer in their sleep and then put them face down in a bathtub to make sure they did not wake up in pain. To make sure they were dead. I am so sorry. I wish I didn't. Words cannot tell the agony. Why did I?

I have been dying since October. I wake up at night so afraid, so terrified that I couldn't be that afraid while awake. It has taken its toll. I have come to hate this life and this system of things. I have come to have no hope.

I killed the children to exchange them for five minutes of pain for a lifetime of pain. I forced myself to do it to keep them from suffering so much later. No mother, no father, no relatives. The fears of the father are transferred to the son. It was from my father to me and from me to my son. He already had it and now to be left alone. I had to take him with me.

I killed Leigh Ann because she was one of the main reasons for my demise as I planned to kill the others. I really wish I hadn't killed her now. She really couldn't help it and I love her so much anyway.

I know that Jehovah will take care of all of them in the next life. I'm sure the details don't matter. There is no excuse, no good reason. I am sure no one would understand. If they could, I wouldn't want them to. I just write these things to say why.

Please know that I love Leigh Ann, Matthew and Mychelle with all of my heart. If Jehovah is willing, I would like to see all of them again in the resurrection, to have a second chance. I don't plan to live very much longer, just long enough to kill as many of the people that greedily sought my destruction. You should kill me if you can.
Mark O. Barton

Having finished in Stockbridge, Barton then waited a few hours before driving into Atlanta. He called his lawyer, Joseph

Fowler, and requested another change to his will. This time he had decided that his widowed mother was to be the sole beneficiary. Furthermore he stipulated that he wanted the children to be buried next to their mother, Debra Spivey, in the event of their deaths. He seemed calm, organised, in control. After all, with his wife and children dead he could no longer leave anything to them. His father had died two years previously, so Barton, ever the loving son and family man, did what any good son would do and made his mother the sole beneficiary of his estate. Certainly, Joseph Fowler was not alarmed by the phone call and the second change to Barton's will in a couple of days. The requests 'did not strike me as being unusual or out of order', he later told reporters.

Then, still just as calm as ever, Barton drove to Buckhead in his black Ford Aerostar van. With him he carried four weapons and hundreds of rounds of ammunition. Looking relaxed in khaki shorts and a pink shirt, he entered the offices of All-Tech just before 3.00 p.m. He asked to see the manager and after a very brief conversation Barton started firing. Armed with a .45-calibre pistol and a 9mm handgun, he stood up and fired point-blank at the manager and his secretary. He moved quickly from the inner office to the main trading room and carried on firing, shooting dead two more people and injuring several others. 'He was shooting anyone just sitting there,' reported Harvey Houtkin, CEO of All-Tech.

From All-Tech Barton crossed the street to the offices of Momentum Securities. There he opened fire again, killing five more people and wounding several more. He was working methodically, shooting victims who were cowering under desks, desperately trying to get away from him. There was nothing random about the violence. Everything was planned: the only things Barton had left to chance had been the electronic deals that had caused him to cross the line in the first place.

Having killed nine and seriously injured a dozen more, Barton quickly made his escape. In the confusion it was not clear what had happened. The police sealed off the area and people in office blocks cowered for hours until it became clear that the spree killer had disappeared. The TV cameras filmed the scene as people sneaked out of doorways or climbed out of windows, silent and afraid of the killer who'd already vanished.

The dead were listed as: Russell J. Brown, 42, Dean Delawalla, 62, Joseph J. Dessert, 60, Kevin Dial, 38, Jamshid Havash, 44, Vadewattee Muralidhara, 44, Edward Quinn, 58, Charles Allen Tenenbaum, 48 and Scott Webb, 30.

Barton had been recognised by enough people for the police to name him as the suspect immediately. When the police tracked his address back to Leigh Ann's apartment in Stockbridge they made the grisly discovery of the three bodies he'd beaten to death.

Five hours later Barton's van was spotted and police forced it over. Barton turned a gun on himself instantly, committing suicide before he could be arrested. The murder weapons and over two hundred rounds of ammunition were recovered from the van.

Barton's death robbed the world of any chance to understand properly what it was that had triggered such brutal violence. What could possibly make a man smash his children's heads in with a hammer? What could cause a man to kill his children so brutally and then surround their bodies with toys? How could a man murder his wife and then pen a note declaring his love for her?

Inevitably, speculation focused on the notes Barton had left behind. The cold, calculating manner in which the letter – time-stamped, dated and addressed formally 'to whom it may concern' – directed its discoverer to the three dead bodies was as shocking as anything else it contained. Nothing could better illustrate the iciness of Barton's personality than the way he listed the locations of his slain family in the same way that other people list items of shopping.

From this Barton moved on quickly to the murders of his first wife and her mother. He was aware that people would immediately link the crimes: after all, not only was he a common factor, but the *modus operandi* was similar. All five victims were beaten to death, the first two with a hatchet, and the others with a hammer. Why deny it? He did not deny the murders of Leigh Ann and his children, so why deny the murder of Debra and Eloise Spivey? Because in some warped way it reflected badly on him. The world would think him a monster for the murders in Stockbridge, but perhaps he imagined that there were extenuating circumstances. However, if he admitted to all five killings then he would be damned for ever. Furthermore, if his innocence of the first murders was accepted then the pressure that was placed on him and that added to his feelings of paranoia and depression was a grave injustice. Barton was, in his own eyes, a victim and in pleading not guilty to the earlier murders he wanted the world to see him as a victim too.

Whatever his reasoning, it remains a fact that Barton was the only real suspect in the murders of Debra and her mother. All investigators into the crime, from the Georgia Bureau of Investigation and the Alabama police to the FBI, were and remain convinced that Barton had cold-bloodedly butchered his wife in order to gain the insurance payments and to be with Leigh Ann.

With the matter of the earlier deaths out of the way Barton returned to his latest killings. 'I hit them with a hammer in their sleep and then put them face down in a bathtub to make sure they did not wake up in pain,' he wrote. His love for his children meant that he wanted to ensure they did not wake up in pain. Like all good parents he wanted to protect his children from suffering, so after smashing their skulls open with a hammer he drowned them in order to spare them any further agony. The mind recoils at the horror of the act and struggles to comprehend the contradictions between the almost tender way Barton described holding the children face down in the water and the reality of what he was doing.

When Barton wrote of 'dying since October' this was clearly a reference to the fact that Leigh Ann had left him. Again he reiterated that he murdered his children because he wanted to spare them any more suffering: 'I killed the children to exchange them for five minutes of pain for a lifetime of pain.'

The next section has puzzled investigators. 'The fears of the father are transferred to the son,' Barton wrote. 'It was from my father to me and from me to my son. He already had it and now to be left alone. I had to take him with me.' This seems to refer to some kind of depressive illness or a form of paranoia. However, there are no details of Barton's father having suffered from depression or any other nervous condition. Clearly Barton did suffer such depression, and his fears were legion. It is possible that he ascribed these same feelings to his father and also imagined that his own son was similarly afflicted. It is significant in that, in his perception, it removed responsibility from him and cast it squarely on his family history. How could anyone struggle against a condition passed down through the generations? A curse with which he was afflicted and which was unbearable enough to cause him to kill his similarly affected son?

There is some evidence that Barton sought help to cope with his depression. Police confirmed that, as well as a number of weapons and much ammunition, they also found a number of capsules of Prozac next to Barton's dead body in the van.

Barton's expressed regret at Leigh Ann's death was followed by the declaration that 'Jehovah will take care of all of them in the next life.' For a man so religious, Barton's life seems to have been remarkably sinful. Aside from murder, there was the alleged sexual abuse of his daughter, profiting from murder, adultery and possibly acts of domestic violence against Leigh Ann. Despite all of this Barton's professed faith in God did not seem to have diminished, nor did he seem to have very much doubt that he would be with his family in the 'next world'.

In the penultimate sentence Barton wrote simply: 'I don't plan to live very much longer, just long enough to kill as many of the people that greedily sought my destruction.' This has been taken to refer to the people running the day-trading firms where he added to his toll of murders. During his attacks at All-Tech and Momentum Securities Barton did not blaze away at random. Eyewitnesses recall that he seemed to be firing at specific people. Some of these, such as the manager and secretary at All-Tech, were clearly people he blamed for his financial losses. In contrast, many of the others were fellow day traders: why shoot them if they were as much at the mercy of the market as he had been?

One explanation is that these were some of the other day traders Barton had borrowed money from. It was common practice for people to lend capital for trades and to expect payment with interest the next day. The day-trading firms have also been accused of acting in this highly dubious manner. It is feasible that Barton blamed these fellow traders as much as the firms for the mess he had got into.

Finally, Barton warned the police: 'You should kill me if you can.'

In the event Barton saved the police the trouble. Unfortunately, though, not before he had murdered nine people and injured many more.

BUFORD FURROW

Los Angeles, USA, 1999

Joseph Santos Ileto was the sort of man who typified the American dream. Born in the Philippines, he emigrated with his parents, brothers and sisters to the United States when he was fourteen years old. For him and his family life was tough, and hard work and determination were essential if they were going to survive and prosper in their new home. Joseph, a keen chess player, attended Schurr High School in Montebello and then studied electronics at East Los Angeles College in order to better himself and help his family. At the age of 39, things were still tough but Joseph seemed happy enough. He was working two jobs, the first at AVX Filters Corporation in Sun Valley, where he was a tester of electrical equipment, and the second as a part-time postal worker.

On the morning of Tuesday, 10 August 1999, Joseph was wearing the distinctive blue uniform that indicated he was a member of the US Postal Service. He had set off from the home he shared with his brother in Chino Hills, Los Angeles. He'd been working for the postal service as a 'substitute carrier' for about two years, and his job was to cover for sickness and holidays, delivering the mail on different routes according to requirements. That morning Joseph was assigned the Chatsworth round in suburban LA.

Sometime towards midday, as Joseph was standing near his van, he was approached by a slightly overweight man with thinning hair and a pencil-thin moustache. The man asked Joseph if he would mind delivering a letter for him. Joseph smiled and said yes. Instead of handing over the letter the man suddenly pulled out a 9mm handgun and shot Joseph twice in the chest. Joseph fell, turned and tried to get away from the man standing over him, gun in hand. More shots rang out and Joseph fell forward as the bullets pumped into his back and head. Nobody else had witnessed the brutal and unexpected slaying.

Satisfied that the uniformed postal worker was dead, the man walked back to the green Toyota car that he'd been driving and then sped off. A post-mortem examination showed that Joseph Santos Ileto had been shot nine times.

Joseph's killer had then calmly driven to the 7-Star Suites hotel in Chatsworth, just across the street from the post office from where Joseph had set off earlier in the day. From there the gunman had disappeared.

In its immediate aftermath the murder received little media attention. The big news was the shooting spree at the North Valley Jewish Community Centre that had taken place about an hour earlier that morning. A lone gunman had marched into the building and opened fire on a group of Jewish schoolchildren attending a summer camp being held there. It would be some time before the 9mm shells found beside Joseph Ileto's dead body could be linked to the neo-Nazi who'd opened up on the group of frightened, screaming children. By the end of the day, however, the link would be made, and with that link came the name of a single suspect: Buford O'Neal Furrow.

Even after a long, hot summer of violence marked by a spate of spree killings, including Benjamin Nathaniel Smith's rampage in Chicago and Mark Barton's murderous outburst of rage in Atlanta, the attack on the North Valley Jewish Community Centre on 10 August 1999 was still a shock. Shortly before 11.00 a.m. a heavy-set, slightly balding white man around forty years old walked into the lobby of the centre. During the school holidays in the summer the centre was usually filled with children, around 250 of them on this particular day in August. He was met by Isabelle Shalometh, the 68-year-old receptionist who had worked at the centre for around thirteen years. She stepped forward to meet the man who, without uttering a word of warning, pulled out some kind of assault rifle and started blasting.

The receptionist was hit instantly. She fell behind the reception counter and managed to crawl into the back office while the gunman carried on firing. Children were screaming and running for cover as he moved through the building spraying bullets in every direction. He moved down the centre of the lobby and along a short hallway. Several children were hit and wounded, and one older girl, a teaching assistant for the summer, sustained an injury to her thigh, a direct hit from the 9 mm semi-automatic assault rifle.

And then, almost before the horror had fully registered, the gunman turned and fled. From start to finish the violence had lasted no more than five or six minutes. But in that time over seventy rounds had been fired and the building was still filled with gunsmoke as the first of the police and paramedics arrived on the scene.

There was chaos on their arrival. A number of the children were seriously injured. They lay in the lobby, covered in blood and cowering, crying from fear and pain. Police sealed off the area quickly and rushed to evacuate the children still inside the building. In all five people had been hit: Isabelle Shalometh, the receptionist, hit in the back and arm; James Zidell, aged six, a dark-haired, articulate child, took a bullet in the heel; Joshua Stepakoff, seven years old, received bullet wounds in his left leg and to the hip; Mindy Finkelstein, a sixteen-year-old high school senior who had acted as a counsellor at the centre for two years, was hit from behind in the leg; finally, the most serious injuries were sustained by five-year-old Benjamin Kadish.

Benjamin had been hit in the stomach and in the leg. His condition looked bad, and paramedics struggled to staunch the flow of blood as the child lay in the lobby. By the time he was rushed to the Los Angeles Children's Hospital he had lost over half his blood. One of the bullets had shattered his left leg, the other had perforated his stomach. Even after emergency surgery lasting over six hours his condition did not look good. After the first round of surgery his prognosis was given as serious but stable, but he was breathing only with the aid of a respirator.

'He's extremely critical,' Dr Charles Deng of the Providence-Holy Cross Medical Centre was quoted by the press. 'He had no blood pressure, no pulse, so that would put you at the most critical condition you could possibly be in . . . We don't even know if he's going to survive the next few hours. Minute by minute now he's very critical . . . one of the most critical cases we've ever seen here.'

For a while it looked as though the gunman had claimed the life of at least one Jewish victim, but more surgery followed, including a colostomy a day after the attack. Later still, pins were inserted into the child's shattered leg but it would be a few more days before he could be taken off the respirator. Despite the seriousness of the injuries, and the immense loss of blood that Benjamin Kadish had suffered, he did manage to pull through in the end, though it would not be until 23 September, more than six weeks after the attack, that the child would be fit enough to return home.

In the immediate aftermath of the horrific attack, there were few clues to go on. The viciousness of the violence aimed at defenceless children and the very nature of the target suggested a racial motive, and it was one that the police did not rule out. 'There was nothing said by the suspect before the shooting,' according to Chief of Police Bernard Parks. 'It was indiscriminate.' But at least they had a good description of the assailant, and Isabelle Shalometh was able to confirm that he was not anyone associated with the centre or who had visited it before.

Despite the hundreds of police fanning through the residential Green Hills district where the centre was sited, and the presence of a number of SWAT teams, the as yet unidentified gunman had gone to ground.

However, about fifteen minutes after the attack 23-year-old Jenny Younsun Choi, an Asian-American, was approached by a 'somewhat heavy-set white male' armed with an automatic assault rifle. He pulled the frightened young woman from her dark green Toyota Corolla and drove off, abandoning a red van he had been driving. The description of the carjacker and the fact that he was armed with an automatic weapon were the first links to the attack on the community centre.

A SWAT team was dispatched immediately and the abandoned red van searched. Inside, police found enough evidence to focus the investigation exclusively on the van's owner. Aside from over two thousand rounds of ammunition, a flak jacket, gas grenades and quantities of freeze-dried food of the type used by survivalists, the police also recovered a number of books and pamphlets on survivalism and neo-

Nazism. One of the books recovered was *War Cycles, Peace Cycles* by Richard Kelly Hoskins, a leading Christian Identity ideologue. 'Christian Identity' is a hard-line form of racist ideology championed by groups such as the Aryan Nations.

The police were able to establish very quickly that the red panel van, still sporting a Washington State number plate, had been purchased on the previous Saturday from a used-car lot in Tacoma. It had been purchased by one Buford O'Neal Furrow, aged 37, for $4000 cash and in part exchange for his pick-up truck. He had then loaded the van with arms, ammunition, survivalist supplies and white-supremacist literature and set off from Washington State to California.

Shortly after the carjacking Furrow had chanced upon Joseph Ileto. The unassuming postal worker was too good a target to resist. Not only was he a non-Aryan, he was also an employee of the federal government, the sworn enemy of the far right. Joseph Ileto paid for these sins with his life, gunned down in cold blood and left to die on the street. Although there was intense speculation in the media that the community-centre shootings and Ileto's murder were the work of the same man, the police initially took a cautious line and would not confirm the obvious hypothesis.

Buford then drove the green Toyota to Chatsworth. The vehicle was spotted some time before 9.00 p.m., parked near the 7-Star Suites Hotel. Within minutes the hotel was surrounded by SWAT teams, armed with sub-machine guns and clad in bulletproof vests, homing in on the only suspect in the North Valley shootings and Joseph Ileto's murder. It was suspected that Furrow was somewhere in the hotel, holed up and ready for a firefight with the authorities. With all the guns and ammunition he'd brought with him from Washington, it was clear that he had declared his own private war.

At around 9.00 p.m. the police moved in, combing through the hotel in search of the lone neo-Nazi. All indications were that he was on his own, though the police were not ruling out the possibility that he'd had support from other people in the planning and preparation of his shooting spree. The meticulous search, with officers aided by sniffer-dog teams, ended about an hour after midnight. 'There's no sign of the suspect right now,' Sharyn Buck, a police spokeswoman, reported to the massed ranks of the media camped out near the hotel. 'We don't know if he was ever in the hotel. All we know right now is we haven't located him.'

The hunt for Furrow went nationwide, with his picture and details flashed across newspapers and television throughout the United States. California's State Governor, Gray Davis, a prominent gun-control advocate, offered a $50,000 reward for information leading to Furrow's arrest. 'This is yet another example of a senseless barbaric act of violence against innocent children and defenceless adults,' he told the press. As the hunt for Furrow intensified, the familiar American debate about guns and gun control raged on. Attention also focused on the racial nature of the crimes, categorised as 'hate crimes' by the press and the state and federal authorities.

With memories of Benjamin Nathaniel Smith's recent 36-hour spree of racist violence still fresh in people's minds, many people were justifiably anxious as to what the gunman's next move might be. He had started out attacking a Jewish target: who was going to be next? Yet again a shudder of fear and apprehension passed through the Jewish community. Only a couple of months previously there had been a series of arson attacks at three synagogues in nearby Sacramento. Nobody had been killed but viciously anti-Semitic leaflets had been left behind to underline the neo-Nazi nature of these attacks. Following the community-centre attack security was stepped up at synagogues, schools and community centres throughout the United States. Irv Rubin, chairman of the Jewish Defence League, talked of the attack as being part of the preparation for what he called 'Holocaust 2000' – a campaign by violently racist neo-Nazi groups to wage race war against all ethnic and religious minorities in the United States. 'They've got to wipe out the Jews,' he explained. 'On their ladder of hate, Jews are on the top rung. They want to see Jews hanging from lamp-posts.'

But it was not just the Jewish community that felt at risk. The sort of person who would use an assault rifle to attack screaming children because they were Jewish would have no compunction about attacking other ethnic targets. The black community shared the same sense of dread as the Jewish one. They too had suffered at the hands of violent racists, and just as synagogues had been arson targets so too had black churches been attacked and burned throughout the United States. Members of the African American community were quick to request that the Los Angeles Board of Education take extra security measures to protect schoolchildren.

Stewart Kwoh, director of the Asian Pacific American Legal Centre in Los Angeles, linked the community-centre shootings to Ileto's death directly, even before it was confirmed by the police. 'We're concerned that this postal worker's killing is linked to this hate-crime spree,' he said. He also pointed out that racist groups do not confine their attacks to one particular minority group. 'And that's something important for all of us to realise. If people think it's just happening to Jewish Americans or Asian- Americans, then that's really an incomplete response.'

While the debate raged on, and the first details of Furrow's life history started to emerge, Furrow himself was calmly making plans for his escape. After abandoning the Toyota in the hotel car park in Chatsworth, around thirty miles north-west of downtown Los Angeles, he had flagged a taxi and taken a relaxed ride into the centre of the city. There he had a haircut and bought himself a new shirt. He moved on to Hollywood where, it later emerged, he had gone looking for a prostitute. Unable to find himself a suitable candidate, he then went into a bar and had seven or eight beers. At around 8.00 p.m., more than an hour before the police announcement that he was the suspect in the shootings, Furrow hailed a cab outside a 7-Eleven store.

Cab driver Hovik Garibyan, an Armenian immigrant to the United States, was asked by his new passenger to drive to Los Angeles International Airport. On the way there, however, the man changed his mind. 'Can you take me to Las Vegas? I don't like to fly in airplanes,' Garibyan recalled his passenger saying. Once they were on their way, driving through the Mojave Desert, the nervous-looking passenger fell asleep in the back of the cab. Furrow remained asleep for most of the four-hour trip and awoke only when Garibyan stopped off at a petrol station to refuel when they were around seventy miles from Las Vegas. Furrow noticed that there was a McDonald's close to the service station. Feeling thirsty, he asked Garibyan to take them to the drive-through. After ordering himself an iced tea he asked Garibyan if he wanted anything for himself. The driver declined.

It was around 11.00 p.m. when they set off again. Furrow was now wide awake and apparently in talkative mood. He asked Garibyan where he was from. The driver replied and asked Furrow why he was going to Las Vegas. 'I'm going to gamble, to play, to enjoy,' came the reply. 'It's a nice city.'

Furrow asked to be dropped off on the Strip, near the New York, New York casino. Driver and passenger even wished each other luck before Furrow hopped out of the cab and disappeared into the night. By then his name and details had been circulated nationwide. Garibyan, however, decided to take advantage of the destination himself, so he parked his cab and went into the casino. He sat down at a poker table and proceeded to gamble away the fare he had just taken from Furrow, and several hundred dollars of his own money too.

Garibyan called it quits at around 5.00 a.m. and headed back across the Mojave for home. When he spoke to a colleague, Boris Krasnov, he described his strange passenger and the journey across the desert to Las Vegas. Krasnov was suspicious: unlike Garibyan he had been keeping up to date with the news on the hunt for the man responsible for the community-centre shooting. Could Garibyan's long-distance fare have been the man the police were looking for?

'I start thinking it's not the usual trip, not every day that you go to Las Vegas,' Krasnov later recalled. He called Garibyan at home later that morning and told him to look at the TV news.

'I just turned on the television and I saw that it was him,' Garibyan said. 'I felt lucky to be alive.'

After being dropped off by Garibyan, Furrow had checked into the Barbary Coast Hotel and Casino in Las Vegas and gone down to play at the tables. He'd gambled a little before turning in to get some sleep. By the time he woke up the next morning his name and face were on nationwide TV. After watching the TV networks for a while he decided, according to FBI sources, to turn himself in because he had 'made a point'.

Furrow called a cab and then rode to an FBI office in Las Vegas where he gave himself up. He was still carrying around $2000 in cash with him. He was quoted as telling FBI officers: 'You're looking for me. I killed the kids in Los Angeles.' As he hadn't killed any of the kids, this suggests that his understanding of what he'd seen on the TV reports was less than perfect.

During questioning by agents Furrow was asked what had motivated his violent spree. His reply was perfectly simple: his action was designed to be 'a wake-up call to America to kill Jews'.

By the time that Furrow handed himself over to the FBI, fuller details of his past were emerging. There was little surprise that he had been heavily involved with several neo-Nazi groups, nor were many people surprised to discover that he suffered from social and personality problems. He came across less as an Aryan superman and more as a social inadequate who had sought refuge in racist politics before finally losing it once and for all.

Furrow was a native of Washington State and had grown up near the small town of Olympia, where his parents still lived. As a child he suffered from a weight problem; he was acutely conscious of it, and it was exacerbated by ill health and a number of allergies. He was the fat kid with glasses who was the butt of everybody else's jokes. It hurt, of course. He became a withdrawn, lonely child, with few friends to help bolster his low self-esteem. As Furrow grew into his teens he withdrew more and more, almost as though he wanted to make himself invisible. 'He wasn't somebody that stood out. He was somebody who nobody knew,' said Loni Merrill, a neighbour from Olympia who had attended junior high school with Furrow. 'He was unassuming. He was just there. Very unobtrusive,' she added. A loner, he would even sit by himself on the bus ride to school every morning.

It is not clear at which point in his life Furrow started to become involved with racist groups, but his involvement went beyond a mere dabbling with dubious ideas. He became a convinced supporter of the Christian Identity movement centred around the Aryan Nations group led by Richard Butler. The Christian Identity movement resembles the World Church of the Creator in that it is virulently racist and neo-Nazi, styling itself as a 'religious' or theological group. Like WCOTC it believes that we are in the midst of a race war, and this violently paranoid world-view informs all of its propaganda and activities. However, unlike Matt Hale's racist pseudo-religion the Christian Identity movement claims that it is acting in the name of Christ. Where Hale bases his theology on the 'holiness' of the 'Aryan race', Richard Butler and other Christian Identity ideologues base their views on readings of the Bible.

Whilst Butler's Aryan Nations group was formed in the middle 1970s, the Christian Identity movement is much older and has its roots in Great Britain. The ideas of the first Anglo-Israelites emerged from the fervid world of occult groups and sects that flourished in the late nineteenth century in Great Britain and the rest of Europe. A number of competing groups put forward the idea that the Anglo-Saxons were descended from the lost tribes of Israel and that the biblical Jews were actually a Nordic race. As for the people known to the modern world as Jews, some groups claimed that these were descended from the unholy union of Satan and Eve while others claimed that modern Jews were the spawn of Satan and the daughters of Cain. But this was splitting hairs: it was clear that the modern Jews were impostors and descended ultimately from Satan. The Anglo-Saxons, on the other hand, were descended from Jesus Christ, a blond and blue-eyed Aryan who had been murdered by the Satanic forces of the Jews.

This bizarre theology never really caught the popular imagination and one would have expected it to die out in time, but occult beliefs have a habit of enduring and this one was no different. Small congregations of Anglo-Israelites managed to survive and even to spread from Great Britain to other parts of the English-speaking world, including the United States. By the 1940s one such group, the Anglo-Saxon

Christian Congregation, was established in Hollywood. Led by Wesley Swift, who had been West Coast organiser for the anti-Semitic populist politician Gerald L.K. Smith, the tiny group attracted little attention. Swift, who immediately after the Second World War had written that 'all Jews must be destroyed', managed to make at least two converts who later went on to greater prominence.

The first was William Potter Gale, a former US Army colonel who had been a guerrilla-warfare expert in the Pacific during World War II. Gale put his guerrilla-warfare training to use in the service of hate politics, and was a founder of the Posse Comitatus movement, one of the precursors of the modern US militia movement. Like the militias, the Posse Comitatus believes that the US federal government is acting unlawfully, that the US Constitution is being violated daily and that paying income tax, social security or having anything else to do with the illegal central government is wrong. Organisations such as the Revenue Service, the Postal Service, the FBI and so on need to be opposed, and several times members of the Posse Comitatus and other similar paramilitary groups have engaged in violent struggles with the state.

Gale also started a church and styled himself Pastor of the Ministry of Christ Church, so as to continue preaching the bizarre gospel of Christian Identity.

Swift's other big success was Richard Butler, who proclaimed himself his heir following Swift's death in 1970. Butler's Aryan Nations group revolves around the Church of Jesus Christ Christian, the central vehicle for the Christian Identity message. Along the way the message that the Jews are the spawn of Satan has remained central, together with the idea that blacks and other non-Aryans were created by Satan out of mud and that they have no souls and are lower than animals. (Incidentally, this idea is one that has been copied by Matt Hale's group, who also like to refer to blacks as 'mud people'.)

The geographic base of the Aryan Nations is at a heavily armed twenty-acre compound in Hayden Lake, Idaho. It is an area popular with far-right groups: sparsely populated, heavily forested, isolated and without large multi-ethnic communities. Not surprisingly, it is home to prominent Holocaust revisionists, militia members, survivalists and racist groups. Butler had built up a fortune working in the aeronautical industry and when the time came for him to make the move from California to Idaho he put his bank account to good use. The compound features a church, printing press, living quarters, guard towers, school, rifle ranges and a heavy shielding of trees. For Butler it is the seed with which to create a white racial homeland, a world without Jews, blacks, homosexuals, anti-fascists, radicals and anybody else who fails to fit the Christian Identity mould.

Once it had been set up, Butler used the compound as a base from which to issue streams of propaganda: pamphlets, books, tapes, videos, pre-recorded sermons to be transmitted by radio. He and his followers set out to infect the world with the violence of their hatred. 'As long as the alien tyranny evil occupies our land,' he has said, 'hate is our law and revenge our duty.'

In the middle 1980s, the compound was also home to an Annual 'Aryan Nations World Congress' at which representatives from the full spectrum of far-right groups would gather together to celebrate the race war they believed they were involved in. Such gatherings would include members of traditional white supremacist groups such as the Ku Klux Klan, neo-Nazis such as David Lane, members of the Christian Defence League, skinheads and others. The purpose of this congress was not just to promote a feeling of comradeship and to boost morale. The aims were practical, too: there was an emphasis on gun training, guerrilla warfare, and unarmed combat. And, of course, it helped to foster links between groups, enabling them to work together and become more effective.

Inevitably, the violent rhetoric gave rise to acts of real violence – the training was there for a reason, after all. The most notorious of these acts of violence were perpetrated by a group of Aryan Nations supporters who called themselves 'The Order'.

Founded by Robert J. Mathews in the early 1980s, The Order were inspired both by Butler's racial creed and by William Pierce's notorious racist novel *The Turner Diaries*.

Their aim was total war, a white revolution that would destroy the Jews and blacks once and for all. They were not interested in any kind of propaganda except propaganda by deed: they wanted violent direct action. Mathews drew around him a small group of fanatical neo-Nazis, all of them ready to go into action immediately. They were going to 'Stand up like men and drive the enemy into the sea,' in Mathews's own words.

The first step in this white revolution was to acquire the guns, ammunition and organisation to get this war going. In the early 1980s members of The Order, including Mathews, carried out a string of armed robberies on banks and armoured cars, netting over four million dollars in the process. But robberies were not enough: the hatred they felt towards minorities needed venting, too. One of their targets was talk radio DJ Alan Berg. Not only was he Jewish, well known and in the media, he was also known for verbally lashing anti-Semites and racists on air. One of these had been David Lane, who had been on the sharp end of Berg's tongue after appearing on his show. Lane was one of those who had joined Mathews's group, becoming a full member of The Order soon after it was created.

On 18 June 1984, Berg was machine-gunned outside his house in Denver. It was an assassination – there was no other way to describe the murder. The DJ's death not only shocked his audience in Denver, but also sent waves of horror throughout the United States. The FBI, already investigating the armed robberies and other violent activities of The Order, stepped up the investigation.

By December 1984 most of the members of The Order had dispersed or had been captured by the authorities. The rest were tracked down to safe houses on Whidbey Island, just north-west of Seattle. While many of the dwindling band of 'Silent Brothers', as they styled themselves, slipped away or prepared to escape, Mathews became more brazen, more grandiose in his schemes and plans. He drafted a declaration of war and talked of fighting his way off the island, even though it was surrounded by over a hundred FBI agents.

In the end Mathews's brother Aryans were captured or gave themselves up, leaving him to face the siege alone. When appeals, including some from his faithful followers, to give himself up failed, the FBI moved in. After a siege lasting more than 36 hours a police helicopter dropped phosphorous illumination flares onto the roof of the house where Mathews was holed up. The house caught fire quickly but still Mathews refused to budge. By dawn the house was a smouldering wreck and Mathews's body could only be identified by using dental records. Later, 22 members of the group were jailed on racketeering charges, and around two-thirds of the stolen money was recovered. The rest had disappeared.

After Mathews's death – and with his death The Order as a distinct organisation also died – Butler told the *San Francisco Examiner*: 'He was a man of the highest idealism and moral character . . . It encourages me because it shows that there are still some patriotic young men left in the country.'

By the time that Furrow became involved with the Aryan Nations, some time in 1989, The Order had already passed into legendary status in the eyes of many on the far right. Despite the violence they had been involved in, and the violence of their demise, there was no let-up in Butler's rhetoric. Indeed, it was this extreme rhetoric that attracted young neo-Nazis to make the pilgrimage to Hayden Lake, and Furrow was one of them.

Furrow had intended to follow his father, Buford Sr, into the Air Force after graduating from high school. However, a knee injury kept him out after he failed to get through boot camp. Following this failure he had then attended a string of different colleges, before finally graduating with a degree in manufacturing engineering from Western Washington University in Bellingham, about ninety miles north of Seattle. Like his high-school career, there was nothing out of the ordinary about his years of study at the university. He was not a student who stood out from the crowd, and even after his name was flashed across the TV networks his old faculty adviser did not recognise him. Following his graduation in 1986 Furrow decided to stay in the Seattle area rather than return home to Olympia, where his parents had remained.

Furrow gained employment with Boeing in Seattle, doing a desk job in one of the non-defence areas of the company. He remained at Boeing from 1987 to 1990, and the only feature of his employment there was that it was so nondescript. Dave Sufia, a spokesman for the company, stated bluntly that there was 'nothing remarkable' during Furrow's period of employment.

It was while Furrow was still with Boeing that he first made contact with the Aryan Nations. There are reports that his first visit to Hayden Lake occurred some time in 1989, though there are no details about what form these first contacts with Butler and his group took. What is not in dispute is that Furrow was deeply attracted to the Aryan Nations, and his involvement deepened very quickly. From being a mere visitor to the compound at Hayden Lake, he was soon dressed in the distinctive paramilitary blue-and-black uniform that marked him out as one of the elite. Despite not having any previous police or military experience he was made a security guard at the compound. As in all such groups the mania for hierarchies and titles meant that Furrow could work hard to prove his worth as a faithful Aryan and gain promotion to the rank of 'lieutenant'. Later, after he gave himself up, he was pictured in *Newsweek* magazine in full Nazi regalia policing one of the World Congresses from the middle 1990s.

It was at Hayden Lake that Furrow first met Debbie Mathews, the unrepentant widow of The Order's founder. After her husband's death she stated that he and another Order member, Gordon Kahl, were 'both murdered because they were brave enough to stand up and fight for God, truth and their race. Their deaths will not be forgotten.' As the widow of a slain 'martyr' to the cause, Debbie Mathews carried, and continues to carry, a great deal of respect within the ranks of the Aryan Nations and other groups. She was described by one anti-racist as the 'Jackie O of the neo-Nazi movement'. Furrow managed to build up a relationship with her and the two of them were married in a ceremony carried out by Butler at the compound some time in 1995 or 1996. The marriage was never formally registered with the authorities, but in the eyes of the far right the ceremony was binding enough.

The marriage proved not to be a happy one, however. Despite Furrow's posturing in uniform and the status that he felt it accorded him, his life was a mess. Outside of the 'white homeland' near Hayden Lake he had trouble keeping a job for very long. Following his departure from Boeing it appears that his temper, always short, was getting worse and landing him in trouble. Unable to cope with stress at work, he'd lose his temper and quit his job. After his marriage to Debbie Mathews he joined her at her home in Metaline Falls, just south of the Canadian border, where she'd lived with her first husband.

The marriage was marked by frequent and violent arguments, and it finally disintegrated some time in the spring or summer of 1998. Mathews had had enough of Furrow and kicked him out. One of their neighbours, Meda Van Dyke, a rancher who lives near Mathews, said, 'I didn't see him a lot. He was pleasant when I saw him. His wife told me he had a violent temper she couldn't put up with.' He moved from Metaline to a trailer park in the Seattle suburb of Lynnwood. His landlady there, Helga Helverson, was very impressed by her new tenant. Speaking about him she said that he 'never said anything about Jews or anybody else. He always was by himself and had no friends in the trailer park. You know, he was a wonderful tenant. He came and did his laundry. He went to work in the morning and he came home. That was all. It doesn't sound like him. He was so quiet. He was supposed to have some kind of sickness that was crippling him. I have no idea what it is. But he didn't seem sick.'

The sickness that Furrow had mentioned to Helverson was of the mental, not the physical kind. His anger, repressed behind a quiet, unassuming façade, was constantly on the boil. There were so many enemies to think about, so many people out to destroy the white race, out to destroy him personally. And things had not turned out the way he had expected them. After marrying Mathews he was seen digging in her garden several times, and it is rumoured that he had been dating Jeannie Yarbrough, wife of Gary Yarborough, another member of The Order who was sentenced to life imprisonment for his part in the murder of Alan Berg. Did Furrow's interest in these two women have anything to do with the hundreds of thousands of dollars that were never recovered by the FBI?

Unable to hold down a job, with a hair-trigger temper and a number of other personality problems, Furrow was going nowhere fast. He took to drinking more and more and, alone in his trailer, he would engage in violent, destructive fantasies. He kept in contact with his parents, but they despaired of their son's ability to cope. Things came to a head towards the end of October 1998.

After a heavy drinking session late in October 1998, during which his moods had swung from dangerously self-destructive to just downright dangerous to everyone else, Furrow had cut himself several times with a knife. One cut had almost taken off a finger. He managed to drive to a hospital where the wound required six stitches. A few days later, on 24 October, he inflicted several more knife wounds to his arms. This time he realised that he was going over the edge and on 28 October he drove to Fairfax Psychiatric Hospital in the Seattle suburb of Kirkland. Furrow's intention was to commit himself for treatment and staff, recognising that he was suffering from an acute mental crisis, persuaded him to hand over his car keys. Halfway through the discussion, however, he clearly changed his mind about what he was doing and demanded his keys back. The hospital staff tried to reason with Furrow but that only served to enrage him. He wanted his car keys back and when this request was refused he pulled a knife.

After the ensuing struggle, during which Furrow had to be physically restrained and the police called, a search of his car found a 9mm handgun, ammunition and several knives. He was arrested and made the following statement to J.R. Hall, a Sheriff's deputy:

I am a white seperatist [sic]. *I've been having suicidal and homicidal thoughts for some time now. Yesterday, I had thoughts that I would kill my ex-wife and some of her friends, then maybe I would drive to Canada and rob a bank. I wanted the police to shoot me. I own a 9mm semi-automatic handgun made by Taurus. I always carry it in the glove box of my car. I also have several knives that I keep in the car.*

Last night, I had some drinks and passed out. This morning I woke up, called work and told them I was going to be gone

*for a while. I had some more drinks. Then drove myself to
Fairfax to check myself in.*

*Sunday, I was feeling suicidal and cut my left index finger
to the bone. Then I drove to Providence Hospital in Everett.
It took six stitches to close the wounds. Today, I cut my left
forearm six to seven times.*

*Sometimes I feel like I could just loose [sic] it and kill
people. I also feel like I could kill myself.*

On 2 November Furrow was formally charged with
second-degree assault for his attack on the hospital staff. In
the normal course of events he should have been remanded
in the county jail. Instead, he was moved from the jail to the
Harborview Medical Centre, which serves as the venue for
psychiatric commitment hearings for cases handled by the
local courts. After assessment Furrow was then transferred to
the Western State Hospital, a state mental institution, where
he remained for six weeks. He was then transferred to the
county jail where he served five months of an eight-month
sentence arising from the assault charge.

The fact that Furrow spent six weeks at a state mental hospital
suggests that the psychiatrists and other professionals who
examined him judged him to be either dangerous and/or unfit
to stand trial. Although he had backed out of the idea of having
himself committed, it was judged that there was no alternative
but to treat him for his illness. Without access to the medical
records it is difficult to verify the exact nature of the psychiatric
problems from which he was judged to be suffering, but for
people in his situation – judged unfit to stand trial and kept
forcibly for psychiatric treatment in a secure mental institution –
such problems usually include an inability to think clearly and
an inability to control their emotions or their actions. There is
often a substantial impairment of mental function and
judgement. Court papers clearly show that Furrow was judged
to be a 'grave risk of danger to himself and society should he be
released'. It was a judgement that accorded with the wishes of
Furrow's family. According to bail bondsman Troy Hunt,
Furrow's parents did not want their son back out on the streets.
'The family wanted him in treatment,' he told the press.

Michael Ryan
(© Mirror Syndication International)

Hungerford, 19 August 1987 (© Mirror Syndication International)

Thomas Hamilton
(© Mirror Syndication International)

Plan of Dunblane Primary School (photographer unknown)

1. ACCESS TO DOUNE ROAD
2. TELEGRAPH POLE
3. MAIN ENTRANCE
4. ENTRY DOOR BESIDE TOILETS
5. ASSEMBLY HALL
6. GYMNASIUM
7. STORE
8. FIRE ESCAPE DOOR
9. HUT 7
10. LIBRARY CORRIDOR

Martin Bryant
(© News Corporation)

The remains of Seascape guesthouse, Port Arthur, set alight by Martin Bryant following an all-night siege
(© News Corporation)

July 31, 1999

Sir

I am interested in relating to you some events I have
experienced. If these events are true then they would
indicate a serious injustice against me. Specificaly:
the denial of due process for me in the investigation of
me as a suspected serial murderer. I use the term "investigation" loosely. It was not so much an investigation
as it was a continuous interference in my life and employment for a period of possibly twenty years.

Three operative terms apply to this situation: First;
rumor control, this was one method by which those investigating me used to create problems for me: Second; Psychological warfare, this was the general mode of operation:
Third; Plausible deniability, the ideas those involved
would proffer in order to divert blame from themselves.

The first experience I had which became a clue to my
future problems occured in July of "79". Soon after reporting
to a deployment site with a U.S. Navy squadron I attended a
social event. While there I was pulled asside by a young
man who was in that squadron and he asked some odd questions.
The questions involved the murder of someone I had no knowledge of. The tone of his questions became almost accus-
atory. This was the first of three similar events which
occured during my active duty with the navy from "79" to "83".
What I eventually began to wonder was if there were any reason for me to be a suspect in any murder. As I now know there
were several abductions or murders of young women in Fort Worth
and Arlington during the "70s" when I lived in the area.

After I moved back to Fort Worth in "84" the odd events
became a major problem in my life and occured both on and
off the job. The seriousness of the events and the humil-
iation I suffered made it impossible for me to keep a job.

The most pronounced situation began soon after I began work
at the Photo-Etch Company in 1986. Shortly after I was hired
as a machinist I was put on the evening shift with another
employee who was hired about a week after me. We were the
only workers at the company during that shift. At some point
around September of that year in the evening I was taking a
break when the other employee walked up to me and made a
somewhat veiled indirect threat. It went like this: "I have a
lot of friends on the police force, in fact I know a woman
police officer who can kick your (deleted) all over the place."
This was the beginning of continuous troubles on the job at that
company. When I attempted to remedy the problems through the
proper channels I got no where. The troubles included minor
physical abuse and general disrespect by another employee

**The first letter sent by Larry Gene Ashbrook to the
Fort Worth Star-Telegram**
(© Fort Worth Star-Telegram)

City Editor Stephen Kaye
The Fort Worth Star-Telegram
400 West Seventh St.
Fort Worth, Tx. 76102

August 10, 1999

Sir

This communication is an addendum to the July 31 letter. It
is obvious that you are uninterested in my story. Therefore, I
find it necessary to amplify certain aspects of it.
Consider one of three situations I experienced where people
, had never met volunteered that they were either former Central
Intelligence Agency employees or were laiason with the CIA
while they were in the military.
In 1987, after being fired from the company I worked for in
July, as I related earlier, I got a job with a forging company
in Fort Worth. On the morning I reported to that company I was
to be indoctrinated into the operations of the machine shop by
the shop foreman. Unfortunately, it was not so much an indoc-
trination as it was a recounting of the mans exploits in Viet
Nam. Particularily his story was about how he worked laiason
with the CIA and his exploits included special forces operations which entailed assissination of enemy political units.
This lecture lasted the entire morning. From eight until
lunch time.
If this were the only time I had ever encountered someone who volunteered such a story I would think nothing of it.
However, since it is one of three encounters and since it falls
within the time period that I am certain that I was being targeted as a suspected serial murderer, then I must consider it
a relevant part of my situation. My employment at this company eventually became impossible and I quit. Not because I
could not work with them but because they did not want to work
with me.
Without belaboring the point with my experiences, I will
call to your attention two stories that have come out of the
news in the last decade. The first involved the Tarrant
County Sheriffs Department. I believe the year was 1991; and
in that year there was a situation which came to light in
which it was found that reserve deputies with the sheriffs department, who were full time U.S. Airforce personel, were also
discovered to be affiliated with the Klu Klux Klan. What I
particularily recall is that when one of those involved personel was interviewed on TV {KXAS CH 5, NBC affiliate} he
directly stated that they were involved in "going after child
abductors." Amy Robinson's abductor perhaps?
The second also involved the sheriff's department. The
year was, I believe, "95" or "96". The story that came out
disclosed that an individual or individuals within the department had had, for some time, a web site that contained the dos-
sier's of suspects in criminal investigations. These files

**The second letter sent by Larry Gene Ashbrook to the
Fort Worth Star-Telegram**
(© Fort Worth Star-Telegram)

According to Christopher Slobogin of the University of Florida, a leading expert on mental illness and criminal law, it is likely that Furrow was treated with anti-psychotic drugs. 'My guess is that they found some evidence of delusions and they treated him with medication and at the end of six weeks they thought OK, this guy's ready to be released . . . so long as he stays on his medication, he's going to be fine.'

While in prison Furrow either continued to take his medication or else his condition had calmed down sufficiently for him to serve his jail sentence without further incidents of violence or aggression. He was released from prison on twelve months' probation on 21 May 1999.

After his release Furrow went back to Olympia to stay with his long-suffering parents. Without supervision or close contact with the psychiatrists and doctors who had treated him at the state mental hospital, it was inevitable that he would stop taking his prescribed medication. As his parents later complained to the press, there was no real support provided once he was released. And without medication his usual problems started to reappear.

Time in prison does seem to have made one crucial difference: on Furrow's release his anger seemed much more focused. Not long after his release he made the trip south from Washington State to California. In Los Angeles he found the time to visit the Museum of Tolerance, run by the Simon Wiesenthal Centre. The museum exists to educate visitors about the reality of anti-Semitism and racism, and includes exhibits on the Holocaust, the Civil Rights movement and on the organisations of the far right in the United States. Given the nature of the museum and the stated aim of the Simon Wiesenthal Centre to confront racism and bigotry, it is no surprise that bomb and death threats against the museum and its staff are frequent. Like all other visitors Furrow would have had to pass through a metal detector to gain entry, and then would have seen the security guards posted throughout the 165,000-square-foot building.

Guides noticed the balding, overweight visitor early on. Furrow seemed uninterested in the exhibits, particularly the ones focused on Auschwitz and the Second World War

Holocaust. This is no big surprise: as a convinced neo-Nazi Furrow would deny the existence of the Nazi death camps and the genocide against the Jews and others deemed subhuman by Hitler and the Nazi Party. Christian Identity, like other varieties of neo-Nazism, denounces the Holocaust as a con by the Jews to guilt-trip the white race and to cover up the fact that the Jews caused the Second World War in which so many God-fearing, clean-living Aryans fought against Nazi Germany.

One tour guide, who refused to be identified to the press, recalled that Furrow '. . . was acting very strangely, almost as though he was scoping the place out.' By the time the security guards had been alerted the furtive visitor had disappeared. He had been inside the museum for less than twenty minutes. An average visitor would take around three hours to tour all the exhibits. 'He obviously didn't come to be educated about tolerance,' Rabbi Abraham Cooper, dean of the Simon Wiesenthal Centre remarked dryly.

According to a report in the *Los Angeles Times*, Furrow also visited two other well-known Jewish sites in the city. In addition to the Museum of Tolerance, he was said to have visited the Skirball Cultural Centre and the University of Judaism. As with the museum, security at these buildings was tight. It was on his way back from one of these reconnaissance missions that Furrow stopped off at a petrol station in the Grenada Hills suburb and noticed the North Valley Jewish Community Centre. For him it was a case of serendipity pure and simple. Here was one Jewish target where security was much more to his liking.

A few weeks later, on the weekend of 4 July 1999, Furrow went back north to Metaline Falls to make one last attempt to patch things up with Debbie Mathews. Perhaps he hoped that the holiday weekend would soften her mood, but it was to no avail. Debbie Mathews clearly did not want him back. While Mathews has refused to make a full statement to the press, a friend and neighbour was clear about what had happened: 'He wanted to get back together with her, but she said "You have way too many problems". I told her I knew she had done the smart thing. I knew he had just gotten out of jail,' the unnamed woman was quoted as saying. 'She thought he finally got the picture and was just out of her life. That's what she really wanted . . . just for him to leave her alone,' she added.

Again Furrow returned to his parents in Olympia. Neighbours recalled him as polite, always smiling and still obviously a great worry to his parents. On Saturday, 7 August he told his parents that he was just going out for a ride in his pick-up truck. They expected him back shortly. However, the short ride turned into something altogether more nightmarish. Furrow drove to a used-car lot in Tacoma and traded his pick-up truck and $4000 for a red panel van. That done, he loaded up the van with the things he'd had with him in his pick-up – and then set off immediately for Los Angeles.

There seem to be few people who knew Furrow who were overly surprised at his subsequent murderous spree. His parents, as one might expect, were devastated. According to Clint Merril, a neighbour for over 35 years, his parents took the news badly. 'They're in shock, just like everybody,' he said. 'They are taking it very hard. They just have no idea how anything like this could happen. No inkling.'

In a rare statement to the press, Debbie Mathews also expressed surprise. 'You bet this is a surprise. I didn't have a clue,' she was quoted as saying. Before Furrow gave himself up, it was claimed that Mathews was afraid that he would be heading for her. He had, after all, expressed violent intentions towards her and it is reasonable to assume that she could have been on the receiving end of some of his bullets had she been around.

Some people not only seemed not to be too surprised at Furrow's actions, but they did not even seem to think that what he had done was terribly wrong or shocking. The Reverend Butler, for example, was quick to find reasons why Furrow had acted the way he had done. Furrow was motivated by 'the war against the white race. There's a war of extermination against the white male.' And, as a good Christian, he was full of sympathy for Furrow's child victims: 'I don't favour hurting children, but I can't get worked up about the wounding of some of my enemies, even though they're children,' he told the *Seattle Post*.

Asked if he accepted any responsibility for what Furrow had done, Butler was frank in his reply to the reporter. 'If a Catholic priest sodomises an altar boy – and they've had a whole string of them – do you blame the church for it? The pope?' What of the other men of violence associated with his Aryan Nations? Apart from the ruthless fanatics of The Order and Furrow, others linked to Butler have included Mark Thomas, Butler's former Pennsylvania state leader, who took to armed robbery to fund an Aryan revolution and Nathan Thill, former Aryan Nations organiser in Denver, who confessed to killing a black man purely because of the colour of his skin, among others. 'I have no control over what people do,' Butler responded truculently. 'I don't espouse violence at all, but it happens. I'm not violent, but I failed Hypocrisy 101 in school.'

Whether Butler espouses violence or not is open to question. Clearly the rhetoric that he uses, the ideas that he promotes and the obsession that he and his followers have with guns suggests that at the very least the matter of 'espousing violence' is in the eye of the beholder. Most sane people would agree that Butler's sermons of hate are violent, and clearly many of his followers have acted on this.

While Butler was being questioned by the press, Furrow was being interrogated by the FBI. He seemed to be in good humour and rather than being tight-lipped he was more than willing to talk to the federal agents. 'He's a regular chatterbox,' one FBI agent stated. Having been arrested in the state of Nevada it would have been normal procedure for the Californian authorities to request that Furrow be extradited to face charges there. Rather than go for an extradition hearing, Furrow decided to play ball, agreed to waive his right to a hearing and was flown to California directly.

It was alleged that Furrow told investigators that he had not meant to target the children at the community centre. He had been aiming at the adults and the children merely 'got in the way'. Presumably the fact that many of the bullet holes left in the walls of the community centre are at child height was also an accident.

On his first court appearance in Los Angeles Furrow looked relaxed as he was brought in for the closed-door hearing.

Flanked by police officers and in handcuffs, he smiled at reporters and was heard to remark to his public defender that 'they all like me'. He was charged with first-degree murder in the case of Joseph Ileto, and five counts of attempted murder arising from the community-centre shootings. The state alleged that Ileto 'was intentionally killed because of his race or nationality'. This additional clause in the murder charge makes it a 'hate crime' in which the death penalty becomes an option. A similar clause – 'because of the victims' religion or ancestry or perceived religion or ancestry' – was added to the attempted-murder charges. Additionally Furrow was charged with the carjacking following the community-centre shootings. Bail, not surprisingly, was refused.

Later, at the end of August, when Furrow appeared before the court, his lawyers told the judge that they would not be entering a plea for their client. The judge, Stephen Hillman, simply responded by saying that the court would enter a plea of not guilty on Furrow's behalf. A trial date was set for October 1999, and in the meantime Furrow would remain locked up on remand.

Inevitably there were questions asked about how Furrow had managed to arm himself so well. The weapon he had used to pepper the lobby of the community centre with bullets was an Armalite AR15 semi-automatic assault rifle, the civilian equivalent of the fully automatic M16 military assault rifle. An automatic assault rifle or machine gun fires continuously when the trigger is held down. In contrast, a semi-automatic fires individual shots as fast as the trigger is pulled. Both types of weapon are deadly and both carry large clips that hold twenty or more bullets. In the case of the AR15 its magazines hold twenty or thirty bullets.

By law Furrow could not have purchased any firearms recently because computer checks would have revealed that he was still on probation on the assault charge against the hospital staff. But as a convinced gun fanatic he had been stockpiling his weapons for a number of years. The provenance of some items in his arsenal proved to be extremely embarrassing to certain parties.

Firstly the Bureau of Alcohol, Tobacco and Firearms revealed that the 9mm Glock semi-automatic pistol that had been used to murder Joseph Ileto had once been a police weapon. It had been sold to a local gun shop after the police in the small town of Cosmopolis, Washington had decided it was surplus to requirements. The local chief of police, Gary Eisenhower, a self-confessed 'gun nut', confirmed the ATF's findings. He described himself as 'stunned' by the discovery. 'We're just devastated,' he said. 'This is not something that we'd like to have notoriety for.'

Also embarrassed was Dick Dyke, president of Bushmaster Firearms, when it was revealed that a central portion of Furrow's AR15 had come from his company. The revelation that Dyke was finance chairman in George Bush Jr's campaign to win the Republican nomination for the presidential elections was enough to cause him to resign his post. The fact that only a part of the AR15 had come from Dyke's company did little to diminish the controversy. It appeared that Furrow, anxious either to save himself some money or simply because he enjoyed tinkering with guns, had put the rifle together himself. However, the central part of the gun, the one with the serial numbers, trigger, pistol grip and the well that takes the ammunition clip, is in the eyes of the law traded as a complete weapon. The last thing that the staunchly pro-gun Republicans needed was a link to deadly assault weapons used for criminal purposes, especially for a crime like Furrow's. 'It certainly doesn't make you feel good when someone comes in harm's way with our gun,' Dyke added.

It is certain that more facts will emerge when Furrow's case finally makes it to court, but even at a relatively early stage it is possible to draw some conclusions.

It does appear that Furrow acted alone. Although he had a history of working in neo-Nazi groups no evidence has been shown to suggest that he acted in concert with others, nor that others were forewarned of what he was about to do. He had already become alienated from Debbie Mathews, and there is little evidence that he had kept up contacts with any other members of the Aryan Nations or other racist groups.

Again and again the image of Furrow that emerges is of someone lonely, embittered, isolated and suffering from severe personality problems. He was the school kid without friends, the student that nobody could remember, the employee who blended into the background. He faced the world with a polite smile that barely concealed the anger and the anguish within. When his landlady could describe him as the perfect tenant, when neighbours described him as pleasant and amiable, they were not being dishonest or disingenuous: they were merely reporting on the façade that he presented to them.

For a man with such low self-esteem to be told, suddenly, that he was important, valuable, a member of the Aryan race and therefore automatically superior to millions of other people, is no mean thing. From being somebody who didn't belong and who had trouble fitting in, Furrow found himself in the midst of a group that proclaimed him a brother and accepted him with open arms. He was even given a uniform and a rank, a place in a hierarchy to which he aspired and that accorded him a degree of respect that he so clearly needed and coveted. Joining the Aryan Nations was like an answer to his prayers. Furrow's self-doubts were whisked away with a liberal dose of hatred, his self-importance inflated and, just as importantly, any distrust that he felt towards the world as a whole could be easily explained and justified. It was no longer his fault: it was the fault of the Jews who ran the world.

Neo-Nazi groups create an aura of paranoia about them. They see themselves as the sole defenders of the white race against alien hordes of Jews, blacks, gays, anarchists, leftists, feminists and other 'enemies' of Western civilisation. They speak the language of war and when the rest of the world reacts with horror and revulsion at this language and their actions they feel vindicated. The paranoia is important as it binds members of these groups together. To a very real degree this overwhelming paranoid sense is deliberately fostered and nurtured. It serves a function for the leadership of such groups and as such it is encouraged in every way possible. In the case of somebody like Buford Furrow, this paranoia feeds their own twisted view of the world, merging with the undercurrent of alienation that they feel all the time.

Where did Furrow's mental illness start and his racism end? Unravelling the factors that made him turn a semi-automatic assault rifle on a group of screaming children is a task as much for psychiatrists as it is for politicians.

We can speculate about Furrow's motives. Although Furrow made it clear to the FBI agents he gave himself up to that he intended his attack to be a 'wake-up call to America to kill Jews', it is difficult to believe that this was his sole reason for carrying out the attack. We all act from a variety of reasons: there is rarely a single overriding motive, especially for an act with so momentous an impact.

Was Furrow acting on the same self-destructive drives that had taken him to a state mental institution months earlier? He was well armed and many police officers expressed surprise that he had not killed more victims and that he had not attacked any other targets. From the number of guns, the amount of ammunition and the other equipment that he had with him, it is clear that Furrow was ready for a siege. He had been expecting to come into conflict with the police and was prepared for it. Prepared, in fact, like Robert J. Mathews had been. If Furrow had gone into battle with the police it is likely that he would have gone the same way as the leader of The Order. In his statement after his arrest for pulling the knife on the health-care workers he had said that he had wanted the police to kill him.

If Furrow had intended to die fighting the forces of the federal government, then his nerve failed him on several occasions. The police were right on his tail after the first wave of shootings. If he had stood his ground a confrontation would have been a few minutes away. Although there were no witnesses to his slaughter of Joseph Ileto, gunshots were heard and the police were on the scene soon afterwards – he could have faced them there and then, but again he chose not to. Either Furrow's nerves failed or a suicidal shoot-out with the ATF was not what he wanted.

The parallel with Robert J. Mathews might offer another explanation, though again this is purely conjecture at this moment. Could Furrow have been planning to emulate Debbie Mathews's first husband? Could it be that in his own mind he imagined that by carrying out an act of terrorism he could prove to her that he was as good as the slain neo-Nazi?

Did he believe, however mistakenly, that he could win his way back into her affections by carrying out an act of pure violence against their perceived enemies?

It is possible that we shall never know the real reasons for Furrow's actions. Perhaps they were not clear even to himself. His behaviour immediately after the shooting spree smacks less of a detailed plan of action and more like the actions of somebody deranged. Perhaps he had no idea what he wanted to do other than to draw attention to himself. Gunning down small children would not give a sane person hero status – unless, of course, that person was so twisted with hatred that killing children became in their warped perception an act of war worthy of the description 'heroic'.

Whatever his motives, it is clear that Buford O'Neal Furrow cut a pitiful figure. He was not the dangerous political fanatic that he might have fancied himself to be. He was not an Aryan warrior doing battle with the spawn of Satan. He was a sad, inadequate figure who committed a series of terrible crimes. At the end of the day he was a pathetic social failure, and he has joined the ranks of those others like him who have used the gun to take out their frustrations on defenceless and innocent victims.

Even before Furrow's case came to trial there was speculation that he was going to plead insanity. It might have been the only hope of saving him from the death penalty. His family were clear that Furrow needed psychiatric help and that after his release from prison none was forthcoming. It was a feeling voiced by Loni Merrill when she told reporters that: 'I could be wrong, but he walked in there and stated he needed help. Then, all of a sudden, the help's not there. I don't believe he ever got the psychiatric help he needed.'

MARTIN BRYANT

Port Arthur, Tasmania, 1996

Port Arthur, on the island of Tasmania, off the southern coast of Australia, is a place long associated with crime and punishment, violence and death. Established on the Tasman peninsula as a penal colony in 1833, it was a locale so fearsome that prisoners at the original settlement felt compelled to commit murder so that they could be sent to Sydney to be hanged. Discipline was harsh, with frequent whippings, beatings and long spells in solitary confinement. By the late 1830s Port Arthur had become a convict town, housing some of Australia's most dangerous prisoners. Shackled inmates, clad in yellow uniforms, worked long, gruelling days in the scorching sun, building houses and roads, wharves and bridges, slowly turning the island wilderness into a true part of the fast-growing nation.

Escape from the prison area was almost impossible, joined as it was to the rest of Tasmania by a narrow strip of land that was always patrolled by guards and savage dogs. Many prisoners tried to swim to freedom. Most either drowned or were shot in the water by the armed guards. In such conditions escape attempts were the acts of men driven to desperation. Failure meant either certain death or vicious punishment to create a deterrent. Escape attempts were punishable by a hundred strokes of the whip, enough to permanently cripple any recipient. Other infractions of the rules were also punished by vicious floggings with a cat-o'-nine-tails or, possibly worse, forced labour in the mines. When Port Arthur was described by many as 'hell on earth' the description was not without justification.

The prison closed in 1877 and in the years that followed fires gutted several of the buildings, including the penitentiary itself and the church originally built by the chain gangs. Seeking to set aside its dark past, Port Arthur was renamed Carnavon, after the beautiful sheltered bay that it faces. By

1927, however, the name had reverted to Port Arthur and the population had dwindled from several thousand to a few hundred.

Today Port Arthur is a major tourist site, a reminder to many of Australia's convict past and violent history. With major government investment, many of the ruins have been lovingly restored or stabilised and the site has undergone major development. It is recognised now as a place of outstanding national significance, an important landmark in Australia's short and often brutal colonial history.

There are stories that the site is haunted, that the lost souls who perished there did not gain their freedom even in death. The tales of ghostly apparitions and unexplained happenings might be dismissed as gimmicks to excite the interest of the thousands of visitors, but the dark past of Port Arthur exerts its fascination even today. However, the events of Sunday, 28 April 1996 would surpass even the grimmest moments in Port Arthur's bloody history.

The weather was good and the fact that it was a Sunday meant that it would be a busy day. As Australia's premier historic site, Port Arthur ranks as one of the country's biggest tourist attractions. The forty hectares of carefully restored buildings, gardens and stabilised ruins, together with the sheer natural beauty of the sheltered bay would often attract over six hundred visitors on a good day: all the indications were that this day was going to be very good.

A guided tour of the area was due to begin at around 1.30 p.m., and a crowd had gathered outside the Information Centre waiting for the tour to begin. It is estimated that there were already around five hundred visitors within the confines of the sprawling historical site. Few people noticed the arrival of a blond-haired young man in a mustard yellow Volvo with a surfboard on its roof rack. The young driver looked like a surfer, too, with flowing golden locks, a tan and the relaxed demeanour of a typical Australian 'surfie'.

Carrying a tennis bag, he wandered into the Broad Arrow Café, next to the car park. There were probably around sixty customers in the café, a few of them eating outside, most of them eating inside the building and some of them browsing in the souvenir and gift shop. The personable young man – witnesses described him variously as being a teenager or in his early or middle twenties – chatted amiably to customers and staff as he ordered a meal and a drink. Rather than eat inside he took his tray outside onto the balcony where he could look across at the rest of the site.

He remarked to customers sitting around him that there were a lots of 'WASPs' about – referring to White Anglo-Saxon Protestants rather than the insect pests – and to others he spoke about the absence of 'Japs', referring to the Japanese and other East Asian tourists who liked to visit Port Arthur in large numbers. Finishing his meal, he picked up his tennis bag and walked back inside the café, still fairly busy serving lunches and cold drinks. He passed through the main restaurant area until he reached the rear wall. He dumped his tennis bag on an empty table, then stood and carefully scrutinised the people around him.

Moh Yee Ng and Soo Leng Chung, both from Malaysia, were quietly enjoying their lunch and were unaware of the young man behind them. They continued to talk and eat while the man carefully unzipped his bag and removed an AR15 semi-automatic assault rifle from it. With the gun slung from the hip – Rambo-style – he took aim and, before anybody knew what was happening, he opened fire. Moh Yee Ng was shot in the neck and died instantly. A second later the gun was trained on Soo Leng Chung and a single shot rang out, the bullet taking most of the tourist's head with it.

Things had happened so unexpectedly and so quickly that people had no time to react. The blond gunman swivelled round quickly to face a group sitting at a table near him. Mick Sargent, Kate Scott and Caroline Villiers, all visitors from Perth, were waiting for a fourth member of their party, John Riviere, to join them. They had just witnessed the murder of the two Asian tourists but things were moving so rapidly that they were still getting to their feet when the killer turned towards them. The third shot hit Mick Sargent – who was facing the gunman – in the head while the fourth hit Kate Scott in the back of the head before she even had a chance to turn towards the gunfire.

After crashing to the ground Sargent realised that his wound was only superficial, despite the blood pouring from it. Unfortunately his girlfriend, Kate, was not so lucky. She was clearly dead, the shot to the back of the head having killed her instantly. Instinctively Sargent lay still, realising that his best chance of survival was to play dead while the crazed gunman continued his murderous rampage.

By this time people were starting to react. Anthony Nightingale, a tourist from Victoria, was sitting near the front of the restaurant. Once the shooting started he jumped up from his seat and started shouting. Some reports claimed that he called out 'No, no! Not here!' The gunman turned towards him and, with his weapon still slung from the hip, took aim and shot Nightingale once in the neck. He was the fourth fatality in only a matter of seconds.

Caroline Villiers, who had been with Mick Sargent and Kate Scott, looked as though she was about to make a run for it. But Sargent realised that the gunman would take her out with a single shot too. So he gestured for her to duck down onto the floor with him instead and to use Kate Scott's dead body as cover.

There was no random spraying of bullets, no wild shooting at anything that moved. The blond gunman was acting calmly and with precision. Not a shot was wasted as he carefully took aim and fired, choosing each victim in turn and then shooting for the head.

The gunman then turned on a large group at the table next to the one at which Anthony Nightingale had been enjoying his last meal. Kevin Sharpe was next: he saw what was happening and flung his arm up, either to protect his wife or himself. He was shot twice, once in the arm and once in the head. Next was Walter Bennet, killed by a single bullet that passed through his neck and caused massive and fatal head injuries to Ray Sharpe. Several more people in the group, including Gary Broome and John and Gaye Fidler, were injured by shrapnel fragments of the bullets that had killed others close by.

Just beyond that table sat Andrew Mills, a resident of Hobart, Tasmania, with a couple of friends of his from

Sydney, Tony and Sarah Kistan. Once the shooting started the group stood up and Tony Kistan tried to push his wife towards the exit. At the same time they wanted to try and reason with the killer, hoping that they could get him to stop shooting. It was a vain hope. The gunman downed the two men, each with a single shot to the head. As Tony Kistan lay dying in his wife's arms he whispered to her, 'I am going to be with the Lord now.' Again, shrapnel from the bullets caused more injuries in those sitting nearby.

While people were diving for cover, or in some cases cowering on the floor covered in blood from bullet or shrapnel wounds, the gunman moved into the centre of the restaurant. To his right were the windows at the front of the restaurant, on his left the servery and an ornamental fireplace, and around him were tables and chairs and groups of shocked and frightened people. Directly in front of him there was a group of three: Carolyn Loughton and her teenage daughter Sarah, and Carolyn's boyfriend Graham Colyer. The gunman lined up Colyer and fired once, hitting him in the neck. As in Mick Sargent's case, the gunman's usual deadly precision failed. The massive wound almost killed Colyer, but somehow he managed to survive and escape the instant death that most of the other victims of direct hits had suffered.

Nothing better illustrates the stunned disbelief of most people in the restaurant than the reactions of Mervyn and Mary Howard, both of whom were sitting at a table in the corner by the door. They had been enjoying an afternoon cup of tea when the shooting had started a few seconds earlier. They were still struggling to work out what was happening when the young gunman turned to them. Mervyn Howard was still clutching his cup of tea when a bullet took his head off. His wife was killed with one shot to the neck and another to the head.

Having taken two shots to kill Mary Howard the killer turned his attention back to the group directly in front of him. Carolyn Loughton was on the floor, doing her best to shield her daughter and certain that Graham Colyer was dead or dying. The gunman approached them and took careful aim. He shot Carolyn in the back at close range but, miraculously, she did not die. Her fifteen-year-old daughter Sarah was not so lucky. She was executed with a single shot to the head.

It had taken the gunman only about fifteen seconds to kill twelve innocent victims and injure many more. It was also abundantly clear that he had no intention of stopping at the first dozen.

Attached to the restaurant was a gift shop, and it was there that some people had managed to take shelter. The gunman paused, turned and decided that his next group of victims was to be in the shop. As the killer walked towards it through the restaurant, Robert Elliott made the stupid mistake of standing up as he passed. In a single, fluid motion the man with the rifle turned and fired twice. Elliot dropped. Wounded in the arm and in the head, he was lucky not to pay for his sudden movement with his life. He survived to tell the tale and to try and work out why he had acted so rashly when everyone else had been doing their best to keep out of the gunman's line of sight.

There were probably about a dozen people in the gift shop and most of them realised that they were in grave danger. One couple, Peter and Carolyn Nash, tried to make a dash for it via a door that led to a balcony, only to find that the door was locked. Two other customers, Dennis Lever and Ron Jary, managed to push their wives and another customer, an elderly woman, behind a screen. Two cousins, Nicole Burgess and Elizabeth Howard, young members of staff, were still standing behind their counter, paralysed with fear and unable or unwilling to move. Ron and Gwen Neander, also gift shop customers, had seen some of the shootings, including those of Mervyn and Mary Howard, and knew that the gunman was headed their way. They ducked down behind a postcard stand near the counter, knowing full well that it was woefully inadequate as cover.

The gunman strode in and shot the two shop girls instantly. A second later he murdered Dennis Lever. Turning slightly he spied Gwen Neander cowering behind the postcard rack. He took aim and, without a second's hesitation, shot her in the face as she looked up at him pleadingly.

Hearing noises from the restaurant, the killer walked back to see what was going on. In the brief lull Jason Winter, a holidaymaker from New Zealand, assumed that the gunman had left the gift shop via a door there. Winter had been hiding near the servery but was worried sick about his wife, son and father-in-law who had been sitting by the window. Relieved that the killer seemed to have disappeared, Winter stood up, turned to tell some of the other people near him that it was now safe and then realised his mistake. As the New Zealander emerged from his hiding place the gunman fired two more shots, killing him instantly. The shrapnel from the bullets also injured Dennis Olson who had been crouching nearby, causing wounds to the hand, chest, head and eyes.

The gunman then took a shot at Peter Crosswell who was covering two friends with his body as they tried to hide under one of the tables. Crosswell was hit in the buttock by a single bullet, a wound that was not life-threatening.

Back in the gift shop a whole group of people were assembled by the locked door leading to a balcony. Unable to get the door open, they were trapped as the killer walked back into the shop. Ron Jary, Peter and Carolyn Nash, Pauline Masters and an unidentified Asian tourist were sitting ducks, facing certain death and with no means of escape. Peter Nash tried to shield his wife's body with his own and was killed for it. Ron Jary and Pauline Masters were killed next. Carolyn Nash survived, thanks to her husband's sacrifice. The Asian tourist was lined up next and was saved only by the fact that the assault rifle had run out of ammunition.

At this point the gunman simply changed the magazine on the assault rifle and decided to leave the café. He had fired 29 shots, leaving a single round in the magazine. By changing the magazine with that round still loaded he was minimising the risk of being caught with no bullets during the changeover. It reduced the time during which he was unable to shoot to an absolute minimum.

In two minutes the killer had emptied his first ammunition clip. The toll was twenty dead and around a dozen injured. For the survivors those minutes were the longest of their lives, a nightmarish 120 seconds when a blond-haired demon had walked among them, arbitrarily claiming innocent lives with deadly precision.

While the gunman had been massacring people inside the restaurant, many others outside had heard the shots and come down to investigate. Regular re-enactments of historical scenes are commonplace at Port Arthur, and some imagined that the volleys of shots from the semi-automatic rifle were actually musket-fire blanks from just such a costumed presentation. A large crowd, many clutching video cameras, were soon making their way towards the source of the shots, hurrying lest they should miss anything.

Fortunately some people had realised that something was not right, chief among them Ian Kingston, the Site Security Officer and also Manager of the State Emergency Service in Tasmania. He was standing in the upper car park when he first heard the shots. At first he was unsure what was going on but as the shots continued he became alarmed and started to run down towards the café. As he got closer he could see dust coming off the walls. He assumed that electrical wiring was shorting and arcing and that this was the cause of both the noise and the dust. When he got to the entrance to the café he was stunned to see two bodies on the floor, covered in blood and clearly both dead.

Kingston stepped into the café and saw one of the staff at the counter, staring open-mouthed at the shocking scene before her. Suddenly the shooting started up again. He vividly described what happened next:

The first thing I saw then was the gun come up. It was a massive gun, big magazine. And then he started shooting people right next to me, only half a metre away. The destruction of the bodies was unbelievable . . . How many were dead and how many were lying down, I don't know. I had time to think that I was going to die. I had time to think that I'd never made a will, that my children would lose their father . . . The girl was still at the servery, still there, frozen. And he's shooting people and getting closer to her and I'm yelling, 'Get out! Leave! Run!' In the finish, he shot a person only metres from her and she ran. She ran out the back door. That saved her life. She would've been shot if she had stayed there.

He got to a point where I could get out. I got out the door and with me I took as many people as I could, but the problem was that every person a few seconds from the café was flocking in. They were flocking in through the front door ... probably thirty or forty people trying to get into the café as I was trying to get people out, the ones that were closer to the door. I had to yell out 'Get out! Get out! There's a gunman in here!' They wouldn't move and in the finish I yelled out 'Fire!' And then they started moving. I said 'Get Out! Fire!' and they all ran. They thought there was a re-enactment going on.

Kingston had witnessed the killings probably just before the gunman turned back to return to the shop. There had been three members of staff working at the counter and the servery, and all three fled at that point through the kitchen. Brigid Cook, who had been working in the kitchens, had heard the shooting and although she had not witnessed anything directly she too fled when the counter staff rushed through.

Cook decided to warn as many people as possible, even though she half feared she would make a fool of herself if there was nothing really going on. From the back door of the café she turned and headed towards the upper car park, waving her arms in the air and trying to attract attention. There were several coaches parked there, with a group of drivers and passengers milling about. Some understood Cook's warning, but others were still moving towards the café to investigate for themselves the reason for the excitement. Closer to the Broad Arrow Café, Ian Kingston was still shouting 'Fire!' and forcing people back the way they had come.

Brigid Cook then turned and headed towards the lower car park. This meant cutting directly across the gunman's line of fire, but she took the chance in order to save as many people as possible from the horror that was unfolding.

Ian Kingston takes up the story again: 'He [the gunman] would have run out – anyone in front of the café he would have shot ... We evacuated everyone we could get easily and quickly from in front of the café and in front of the Information Office ... We hid them out of sight up Jetty Road, the road to the toll-booth. When we got up Jetty Road far enough, we took them into the Government Gardens [the area to the left of the road]. We had them just at the corner of Jetty Road when he came out of the café.'

The gunman emerged from the café at around 1.50 p.m. He stopped and took aim at the crowd fleeing up Jetty Road. He fired several shots but his aim this time was not so true and nobody was hit. He even fired at a building worker operating machinery at one end of the site, where renovation work was still taking place. The panicked crowd dispersed, some seeking shelter in the bush by the side of the road or behind the Information Centre, others following Ian Kingston up towards the toll-booth that marked the entrance to Port Arthur.

Perhaps missing his latest batch of targets caused the gunman to rethink his strategy for his next move was to head towards his car parked in the lower car park. He had come ready with ample supplies: three high-powered rifles, stocks of ammunition, handcuffs, containers full of petrol and fire lighters. It emerged later that on the way to the Broad Arrow Café he'd even stopped off to buy himself a lighter as he didn't own one.

Brigid Cook had by this time reached the lower car park. There were three coaches parked there, all of them with the driver's cabs facing the café. She had been warning as many people as possible and was at the last of the coaches when the killer reached his car. He looked across at the coaches and saw Royce Thompson, one of the drivers, running for cover. The gunman killed him with a single shot to the back. He then proceeded to target whoever else crossed his sights. Brigid Cook was still ushering a group to safety when she was shot. The bullet passed through her right leg and entered her left. She fell back against one of the rear wheels of the coach, where she was later helped by another of the drivers who had first-aid training.

Some people tried to take cover inside the coaches. Yvonne Lockley and Winifred Aplin, on holiday from Adelaide, were shot as they clambered into their coach. Yvonne was injured, Winifred Aplin was killed. The killer fired at Neville and Janette Quin, missing Neville but hitting and injuring Janette. Next he turned on Douglas Hutchinson, a passenger on the last bus, hitting him in the arm.

Having finally arrived at his car, the gunman dumped the AR15 and selected his .308 SLR (self-loading rifle). He tested the new gun by turning and firing across towards the Broad Arrow Café again, and out towards the water. People up by the jetty near the car park were stunned to see the gravel near them suddenly flying up. Some even imagined that this was a special effect designed to heighten the Port Arthur experience.

There were more bursts of gunfire as the killer moved towards the coaches. None of his shots found their targets until he came across Janette Quin lying on the ground, suffering from the injuries he had just inflicted on her. Mercilessly he took aim and fired again, clearly intending to finish her off for good.

As had been the case in the café, things were moving so quickly that people hardly had time to respond. There were still people sitting in their seats on the coaches, unable to grasp what was happening or why. The gunman seemed relaxed and in control of the situation: there was nothing panic-stricken about his behaviour. He moved from place to place, deciding on a victim, taking aim quickly but efficiently and firing. If he experienced any fear of capture or death at the hands of the police he didn't show it.

The killer climbed aboard one of the coaches only to find that it had already been deserted by driver and passengers alike. Finding no targets he simply looked through the window at the adjacent coach where Elva Gaylard was still in her seat. He fired through the coach windows, killing her with a single shot. Gordon Francis, a passenger on the same coach as Gayland, ran down the aisle to shut the door before the blond spree killer tried to get on. He knew that once the killer boarded the coach there would be no escape for any of them. The gunman took a shot and injured Francis in his shoulder.

Meanwhile Neville Quin had become separated from his wife in the panic and confusion. Fearing the worst he started looking for her, moving carefully around the coaches, aware that the maniac gunman was still hunting for victims. Neville found Janette lying on the floor, cold to the touch, unconscious and obviously dying. While Neville tried hopelessly to do something to help her he heard an explosion of sound and realised that a shot had been fired at him. When he turned he saw the killer taking aim once more. Neville scrambled to his feet and made it to the front of the coach, but the gunman was in pursuit, firing shot after shot. For a second Neville thought he'd got away after scrambling onto the coach and hiding, but the killer spotted him and followed.

'No one gets away from me,' he was told. Then the gunman fired again. The shot entered Neville Quin's neck, but his assailant was wrong, Neville did get away as the wound later proved not to be fatal. A few minutes after the killer left the coach to seek his next victim, the seriously injured man staggered off the coach and crawled to his dying wife.

Having finished with Neville Quin, the gunman then took a few more shots at other people before climbing back into his car and heading up the road towards the toll-booth at the entrance to the site. For those left behind, the scenes of bloodshed and mayhem were unbelievable. Doctors and nurses, off-duty policemen and others among the visitors who had training in handling emergencies emerged slowly to try and treat the injured. There was still a great deal of fear: nobody knew where the gunman had gone and many were not even sure whether the killings were the work of one lone maniac or of some kind of armed group.

In his account Ian Kingston ably expressed this air of confusion and fear. Describing his journey back towards the café after herding people to safety, he said: 'I was petrified that any second he was going to jump out from behind a tree and shoot me – getting from the Parsonage back to the café was the most fearful time in my life . . . Where was he? Was he there? It was dead silent. I could hear a little bit of activity at the café, but nothing much. So I ran back down, dodged from tree to tree in case he was still lurking on site with a gun. I finally got back. Went to the café. Couldn't believe what I'd seen . . .'

A number of people had rung the police, including Wendy Scurr, one of the tour guides who had first phoned from the office in the Information Centre soon after the shooting started in the café. At first she had trouble convincing the police that there really was a gunman on the loose, but her call was soon confirmed by a number of others. In the end Scurr simply held the phone out towards the sound of the firing so that the person at the other end of the line could hear the shots for themselves.

Up at the toll-booth nobody knew what had been going on. They had heard the shots but had no way of knowing what they meant. When two more cars arrived at the entrance to Port Arthur, Aileen Kingston, who was on duty, took the entrance money and waved the cars in. The first car, a BMW, belonged to Mary Nixon, a native of Tasmania who had with her three elderly friends from the mainland: Jim Pollard (who was doing the driving), Robert Saltzman and his wife, Helene. The second car contained a holidaying couple from New Zealand, identified only as the Buckleys.

While the large group that Ian Kingston had directed up towards Jetty Road had largely taken cover behind the trees at the side of the road or behind the Information Centre, a smaller group who had set off earlier had decided to carry on up the road towards the site's exit. The group included four friends from the mainland and a local mother, Nanette Mikac, with her two small children, Alannah, aged six, and Madeline, aged three. As they neared the toll-booth they could look back towards the lower car park where the gunman was still stalking around the buses, shooting at will.

When they heard a car coming up the road from the site towards them the group must have sighed with relief, imagining that help was at hand. The five adults had been struggling up the road with the children and the chance for a lift to safety was just what they needed. 'We're safe now, Pumpkin,' Nanette told the six-year-old. The car stopped a little way from them, on the opposite side of the road. Nanette walked towards it and John Boskovich, also part of the same group, also stopped and turned back.

The blond man who emerged from the car put his arm on Nanette's shoulder and told her to get down on her knees. He repeated the order three times. 'Please don't hurt my babies,' the poor woman cried.

One of the group cried, 'It's him' – and then John Boskovich saw the gun. It was too late to save Nanette and the children. While everybody else turned and ran, Nanette Mikac and three-year-old Madeline were shot at point-blank range. Alannah fled into the bush and tried to hide behind a shrub, but the gunman was heartless. He chased the six-year-old and executed her in the same callous manner as he had her mother and sister.

As the two newly arrived cars moved down into the site they stopped when a man ran towards them and flagged them down. Breathlessly he warned them that there was a gunman on the loose. Both cars reversed immediately and drove back the way they had come, towards the toll-booth. There they stopped and the Buckleys got out of their vehicle to ask Aileen Kingston for an explanation. As they did so they heard a noise, turned and saw the gunman cold-bloodedly execute Nanette Mikac and her children. The Buckleys had no time to get back into their car to escape. Instead, they ran out into the main road beyond the toll-booth where they were picked up and whisked to safety by a passing motorist.

The group in Mary Nixon's car had not witnessed Nanette's execution and were probably at a loss to understand what was happening. When a mustard yellow Volvo pulled up beside them they had no idea who the young blond driver was. When he walked over and demanded that everybody get out of the car because he wanted it, there was consternation. Robert Saltzman climbed out of the car to start arguing. The argument did not last long. The younger man simply turned, walked back to his Volvo, grabbed his .308 SLR and shot Robert Saltzman dead.

Instead of simply obeying the obviously armed and dangerous young man, Jim Pollard got out of the driver's seat and crossed the road towards him. Pollard's fate was to join his friend in death as a single shot rang out. The gunman then calmly walked over, opened the rear passenger doors of the BMW and shot Helene Saltzman and Mary Nixon, pulling their bodies out of the car and onto the road.

The Mikac murders were witnessed by Debra Rabe who had turned onto the road leading to the Port Arthur site. She had been signalled to turn back by Mary Nixon even before Robert Saltzman had been gunned down. She reversed quickly and headed back up the road towards the petrol station at the junction of the Port Arthur road and the main highway.

Having acquired the BMW, which was more to his fancy than the Volvo – to which the police would have been alerted in any case – the blond killer then transferred his belongings to his new car. Aside from the guns and ammunition he made sure that he took some of the containers of petrol and the two pairs of handcuffs.

Another car turned onto the road towards the site. The occupants could see the dead bodies lying sprawled on the ground, and they could see the gunman running between the Volvo and the BMW. They backed away quickly but not before he managed to fire at them, shattering the windscreen but fortunately not hitting anyone. They headed directly for the service station near the road that led into the site. To Debra Rabe's horrific report of the murder of Nanette Mikac and her children, they added their report of the murder of the people in the BMW. The two cars then headed off, making a getaway while they still could.

Those left behind at the service station rapidly prepared to join the fleeing cars or else sought cover. Glenn Pears, a Tasmanian who lived in Sydney, had returned to the island for a family party and had brought a fellow lawyer, Zoë Hall, with him. As they rushed to get into his white Toyota Corolla, the BMW zoomed up and blocked their exit. An eyewitness, Jim Laycock, described the events that followed. 'He [the gunman] just blocked their exit and then pulled or forced the man out of the car and threatened him with the rifle. The guy was saying, "Don't shoot, don't shoot. Everything's OK." Then the gunman yelled at him to get in the boot [of the BMW] . . . then slammed the boot and he just went and shot the woman. It was the quickest shot, she just went. It smashed the window, went straight through, straight in the heart . . . it was the most frightening two minutes of my life, but at the time you don't think about that.'

Zoë Hall had been shot three times and killed.

With a hostage stashed in the boot of the stolen BMW, the gunman drove in the direction of the Seascape guest house, a picturesque cottage in landscaped gardens next to the sea. As he approached the entrance to the cottage he cut sharply across the road and jumped out of the car. Another car that was towing a trailer was just passing and he fired a couple of shots at it which went wide. The driver simply assumed that for some reason the blond driver was firing blanks.

A second later another car turned the corner towards the Seascape. The driver, Linda White, saw a young blond man with a gun and thought that he was out hunting rabbits. As she watched him, however, he raised his rifle and fired directly at her. The first bullet hit the bonnet and shattered the windscreen. One of the next two or three shattered her arm. She managed to keep control of the car as she took the corner but then the vehicle stopped. Another bullet had severed the accelerator cable.

The people in the car following Linda White's vehicle had witnessed the shooting, but before they had time to react they too became targets. A bullet smashed their windscreen, causing numerous injuries to the driver, Doug Horne. The car took the corner and came to a stop. As passenger Neville Shilkin took the wheel they were joined by Linda White and her passenger, and together they managed to make an escape.

The driver of the next car slammed it into reverse as soon as he saw what had happened to the vehicle in front. Again gunfire rang out and a windscreen splintered but nobody was hurt. The gunman's aim was better the next time. He fired at a car belonging to Simon Williams and his wife Susan. Both suffered serious head injuries but they were lucky: they lived.

The sport of shooting at passing cars seemed to pall fairly quickly for the young killer. Perhaps the ratio of kills was not high enough compared to the carnage he had created in the café. He jumped back into the stolen BMW and drove down to the cottage. There he opened the boot, dragged Glenn Pears out and snapped the first pair of handcuffs onto him. He then forced his unwilling and frightened hostage into the cottage and used the second pair of cuffs to secure him to some immovable object, probably the post at the foot of the staircase.

Having immobilised his hostage the gunman went back outside, retrieved his guns and then used some of the petrol he'd been stockpiling to set the BMW alight. It signalled the end of the spree and the start of the siege.

The first local police had started to arrive. The messages radioed to them had been getting more and more fantastic, with spiralling body counts and confusion over which car the assailant was driving. As Constable Paul Hyland neared the Seascape he saw the damaged vehicles, including one parked outside the Fox and Hounds hotel where many of the car passengers and drivers were taking refuge. He too called at the Fox and Hounds where the witnesses told him what had happened. From there he drove nervously towards the Seascape where he was joined by a second police officer, Constable Gary Whittle. Looking across to the cottage they could see black smoke billowing into the air as the BMW went up in flames.

The two men decided that they needed to set up road-blocks to stop any more cars approaching the cottage. Two more policemen, Pat Allen and Perry Caulfield, sharing a single estate car, were on their way. Perry Caulfield armed himself and was dropped off at the Fox and Hounds in case he needed to defend it if the gunman decided to launch a one-man attack on the place. Pat Allen took the car and headed towards the Seascape. As he approached it he realised that he was on the same side as the cottage, in direct line of sight of the killer. He turned rapidly and reversed at speed along the road towards the cottage and the other two police officers, thus placing as much of his car as possible between himself and the gunman.

This precaution probably saved his life, for as Allen neared Gary Whittle's car the shooting began. Several shots were fired. Some hit the car but missed Allen. He stopped, grabbed his radio, then scuttled out of the car and into the ditch at the side of the road, next to Gary Whittle.

The gunman had found himself a whole new armoury inside the house. And from his vantage point he had a clear view of the road. He could see where the police officers were huddled together and was easily able to keep them pinned down, firing repeatedly any time one of them moved. The officers were certain that they were going to die, but there was nothing they could do to escape.

The biggest police operation in Australia's history was by now moving into gear. Members of the Special Operations Group (SOG) were on their way, and dozens of other police officers were quickly arriving at the scene. Their first aim was to ensure that there could be no escape for the lone gunman, who was believed to be holding two other hostages as well as Glenn Pears. The owners of the Seascape, David and Sally Martin, were believed to be still in their cottage and at the mercy of the lone gunman.

Conditions around the cottage were not helpful to the police operation. The Seascape commanded excellent views of the surrounding area, allowing the gunman to have full views of the road and part of the adjacent highway. Also, because of the geography of the area, radio transmission was extremely poor, hampering communications and at one point forcing the police to use runners to pass messages between different groups. It meant that an all-out attack on the cottage was out of the question. Not only would it have meant possible injuries and fatalities among the SOG officers but it would also have given the killer time to execute all three of the prisoners he was thought to be holding.

There was no choice but to negotiate, and that task fell to a team headed by Sergeant Terry McCarthy. Communication was established with the gunman by talking with him on the cordless phone in the cottage. It was confirmed that the blond spree killer was Martin Bryant, a 29-year-old with a history of behavioural problems. In the course of the next six hours McCarthy kept Bryant talking, trying to get him to release his hostages unharmed and to give himself up. At one point Bryant demanded a helicopter in return for the three lives he was holding hostage.

As darkness fell, over two hundred police officers were involved in the operation, but they were stymied by Bryant's superior position inside the cottage. Eventually the battery on the cordless phone gave out and silence fell. The six hours of negotiation had made no progress towards resolution.

Throughout the night the police were kept at bay as Bryant fired at anything that moved. With access to the roads severely limited, helicopters were being used to ferry the dead and injured and these too became targets. At one point officers Gary Whittle and Pat Allen were rescued by members of the SOG who helped them escape from the ditch where they had lain for over eight hours. In marked contrast to Bryant's earlier marksmanship, the 250 rounds that he fired during the siege caused no major damage and no injuries.

Finally, after about twelve hours, smoke started to rise from the cottage. Soon the whole place was ablaze, and it appeared that Bryant had decided to kill himself and his hostages rather than give himself up. Suddenly, however, a blazing figure ran out, pulling at his burning clothes. Police rushed forward and doused the flames to discover that the fiery form was that of Martin Bryant. Nobody else was left alive in the cottage.

Glenn Pears had been executed by Bryant at some point during the siege. The Martins, it later transpired, had been murdered by Bryant before he'd even arrived at the Broad Arrow Café. The Seascape was both the start and finish point of the murderous spree that involved thirty-five deaths and numerous injuries.

Police could not even enter the burning house to search for the bodies of the victims as the fire ignited the ammunition left behind and bullets were still firing at random. Bryant was arrested, put under armed guard and taken to the Royal Hobart Hospital to be treated for his severe burns. He was to remain in hospital for several weeks under permanent armed guard, following a spate of death threats directed at him by outraged Australians.

On 1 May, in a hearing at the hospital, Bryant, drugged, groggy and hardly conscious, was charged with the murder of Kate Scott. Later he was charged with an additional 34 counts of murder, nineteen counts of attempted murder and numerous charges of causing grievous bodily harm, wounding, aggravated assault and two cases of arson. In all, he was charged with a total of 72 offences.

The shock of the story stunned not only Australia but the whole world. The scale of the violence and its sheer ruthlessness was stunning. The harrowing scene of the murder of Nanette Mikac and her two daughters was reported the world over. Wendy Scurr, a trained nurse with over thirty years of experience, described the horror of the carnage in the café where she accidentally trod on skull fragments and saw bits of brain smeared across walls and lying in plates of food.

With the shock came the details of Martin Bryant's life. The picture of the young blond was flashed across the world, his long hair, pale skin and blue eyes making him look more like an Aussie soap star than a deranged maniac. And yet 'deranged maniac' was the tag that stuck to him as neighbours recalled his odd behaviour, manic-depressive mood swings and occasional aggression.

Born on 7 May 1966, Martin Bryant revealed very early in his life that he was of extremely low intelligence and suffered from a number of behavioural problems. With a measured IQ of 66, it was estimated that this put him in the bottom one or two per cent of the population. This low figure, confirmed in numerous assessments when he was a child and an adolescent, was described by Professor Paul E. Mullen, a Forensic Psychiatrist, as putting Bryant on 'the borderline range between intellectual disability and the dull normal individual'.

Predictably, Bryant's school career was characterised by constant behavioural problems. He suffered learning difficulties and speech problems that put him in remedial classes, adding to the already considerable alienation between him and his peers. He was also frequently disruptive in class, leading to suspicions that he suffered from hyperactivity. This was treated with drugs that had little or no effect on his behaviour. Bryant lacked friends: his frequent attempts to make them were rebuffed and the resultant feeling of constant rejection was something that was to stay with him for the rest of his life. He was also bullied to some extent, constantly the butt of the joke and on the receiving end of a good deal of verbal and, occasionally, physical abuse. As he himself stated later: 'I was hazed and knocked around all the time. No one wanted to be my friend.'

In August 1977 Bryant was suspended from his primary school and had to undergo psychiatric assessment. During this assessment it was noted that he enjoyed torturing animals and tormenting his younger sister and other young children, and that he took great pleasure when other children suffered difficulties at school. By the time he moved to high school a great deal of remedial work had been done with him and his behaviour had improved considerably. Bryant was placed in a special educational unit where his problems were acknowledged and he received additional support. There was no change socially: he was still isolated from everyone but his immediate family, no matter how hard he tried to remedy the situation.

Bryant's problems were exacerbated by his appearance. He was a good-looking young man: he looked 'normal', which created social expectations in those who encountered him. When these expectations were not met, he felt extremely hurt by the rejection that inevitably followed. After leaving school he was examined, in 1984, to ascertain whether or not he qualified for a disability pension since his problems made it impossible for him to seek work. It was at this time that the possibility was first raised that Bryant might be suffering from a form of schizophrenic illness. The clinical psychologist who examined him, Dr Cunningham-Dax, concluded that he was 'intellectually handicapped and personality-disordered' and the pension was granted. The tragedy of Bryant's condition was that he was not so severely impaired intellectually that he did not understand that he wasn't as bright as everybody else. He was, in fact, painfully aware of his inadequacies, and always felt inferior when meeting other people. So it is no surprise to learn that he suffered from a low level of self-esteem.

Bryant's mother took the possibility of schizophrenia and ran with it. She reported to other doctors in subsequent years that her son was a paranoid schizophrenic, though he had never been formally diagnosed. In fact, in the report on Bryant that he compiled for the court case after the massacre, Professor Mullen explicitly rejected the possibility.

Bryant's social problems did not disappear after leaving school. He still had no friends, and without being able to gain regular employment there were few social arenas in which he could engage with other people. Occasionally he would be employed to do odd jobs – tidying up or doing some simple gardening – and it was at one of these that he first met the person he described as his 'only true friend'. Helen Harvey, a wealthy middle-aged woman, first employed Bryant to help around the garden but soon warmed to the lonely young man. She took a motherly interest in him: reportedly, she told neighbours that '. . . she had looked after him for years, that she was like a mother to him and that his parents couldn't handle him.'

Bryant and Harvey lived together for a number of years, though there was no evidence of their having a sexual relationship. In October 1992 they were involved in a car accident in which Bryant was seriously injured and Harvey was killed. With Harvey's death, Bryant inherited upwards of $500,000 and several properties. He was now rich, but his intellectual disability was such that he did not really appreciate it. The money was placed into a trust that gave him a generous monthly allowance but stopped him squandering his new-found wealth.

Less than a year later Bryant's father, who had been suffering from depression, committed suicide. Although Bryant claimed to have had a good relationship with his father, and there is ample evidence to support this, some observers said that he reacted to the death with marked indifference. Neighbours asserted that minutes after being told of his father's death Bryant was out 'nonchalantly mowing the lawn'. Much later, after the Port Arthur massacre, there was much unsubstantiated speculation in the press that Bryant had actually murdered his father, had murdered Helen Harvey to inherit her wealth and was linked to a series of unsolved murders.

While Bryant's intellectual abilities were severely impaired, there was no evidence that he was suffering any lowering of the libido. His first sexual encounters were with prostitutes and escorts, whom he would visit about once a month. Later he managed to form relationships with a number of young women, including one sixteen-year-old girl. It was also reported that Bryant had an interest in hard-core pornography, including videos depicting bestiality. It is known that during his only trip to Amsterdam he had spent many hours visiting the red-light district and sex shops. On his return to Australia he was stopped by Customs who seized a number of videotapes, including one that featured sex between women and animals. Neighbours reported also that Bryant slept with his pet pig, though there was nothing in the psychiatric reports to suggest that there was anything sexual about this. However, some of the more salacious newspaper reports hinted that there was something unnatural going on.

Also widely reported at the time were Bryant's interests in survivalism and violent horror videos. For example, it was reported by some tabloid papers that his favourite film was one of the *Child's Play* series of schlock-horror movies, which feature a doll called 'Chucky' who comes to life and carries out a series of gruesome slaughters. The films have become notorious in recent years as they have become associated with a number of high-profile cases of murder by children, including the James Bulger case in which two young boys beat a younger child to death after luring him away from his mother. However, in conversations with Professor Mullen Bryant admitted to watching violent action videos but claimed that he did not like horror movies as they frightened him. Rather, he claimed that his favourite video was *Babe*, perhaps because he had his own pig.

There is no doubting Bryant's interest in survivalism, guns and violence. He is known to have regularly purchased survivalist and gun magazines that featured articles on weapons, tactics, militia activities, ammunition and so on. What he managed to make of these magazines, given his low IQ, is not known. But it is known that he had a good detailed knowledge about weapons, and he admitted that his interest in the subject had been growing rather than diminishing. Certainly some people have suggested that Bryant gleaned enough from these magazines and action videos to be able to meticulously plan and carry out the massacre, which, if true, was certainly a remarkable achievement for someone with such a limited intelligence quotient.

The break-up with his sixteen-year-old girlfriend had affected Bryant badly, making him severely depressed. He had begun to realise that things were not going to change for him. Without a girlfriend, without Helen Harvey and without his father, he felt totally on his own. He wanted to be liked, to have friends, to have a future, but instead his life was filled with the pain of repeated rejection.

For example, Bryant had travelled abroad – to the UK, the US, New Zealand and Thailand as well as to Holland – with the intention of meeting people, yet here too his efforts at socialising failed miserably. He tried to strike up conversations in bars and cafés, but people simply moved away, ignored him or else extricated themselves from the situation very quickly. In a telling statement, Bryant admitted that the most successful parts of his excursions outside Australia had been the flights. On the planes, strapped into his seat, he had been able to have conversations with the passengers sitting next to him as there was nowhere else for them to go.

Although Bryant had found a new girlfriend in the months before the massacre, his depression did not lift. One of the characteristics of his personality was to brood about past slights and disappointments. He had a long memory, and would run through incidents over and over again, becoming increasingly angry and agitated. The years of rejection had also caused him to become deeply suspicious of strangers. Although he did not imagine that there was an all-out conspiracy against him, he did believe that people were talking about him, looking at him, conspiring to harm him. In the words of Professor Mullen, he nursed the 'conviction that people wanted to hurt or harm him'.

Increasingly, too, Bryant had been thinking about how he could 'get even' with the people who he imagined were against him. He bore grudges against the Martins, owners of the Seascape and the first victims in the massacre. The Martins and Bryant's father had both wanted to buy a particular farm near Port Arthur. The Martins eventually purchased the property, causing great disappointment to the Bryant family. Bryant believed that the Martins had acted unfairly in acquiring the property, and that his father's disappointment was a major contributing factor to his depression and eventual suicide. After he had inherited Helen Harvey's money Bryant had attempted to purchase the property but his offer had been rejected.

Bryant, Professor Mullen concluded, was not mentally ill. Nor was he especially manic. There was not even evidence of a depressive illness, despite the family history of such affliction. It meant, of course, that Bryant was fit to plead a case. Insanity or diminished responsibility were not options that he would be allowed to exercise.

In his statement to the police, Bryant was adamant that he had not carried out the massacre. He denied ever being at Port Arthur, and claimed instead that he had been surfing that day. He admitted carjacking the BMW, but not shooting anybody. He admitted taking a hostage but could not remember clearly what had happened to him. He admitted setting fire to the stolen car and claimed that it was how he had received his own severe burns. He admitted having guns, but not all the guns that were said to have been used at Port Arthur. He admitted having the guns without a firearms licence, but claimed not to have spent much time firing them or practising shooting.

Bryant's wounds were healing slowly and by July 1996 he was in a prison hospital cell. He was still refusing to admit to the horrendous crimes with which he had been charged and was still insisting that he was guilty only of the carjacking and that he had not been at Port Arthur that day at all. On 13 July Bryant attempted suicide, trying to hang himself with his bandages. The attempt was foiled by prison guards who had him constantly under surveillance.

Two months later Bryant appeared in court, behind bulletproof glass. He was formally charged with 72 offences. To everybody's shock and amazement, he pleaded not guilty to every single charge. His protestations of innocence served to reignite public anger. Many people felt that he was making things even more difficult for the survivors of the massacre. 'You're a bloody coward!' one man, who had lost a brother in the massacre called out in court.

In the subsequent weeks great pressure was brought to bear on Bryant. It was rumoured that at one point his mother and his sister, the only two people in the world willing to visit him and retain some contact with him, both threatened suicide. Six weeks later, in the first week of November, Bryant appeared in court again. To audible sighs of relief he pleaded guilty to all of the charges, having changed his mind. Yet even now there was anger in court as Bryant giggled and laughed as he admitted his guilt. At one point even his own lawyer tried to shut him up.

No motive had been offered for the massacre, and in the wave of relief that followed Bryant's change of plea to guilty few seemed particularly concerned at this omission. Rod MacGregor, co-ordinator of the Port Arthur Recovery Centre set up to help those suffering from the shock and trauma of the incident, remarked: 'It's sort of an end to a chapter and a closure for them. They can put it behind them and go on with their lives.'

Prior to sentencing, the Tasmanian legislature passed a law allowing the seizure of Bryant's considerable assets. These, along with the hundreds of thousands of dollars donated by members of the public, were to be used to aid the victims' families.

There was little surprise when Chief Justice William Cox of the Tasmanian Supreme Court, in front of a packed courtroom, sentenced Martin Bryant to 35 life sentences. 'It is difficult to imagine a more chilling catalogue of crime,' the judge said, recommending that Bryant should never become eligible for parole as he would always remain a danger to society.

According to Bryant's lawyer, his client was 'happy' with the sentence. The lawyer also claimed that he had been told the motive for the attack, but that his client had not given him permission to discuss this. It was, therefore, confidential and would remain so until Martin Bryant changed his mind.

The sentence, which effectively means that Bryant will spend the rest of his life in prison, was little consolation to many of the families of victims or survivors. Glenn Pears's brother, Philip, told CNN that: 'Perhaps the sentence is just in the eyes of the community. But it's little compensation for the families of the 35 victims.' Carolyn Loughton, who had watched her fifteen-year-old daughter being murdered, was more forthright. 'I think that all Australians should look at the debate on the reintroduction of capital punishment for mass murder,' she said.

This widely voiced desire for Martin Bryant's extinction was almost fulfilled on the first anniversary of the massacre, on 28 April 1997, when he made another attempt at suicide. Using pills supplied by another inmate, he took an overdose after having failed to put together a noose made from the prison-issue cotton sheets. The attempt was as unsuccessful as his first, and after a brief flurry of publicity around the date of the anniversary the survivors and those affected by the massacre were left to get on with their lives once more.

One would expect the story to end there. The story was done and dusted and Bryant had earned himself a place in the hall of infamy: a monster beyond the pale, unworthy of sympathy or understanding. And yet the story refuses to lie down. Questions are being asked and doubts raised about Bryant's prosecution.

Firstly, there are a number of inconsistencies in the story as described above. By itself this should not surprise anyone. Things happened quickly, people were in shock, and so it would be strange if all accounts of the events of the day tallied completely. The police took over six hundred statements in order to construct a version of events that could be used as the basis for the prosecution case. However, some of these inconsistencies are quite serious. Many of the witnesses – including, for example, Wendy Scurr – dispute the police version quite strongly. The timings are out, for one thing, by several minutes. The police stated that the killings in the Broad Arrow Café took around ninety seconds. By Scurr's reckoning this is out by a factor of four or five. Why the big difference?

Secondly, by applying pressure through Bryant's family, the prosecution ensured that Bryant changed his plea to guilty, thereby avoiding a lengthy trial. The ostensible reason was to spare the victims and the families of victims any more trauma. Yet this also meant that the prosecution case was never examined in open court. Were there any positive identifications of Bryant as the perpetrator of these horrific crimes? Why were Wendy Scurr and a number of other witnesses denied the chance to give evidence? In fact, Scurr was told early on in the case that her evidence was not required, before Bryant had even changed his plea. As one of the people who had phoned the police during the massacre she was a key witness to the timetable of events that unfolded that day. Why were the police so intent on denying her a voice in court?

Questions were also raised about Bryant's shooting ability. Clearly the gunman in the Broad Arrow Café was someone skilled in the use of a semi-automatic assault rifle. Firing from the hip, the killer had been able to score accurate and deadly hits again and again. Although he was in a confined space, he was not shooting point-blank but from a distance of around four metres. He was also shooting at the head, a much smaller target than the chest, for example. Many people have questioned the veracity of the prosecution account simply because they doubted that anybody could shoot twelve people in fifteen seconds with such devastating accuracy.

Clearly this is a perplexing point. There is no evidence that Bryant was a particularly good shot, yet he was said to have achieved a kill ratio that many trained marksmen could not hope to equal. Furthermore, the *modus operandi* of the attack matched that used by special-forces personnel when trying to secure a given environment. The aim is to kill as many people as possible in as short a time as possible. In these military or terrorist scenarios it is assumed that the opponents are armed and wearing body armour so therefore it is better to aim at the head, even though it is a smaller target.

Finally, the absence of motive and the fact that Bryant would only admit to carjacking the BMW is said to be significant. In all of the police interviews and in his sessions with psychiatrists (including Professor Mullen), Bryant denied being in Port Arthur on the day of the massacre. Having changed his plea to guilty, why did he not explain his actions or give the police a full confession? Why did he deny that one of the guns used in the massacre was his?

These and many other questions were raised by Joe Vialls, an 'independent investigator' who first came to prominence when he claimed that WPC Yvonne Fletcher had not been killed at the Libyan Embassy Siege in London in 1984 by a bullet fired from an embassy window, but that she had been assassinated by a shot fired from a building owned by an American multinational. This claim was dismissed at first as just another conspiracy theory, the product of an imagination working in overdrive. According to Vialls, the murder of Yvonne Fletcher had been an elaborate 'psy-op' designed to mould public opinion and whip up anti-Libyan feeling. Her murder provided one of the pretexts for the US bombing of Libya a short while later.

The theory was easily dismissed but Vialls worked at it diligently, analysing film recordings, working on times and dates and so on, until he claimed to prove that Fletcher's murder could not possibly have been committed by anyone in the embassy. Many months after her murder, and months after the inquest into her death, a piece of amateur film that purported to show her murder mysteriously surfaced. This film was accepted as genuine and was broadcast by the BBC as such. Vialls analysed the film and using measurements of the position of the sun, as shown by the shadows cast by objects in the film, allegedly proved that it could not possibly have been filmed on the day of Yvonne Fletcher's murder.

Vialls's evidence was compelling enough to cause many sceptical people to question the accepted wisdom that Fletcher had been killed by the Libyans. Eventually he was contacted by British television's Channel 4 *Dispatches* series who wanted to make a film about the case. He co-operated with the prestigious documentaries company, only to find that they backed down at the last minute. His name was removed from the credits of the programme and much of his analysis was not even used.

In Bryant's case, new video footage mysteriously appeared the day before he was sentenced. The film was said to have been shot by an American tourist, and it purported to show Bryant in the act of carrying out the massacre. Like the film in the Fletcher case, it was broadcast on television as the real thing, in this instance on the night before Bryant was due to be sentenced. Why did it take so long for the film to surface?

This is a major question that needs to be addressed. Many other people had taken snatches of video on that day: they had all been handed over to the police or the press. Indeed, anyone with film of Bryant in the act would have been able to name their price since the media networks were hungry for it. It is difficult to understand how somebody could sit on the film for so long. It just does not make any sense.

Vialls noticed that in this piece of film the sky was overcast and cloudy. Yet on the day of the massacre it had been a sunny, cloudless day. Other videos shot on the day showed a clear sky: why was this one different? The video also shows a man, presumed to be Bryant, running away from the Broad Arrow Café carrying a package, believed to be his weapons, under his arm. Yet Vialls claimed that analyses showed that the package was over ten inches too short to be the AR15 or the other gun used during the massacre. The blond man in the film is also not conclusively shown to be Bryant. Again, the identification is taken for granted rather than proved definitively by this film.

On looking further into the case Vialls became convinced that something else was not right. He discovered that the two officers who should have been closest to Port Arthur during the massacre were, in fact, on the other side of the island. They had been called out to look for a reported stash of drugs. An anonymous caller had, according to Vialls, phoned in a report that several large jars of heroin had been seen near Saltwater River, on the other side of the Tasman Peninsula. On arriving at the scene the police officers discovered several glass jars of soap powder. Graham Scurr, Wendy Scurr's husband and an attorney, pointed out that it 'would be hard to select a more suitable remote location if specifically decoying the two policemen away from Port Arthur'. Vialls also discovered that no such decoy call had ever been made in Tasmania before. Within minutes of the officers arriving at Saltwater River the shooting started at Port Arthur, and they were faced with a thirty-minute drive back to the historic site, by which time the massacre was over.

Vialls also pointed out that there was no fingerprint or DNA evidence linking Bryant to the Port Arthur site. The gunman was alleged to have eaten a meal at the Broad Arrow Café: surely some kind of mark would have been left behind? Given the chaos that he left in his wake, of course, it may not be so strange that the traces had disappeared, but to Vialls it was another significant fact.

Finally, it was pointed out that Tasmania's emergency regulations, which cover important incidents such as major accidents or terrorist activity, specify that the swing bridge at Dunalley, which links the Tasman Peninsula (where Port Arthur is located) to the Tasmanian mainland, should be closed. The idea is to stop traffic coming into the peninsula and thus complicating operations. It is a plan that Wendy Scurr was more than familiar with. But in the case of the massacre, while other parts of the emergency plan were put into action this one was not. The bridge was left open, allowing people to come into the area and, more importantly, to leave it.

There were several more inconsistencies and anomalies that Vialls, the Scurrs and others pointed out. At the very least they suggested that the events of the day were not as clear-cut as the authorities had suggested. To Vialls it was suggestive of yet another state-sponsored 'psy-op', with Bryant an innocent victim, selected – because of his low intelligence – as the fall-guy destined to take the rap. In Vialls's own words, 'Just like Lee Harvey Oswald in Dallas, Martin Bryant was a perfect patsy.'

Vialls theorised that the massacre could only have been carried out by a skilled operative from one of the world's elite special-forces units. His persuasive analysis took in the kill rate, the dead-to-injured ratio, the timing, the recoil of the weapons and much more. Vialls could not see how a man with little shooting experience and an IQ of only 66 could wreak such havoc in such a short time in such an enclosed space. Martin Bryant was not the murderer, he concluded: it had to be an armed specialist brought in from outside for so many innocent civilians to have been killed. This same operative carried on the massacre outside of the café and out to the Seascape guest house. At that point Bryant, whose marksmanship was said to be poor, was set up to take responsibility. The theory also neatly explains why the 250 rounds that Bryant fired from the guest house were so far off the mark.

In Vialls's words: 'Whoever was on the trigger that fateful day demonstrated professional skills equal to some of the best special-forces shooters in the world. His critical error lay in killing too many people too quickly while injuring far too few, thereby exposing himself for what he was: a highly trained combat shooter, probably ranked among the top twenty such specialists in the Western world.'

But what of the motive? Yvonne Fletcher was murdered, according to Vialls, in order to ready public opinion for the bombing of Gaddafi's Libya. What possible reason could there be to slaughter 35 people in sleepy Tasmania? Vialls had an answer there, too. Twelve days after the massacre the Australian federal government announced drastic new gun laws that severely curtailed the availability of assault rifles, machine-guns and shotguns. The new gun controls included setting up a national register of ownership and increased checks on the import, sale, possession and resale of firearms.

After the massacre the public was virulently against gun ownership, and the new controls were put swiftly into practice. Over 400,000 firearms were impounded by the government, and these were to be melted down. According to Vialls, this was precisely the outcome that those behind the massacre were after. This massive disarming of Australia, he claimed, put the country's national security at risk. In case of war or invasion, these weapons held by ordinary Australians would no longer be available to fight the invading forces.

Vialls's arguments were soon picked up by sections of the Australian far right. Groups with links to Christian Identity churches, Pauline Hanson's racist 'One Nation' party, anti-Semitic organisations and Christian fundamentalists all adopted his arguments. The responsibility for the massacre was assigned to the 'New World Order', the secret government that supposedly runs the world and has nominal leaders such as President Clinton dancing to its tune. As to the identity of the 'invaders' who would stroll into a disarmed Australia, one must look eastwards to Japan and inwards to the racial paranoia of white Australia.

As in the United States, the massively powerful gun lobby in Australia has an overwhelmingly right-wing agenda. Despite the horror of the Port Arthur massacre, they feel that they are under attack and that their right to bear arms is a fundamental and inalienable human right. Sections of this pro-gun lobby also took up the conspiracy theory. Not only did it mean that the new gun-control laws were deliberately planned in advance, rather than being a reaction to the violence of the massacre; it also meant that the blame for the violence lay not with the ease with which Bryant had acquired his deadly weapons but with the government conspirators who had set up and executed the massacre.

In July 1998 the new One Nation MP for Queensland, Jeff Knuth, told the Australian Parliament that the massacre was 'only the excuse to slap Australians with extremist laws long hidden away in the dark bolt-holes of Canberra waiting for the day they could scare Australian lawmakers into passing laws hatched in a faraway foreign capital. We now know Port Arthur had nothing to do with it.'

The story continues to grow and mutate. In some versions of the theory Martin Bryant is completely blameless, a simpleton tricked into pleading guilty to crimes he did not commit. In other versions he actively worked with the unknown forces who carried out the murders – which explains why he was not killed at the Seascape – and he has since been double-crossed by the government. In some versions Bryant carried out the murders, in others it was someone else.

Another variant of the conspiracy theory suggests that Bryant was 'brainwashed' like the Manchurian Candidate in the novel and movie of the same name and that he was 'programmed' to go on the rampage. This theory also posits the possibility that Bryant suffers from 'multiple-personality disorder' and that it was one of his alter egos that was programmed to carry out the massacre. This other personality had the intelligence and the training to carry out the massacre. Indeed, this other Martin Bryant planned the massacre down to the minutest detail with military precision. And who would have carried out this programming? The psychiatrists with whom Bryant had come into contact as a difficult child and teenager. In particular Dr Cunningham-Dax, who is accused as being part of an international conspiracy run by the British-based Tavistock Institute. This theory links Bryant to Thomas Hamilton and the Dunblane Massacre rather than to the Kennedy Assassination, but the ultimate beneficiaries are pretty much the same: the shadowy New World Order who aim to destroy the nation state and create instead an unelected international government.

There are certainly glaring inconsistencies in the Port Arthur story, and it is difficult to believe that someone like Bryant was able to carry out such a gruesome act so successfully. But it is also hard to believe the alternative conspiracy theories. Joe Vialls continues to work on the case and is pressing for a Royal Commission to look at the case. If this is ever convened then new light may be shed on the harrowing details of the Port Arthur massacre. Until then the questions remain open.

LARRY GENE ASHBROOK

Fort Worth, USA, 1999

The last case we shall look at in detail, that of Larry Gene Ashbrook, embodies many of the common themes that have recurred again and again in this examination of the life histories and personalities of modern spree killers. That Ashbrook's rampage also occurred in 1999 – the year in which Eric Harris and Dylan Klebold killed twelve of their fellow students, a teacher and then themselves at Columbine High School, Benjamin Nathaniel Smith killed two in his racist spree in Chicago, Mark O. Barton killed his family before going on a shooting spree through the financial district of Atlanta and Buford O'Neal Furrow attacked the North Valley Jewish Community Centre before killing Joseph Ileto – suggests that the incidence of such violence is rising fast rather than diminishing.

Ashbrook, aged forty-seven, the youngest of four siblings, was a strange and lonely child. He was considered by many to be a troubled boy, though there is no record of him undergoing any form of psychiatric assessment or having major behavioural problems at school. 'He was always a strange kid,' one neighbour later recalled. Jane Lee also remembered that Ashbrook had forced her elder sister, who was younger than he was, to eat insects.

After school and college Ashbrook joined the US Navy, working in anti-submarine units in Texas and Florida. He signed up for two stints in the Navy, lasting in all just under eight years, between 1972 and 1983. His career could hardly be called a success, and although he managed to reach the rank of aviation warfare systems operator, it took him twice as long as other recruits to get there. 'This kid was going very slow,' said William R. Whitley, a retired naval commander in Jacksonville, Florida. 'It very well could have affected him. He probably saw people around him learning much faster than he was. The peer pressure on him was probably tremendous.'

Despite his problems, Ashbrook received security clearance to take up his post. This would have included a thorough background check by the FBI. Apparently nothing untoward was discovered, suggesting either that he was very good at covering up or, more likely, that his personality problems were relatively minor at the time.

Ashbrook's naval career, although progressing slowly, was cut short in December 1983 when he was dishonourably discharged for marijuana use. It was not his first bout of trouble for using the drug. He had previously been arrested for possession in 1971, but the police never filed charges and the matter had been allowed to drop.

After being thrown out of the Navy, Ashbrook drifted from job to job, but it was clear that his problems were getting worse. Unable to hold down steady employment he depended on his elderly parents for financial support. Four years after the death of his mother, Ethel, he moved back to Fort Worth in 1994. There he moved into the family home of forty years, which he shared with his elderly and long-suffering father, Jack. Ashbrook took the death of his mother badly. 'Before she died, Larry still had it together. After she died, he went mental,' said Karen Ivey, a neighbour of the family for almost twenty years.

There are suggestions that shortly after this period Ashbrook flirted with a number of groups on the far right, including the Ku Klux Klan and a shadowy Christian Identity sect called the Phineas Priesthood. This story originated with John Craig, who has extensively studied the American far right, and who claimed that he met Ashbrook in 1996 when Ashbrook had boasted of his membership of the group that advocates the murder of Jews. There were rumours that Buford Furrow was also a member of this self-elected Priesthood, though this too has not been confirmed. The police have so far failed to confirm these allegations, though there is some evidence that Ashbrook had had contact with the Klan at least.

While living at home with his father, Ashbrook's behaviour steadily deteriorated. He was frequently abusive to neighbours, shouting and screaming at them, and on at least three occasions he exposed himself to them. Karen Ivey recalled one of these occasions. 'We were sitting there laughing, and he pulled up and he said, "What are y'all laughing about?" and he exposed himself, shook himself at the neighbours, put it back in his pants and went in the house.'

'Everybody thought he was sort of strange,' Venita Hord, also a neighbour, told CNN. Another neighbour, Tim Walker, concurred. 'You could see it. He was always talking to himself,' he said. 'He would be as close as you and I, and you could see him carrying on a conversation with himself.'

There were also numerous reports that Ashbrook was often violent, and that he had physically attacked his elderly father. A number of people have described seeing Jack Ashbrook bruised or scratched, and when asked about these marks the elderly man would admit, with an embarrassed smile, that the injuries had been inflicted by his weird and unpredictable son. Despite this, many neighbours considered Larry Ashbrook to be merely a bit weird but not dangerous.

The principal feature of Ashbrook's personality disorder was a marked paranoia. He was convinced that his neighbours were talking about him, that there was a conspiracy directed at him, and that people were out to get him. Although paranoia is a common part of the psychological make-up of a spree killer, in Ashbrook it reached such an extreme level that his own brother, Aaron, referred to him as 'a paranoid schizophrenic'.

Despite this extreme paranoia, nobody seems to have attempted to tackle it in any systematic way. Ashbrook was not referred to any psychiatric specialists, and there is no evidence that his mental illness was ever formally diagnosed. Certainly, despite initial police reports to the contrary, there is no evidence that he was receiving medication. Nor does it appear that he ever came into contact with local mental health officials.

His father died in July 1999 and Ashbrook's behaviour deteriorated still further. He was violent and out of control, and without his father to try and keep him in line things rapidly went downhill. His brother became so concerned that he armed himself with a twelve-gauge shotgun to protect himself. He also called the police on occasion, though no action seems to have been taken as a result of his complaint.

Ashbrook saw a vast conspiracy arrayed against him that included the CIA, the police, work colleagues and psychological-warfare specialists. He also became convinced that he was being targeted for investigation as a serial killer and a paedophile. Such a delusional world-view is consistent with paranoid schizophrenia, so perhaps his brother's assessment was not so far from the truth after all.

The best evidence that we have for this conspiracy theory that so consumed Ashbrook is from his own hand. On 31 July 1999, less than two weeks after his father's death, Ashbrook wrote the first of two long, rambling letters to Stephen Kaye, the City Editor of the *Fort Worth Star-Telegram*. In this first letter, he related a series of events, including being bullied at work and his troubles finding employment, and then alleged that he was being investigated as a serial killer. He even claimed to have been drugged in a bar by a number of men who were police officers. Finally, he detailed his attempts to have his case investigated by the FBI and by the press and television. He talked of 'rumour control', 'psychological warfare' and 'plausible deniability' as being the three techniques employed against him.

The second letter arrived on 10 August, and continued where the first letter left off. 'It is obvious you are uninterested in my story,' Ashbrook stated bluntly in the first paragraph. The letter then went on to relate more of his problems holding down a job and the allegation that somehow the CIA were involved in his case. Nowhere, though, was there any suggestion why anyone would want to ruin his life by suggesting that he was a serial killer. 'It is apparent to me that the suspicions against me have been widely disseminated . . .' he stated in his closing paragraph.

As Stephen Kaye reported in his newspaper, 'There were outlandish things in these letters. The first letter rambled. It was hard to follow. It didn't seem very plausible. My immediate reaction was that there was not much we could do for him.'

Newspapers often receive such weird, paranoid missives. Kathy Vetter, the Managing Editor of the *Star-Telegram* confirmed that 'I see letters like that two and three times a week. They are often from people who feel they're being persecuted. Unfortunately, you just can't look at these things and see danger. I wish I could do that, because if I had that ability, those things would go to the cops every time. But 99.99 per cent of them are just people who want to vent. Never before in my career have they turned out to be anything, and it's hard to believe that they ever will again.'

Ashbrook was more persistent than many of these other letter writers. About a week after the second letter he turned up at the offices of the newspaper to talk to Stephen Kaye in person. The delusional tone of the letters suggested that Ashbrook was some deranged crazy with mad, staring eyes, muttering oaths out of the corner of his mouth. In fact, he was presentable and coherent.

'Frankly, he was just the opposite of someone you'd be concerned about,' Kaye said. 'He was very cordial. He was very apologetic for bothering me. I kept saying: "You're not a bother; I just can't do anything for you. These are hard things to prove that are in your letter."'

Kaye suggested that Ashbrook should seek a lawyer to help him prove his case. There was nothing that the newspaper could do to help him, he explained.

'He [Ashbrook] said, "I'm sorry to take your time up,"' Kaye said. 'He couldn't have been any nicer.'

Nice as he appeared, Larry Gene Ashbrook harboured an anger and an aggression that he was finding more and more difficult to control. While his father had been alive the damage that Ashbrook inflicted on their home could be patched up after the explosions of violence. Left to his own devices the house was beginning to look like it had been hit by a wrecking crew. He'd punch holes in the walls, trash family photographs, smash doors.

Ashbrook was still unemployed and had been for some time. He was also lonely. He had never married and there is no evidence that he was ever involved in any long-term relationships. Without friends or colleagues, he had been depending on his father for company as much as anything else. Certainly his relationship with the rest of his family appears to have been rather strained.

Just as importantly, without his father to support him, Ashbrook was running out of money. It had been a long time since he'd worked, and to a great extent he had been living off his parents for some time. With both parents gone he had no source of income.

Ashbrook expressed concern about his financial problems to Fort Worth's Chief of Police, Thomas Windham. Ashbrook had called Windham on a number of occasions to talk about the conspiracy against him. Windham, who fielded a number of such calls every week, recalled that Ashbrook did not appear outwardly deranged. 'I didn't make anything out of it other than here's a guy who lost his job,' Windham said. 'He always seemed like a nice enough guy to me. It's an understatement now to say that's a misperception of him, but nothing in those conversations would ever signal he was a violent individual.' Their last conversation took place shortly after Ashbrook's father had died. Windham recalled that Ashbrook had said: 'All he left me was debts. I don't have a job. I haven't worked for years and I guess I'm going to lose my house because it's not paid for, and I don't have any way to pay for it.' Windham added that Ashbrook '. . . wasn't angry, and he really wasn't distraught. It was just a voice of concern.'

The rest of Ashbrook's family talked it over with him and they made it clear that they could not afford to support him. Furthermore, in his will their father had stipulated that his estate was to be shared equally between his four children. What this amounted to in practice was that the house was to be sold off and the money divided between them. The modest single-storey house was probably worth no more than $20-25,000, not enough for Larry Ashbrook to buy himself another place. How he reacted to this news is not known, but the fact that his brother sought a firearm to protect himself and his family suggests that Ashbrook's resentment was likely to lead to an explosion of violence.

When that violence erupted, no one was prepared for the extent of it. Nor was the target one that could easily have been predicted. On 15 September 1999, at around 6.30 in the evening, Ashbrook, dressed from head to foot in black, climbed into the beat-up old Pontiac sedan that he drove and backed out of the driveway of his home. A neighbour was passing and Ashbrook politely waited to let the man go before continuing on his journey.

Ashbrook headed west along Interstate 20 for about ten minutes before pulling off and heading for the Fort Worth suburb of Wedgwood. At around ten to 7 he parked his car in a disabled-parking space near the main entrance of the Wedgwood Baptist Church. The *Star-Telegram* described the church as 'nestled in the heart of a middle-class neighbourhood of brick homes and soaring shade trees.'

Across the street from the church, in Wedgwood Park, a group of schoolchildren were playing soccer. Supervised by a number of parents and teachers, the kids were playing a practice match. Ashbrook, it is alleged, sat on the grass and watched the children, staring at them intently as they played. Some of the parents grew concerned by the presence of the stranger, fearing that he was a paedophile. According to Detective Michael Carroll, 'No one recognised him. No one knew who he was. It made them concerned,' he said. 'He was there through the end of the practice. As far as I know, he didn't talk to anyone. He just sat there.'

By the time the soccer match was over, the stranger had disappeared. Not long afterwards the shooting began inside Wedgwood Baptist Church.

There were over 150 young people in attendance at the Wednesday evening service at the church. Some were there to take part in the annual 'See You at The Pole' prayer event, others were there for choir practice. A Christian rock band, 'Forty Days', was on stage and the programme was due to include a number of skits and performances once the band had finished. The mood was relaxed, festive.

Still wearing his dark glasses and smoking a cigarette, Ashbrook entered the church foyer at around 7.00 p.m. He exchanged a few words with some of the adults at the door and one of them, Jeff Laster, aged 36, asked him to put out his cigarette. Ashbrook's reply was to pull out a Ruger 9mm semi-automatic pistol from his waistband and shoot Laster in the stomach. Laster's legs gave way and he collapsed to the floor, seriously injured.

Sydney Browning, director of the children's choir, and her friend Jayanne Brown were seated nearby. Ashbrook simply pointed the gun at Sydney and fired again. The single shot that hit her was enough to kill her. The bullet also hit Jayanne but she was lucky: the shot merely grazed her head. 'I knew I'd been hit because there was a very hot feeling,' she told the press later. 'I put my hand up and thought, "Dear Lord, is this how it feels to die?"'

Now that Ashbrook had started, he knew that he had to carry on. It was as though there was an internal momentum to the events now unfolding that he could not resist. He moved through the foyer and into a hallway leading to the interior of the church. Along the way he met Shawn Brown, a 23-year-old theology student, walking along the hallway towards the foyer. Ashbrook fired again. Shawn stumbled, tried to stagger away but collapsed. In only a matter of seconds Ashbrook had killed two people.

Kevin Galey was also in the hallway. He had heard some shots but assumed that there was a skit going on. When he saw Ashbrook he believed that the man was firing paintballs. When Ashbrook took aim at two women nearby, Galey stood between the gunman and his intended victims. Galey's accidental heroism meant that he took a shot in the chest. At first he thought that the blood oozing down his front was simply paint. When Ashbrook changed the clip in his gun the terrible truth suddenly dawned and Galey collapsed.

Moving on down the hallway Ashbrook passed a window that looked into the inner sanctuary of the church. From this vantage point he had a clear view of the rows of pews arranged in a semicircle that faced the main stage. Many of these pews were occupied by the teenagers and their parents, watching the band that was still performing. The view was too good to resist. Ashbrook raised the gun and fired again, shattering the window and spraying glass in all directions.

However, rather than causing chaos and making people dive for cover, the shooting seemed to have no effect on the churchgoers. The reason? Many simply assumed that the weird-looking guy in dark glasses was part of the evening's entertainment.

'I heard some noise out in the hallway and turned around to look back, and I saw this guy with a gun through the window in the doorway,' Ben Killmer, a seventeen-year-old high-school student, told the *Star-Telegram*. 'I saw the gun in his hand. I saw him shoot through the glass and the glass fly.'

Killmer's remarks were echoed by many others who saw and heard the shots but could not believe that anything untoward was happening. Ashbrook had been looking for a reaction and this was clearly not it. Suitably enraged, he continued on down the hallway to a set of double doors. Shawn Brown had managed to make it that far and no further. Ashbrook ignored Brown's body and entered the sanctuary.

Ashbrook announced his entry by banging hard on the door to get people's attention. Then he started shooting. 'Religion is bullshit,' he screamed as he fired at random. 'I can't believe you people believe this shit.' He paced up and down the back row of pews, choosing his victims at random, taking careful aim at them and then firing.

Many still thought that they were watching a skit. 'We thought it was a joke,' said fourteen-year-old Kristen Dickens. 'We were singing and he told us to shut up. I thought our pastor was playing a joke on us.' Aaron Bray, another high-school student, was shot at but he too thought it was some kind of elaborate put-on. 'We never knew if it was real or part of the show,' he said. 'Some people up in the balcony were giggling, some even laughing. There was no screaming.'

It was no joke for Justin Laird, celebrating his sixteenth birthday. He was one of the first of those in the sanctuary to be shot by Ashbrook. His parents grabbed him and dragged him out of the line of fire, unaware of the severity of his wound. The high-school football player had suffered a serious spinal injury that paralysed him from the chest down.

By this time some of the people were diving for cover. The message was finally getting through, though events were happening too fast for anybody to be sure of anything. Somebody called the police and when asked if anybody had been hurt responded: 'I don't know. There's a rally going on here. I don't know what else is going on. It may be a, well, if it's a skit or something I don't know about it, but I'd rather have you on your way than . . .'

Ashbrook spotted the person making the call, took aim and fired. The shots missed and the caller fled, the noise of gunfire confirming that the shooting was for real after all.

While one person had been calling the police, two others had been videotaping Ashbrook. Both the tapes caught about a minute of Ashbrook's spree before finishing abruptly. After the event, Police Chief Ralph Mendoza described what was on the tapes, which mainly showed people diving for cover. 'He's kind of pacing slowly, holding his hand out with the gun out,' Mendoza told reporters. 'What I saw on the film was one handgun firing. It was not rapid. It was slow, methodical, picking [his targets], aiming and shooting. He did not seem to be panicked . . . He took his time . . . He randomly stood there and fired shot after shot after shot.'

Justin Ray was one of the people taping Ashbrook. He was soon spotted by the gunman, who simply turned the gun on him. The seventeen-year-old was hit and killed instantly. He was still clutching the camera when police retrieved his body.

When the gun emptied Ashbrook simply loaded up again and continued firing. At one point he stopped shooting long enough to toss a pipe bomb down the aisle towards the stage. It exploded harmlessly in the space in front of the stage. Aaron Bray recalled, 'I heard a big bang. At first, I thought he was close to me and had shot. But I guess now that that's when the pipe bomb went off. A piece of shrapnel came down and hit me on the back of the neck, but it didn't hurt.'

Ashbrook continued firing while people tried desperately to escape. Some hid behind pews, others tried to make for the exits. Joseph Ennis, a teenager, was hit and killed. So too was teenager Cassandra Griffin and 23-year-old Susan Kimberly Jones. Others such as seventeen-year-old Mary Beth Talley were hit and injured while trying to protect friends. Among the most seriously injured was Kirsti Beckel, fourteen years old, who was to die of her injuries shortly before midnight.

Inside the sanctuary Ashbrook was stalking around shooting at will. Outside there was pandemonium. People were screaming, police and ambulance officials were rushing to the scene and parents with children inside were frantic with fear and worry. The first police were on the scene within a few minutes.

Realising that his time was up and that the police were only seconds away, Ashbrook moved to the back of the sanctuary and sat down at one of the pews. Then, calmly, he placed the gun to his head and fired. He had killed seven and injured seven before taking his own life. Then, after a second of absolute silence, everybody made for the doors to get away from the scenes of carnage. There was broken glass everywhere, bodies sprawled here and there, blood splattered on the walls. It was over, at last.

Later, when police searched Ashbrook's home they discovered that the place had been comprehensively trashed that same day. Concrete had been poured down the toilets, pictures smashed, a Bible was recovered with the pages torn out and flung around the room, holes had been gouged out of the walls. In his rage Ashbrook had tried to destroy everything he could, to wipe out every image of normality that existed in the run-down wooden house. And yet during that same day he had mowed the neat little lawn at the front of the house, watered his plants in the garden and tended his fruit trees. Inside there was mindless destruction, outside was a picture of suburban normality.

A number of journals were recovered that were full of Ashbrook's paranoid scrawlings. The world was a conspiracy against him, and in the privacy of his notebooks he had wailed and screamed against it. There was nothing new to add, though. His letters to the press had been of the same type and tempo – blaming an uncaring and hostile world for all of his misfortunes.

Why the church? It was a question that people asked again and again. Why pick on that particular church? What was Ashbrook's problem with religion? It emerged later that about a month before his attack Ashbrook had been seen at another church. When questioned there he had asked about exorcisms and then pretended that he had been looking for a friend. It appears that his choice of the Wedgwood Baptist Church was random. He had no connection with the church, no grudge against its members or anyone connected with it. The only thing that might have attracted him to it was the prayer service that had been widely publicised.

Although it is impossible to be certain, there does not appear to have been any overtly political or religious motive behind the violence. Allegations of Ashbrook's involvement with racist political groups may or may not be true, but there really is no evidence to suggest that there was any connection to the actual violence. The only thing that suggests itself as a possible motive was that Ashbrook's own father was a deeply religious man.

Jack Ashbrook was a Christian who tithed part of his salary to his church. We know that after his father's death Larry Ashbrook was left without any means of support. Could it be that he blamed the church for taking money that should have been left to him? In destroying the interior of the house that he had shared with his father, Ashbrook was venting his rage at his family and at the memory of his father. It is possible that the same feeling of rage led him to massacre seven innocent victims, as though in killing them he was finally striking back at the hostile world that had long rejected him.

In an effort to explain the ferocious violence, some police officers initially suggested that Ashbrook had been misusing medication. Some reports suggested that he had been taking his father's pills, others that he had been on Prozac. Later these statements were retracted. No Prozac was found on the scene or at his house. Medical reports later confirmed that Ashbrook was clean, there were no signs of any drug-taking. It would have been easier to understand if he had been doped up, but the truth was that Ashbrook was stone-cold sober.

Sober maybe, but was Ashbrook in control of his actions? The characterisation of him by his brother as a 'paranoid schizophrenic' may be close to the truth. According to the American Psychiatric Association's *Diagnostic and Statistical Manual of Mental Disorders (DSM-IV)*, the diagnostic criteria for paranoid schizophrenia are:

A. Preoccupation with one or more delusions or frequent auditory hallucinations.

B. None of the following is prominent: disorganised speech, disorganised or catatonic behaviour, or flat or inappropriate affect.

Ashbrook's delusions were confirmed in his letters to the press and in his journals. It has also been reported by numerous acquaintances and neighbours that he would frequently talk to himself. These conversations with himself are evidence of auditory hallucinations: in blunt terms, he was hearing voices. His speech was not disorganised: he could be coherent and polite and appear outwardly normal. The violence that he displayed before his attack on the church was not evidence of disorganised behaviour. If anything, it was evidence of a very organised set of behaviours.

It could be that no further explanation is necessary. If Ashbrook was indeed mentally ill, then the form of his illness may be all that we need to know. Of course, this raises the question 'How many other spree killers are mentally ill?'

For the worshippers of Wedgwood Baptist Church such questions are irrelevant. For many of them their faith is enough to get them through the horror of this tragedy. On the night of the shootings the following message was posted on the church's website:

We serve an awesome God!
We don't understand why these things happen. An incomprehensible tragedy occurred this evening at Wedg-wood Baptist Church. A large group of teens were holding a rally in the church's worship centre, a follow-up to this morning's See You at the Pole event. Many attending were visitors. Shortly before 7 p.m. a gunman entered the building near the youth rally and began shooting.
The following results are known:
* 8 dead (including the gunman)
* 7 injured
* Everyone else – changed!
God, we don't understand. But you don't call us to understand . . . just to serve.
We still serve an awesome God!
11:30 p.m., September 15, 1999

OTHER SPREE KILLERS

Judged solely on the cases that have been detailed in previous chapters, it might appear that spree killing is both a relatively new phenomenon and one that is confined to the United States, Britain and other English-speaking countries. In fact, like serial killing – and, indeed, any other form of criminal activity – spree killing occurs in many countries and cultures and has done so for as long as people have had access to weapons.

Although space does not permit us to look at every case in detail, a small number of cases in non-Western countries are worthy of consideration as they cast more light on some of the other cases already discussed. The aim here is to establish common themes, where they exist, in order to draw general lessons from the phenomenon as far as possible.

In the two clear-cut cases of neo-Nazi spree killers – Benjamin Nathaniel Smith and Buford Furrow – the Jewish community was a primary target. Although both men were driven by a hatred of all non-white minorities, both of them subscribed to racist beliefs that singled out Jews as the ultimate enemy. In fact, both Matt Hale's World Church of the Creator and Reverend Butler's Aryan Nations group refer to blacks and Hispanics as 'mud races' and view them with nothing but contempt, and both of them view the Jewish community as their direct and implacable enemy. The Jews, they insist, are Satanic forces with a mission to destroy the 'Aryan race', and the 'mud people' are simply tools of the Jews, a biological weapon to 'mongrelise' the White race through interracial sex and mixed marriages.

However, we should not fall into the trap of viewing such fanatical racism as purely the product of neo-Nazi ideology and/or racial paranoia. Unbridled racism and hatred can occur in any community, even those that have historically been at the receiving end of it themselves. Such is the case with Dr Baruch Goldstein, an American-born Jew who emigrated to Israel, to the occupied West Bank. A follower of the late Meir Kahane and the extremist Kach movement, he moved to the settlement of Kiryat Arba, near Hebron. Tensions between the armed Jewish settlers and Palestinians are always high, and these are exacerbated by the activities of zealots and extremists on both sides.

Seven thousand people live in Kiryat Arba, described by Patrick Cockburn in the *Independent* as 'a fortress-like suburb on the eastern side of Hebron, a Palestinian town with a population of 100,000.' With 'electrically-operated sliding steel gates at its entrance', a sizeable portion of its population comes from the United States. Recruited by extremists such as the successors to Rabbi Meir Kahane, these settlers do not arrive in Israel with the intention of settling within the legally recognised borders of the country. Instead they move directly to the hot spots, to the occupied territories where they come face to face with the Palestinians. They come to Israel to engage in conflict, to take part in what they believe is a religious quest that is part of their destiny.

The settlers of Kiryat Arba view the occupied West Bank as historically part of the holy land of Israel. The Palestinian Arabs are viewed not as the native population but as vermin to be excluded, pushed outside the borders of Israel once and for all. Armed to the teeth, arrogant and dogmatic, these settlers view any moves aimed at moving towards peace as betrayal. There can be no peace with the Arabs, only war. However, the settlers are not stupid. No matter how fanatical or dogmatic they may be, they understand that they cannot by themselves 'drive the Palestinians into the sea'. They need the support of the rest of the population of Israel and, to a degree, the support of international public opinion – especially American public opinion.

The most direct way to get that support is for the settlers to portray themselves as victims. If they are seen as armed invaders then there will be little support for them. If they are seen as a Jewish population under siege by hostile Arabs, especially by hostile Islamic fundamentalists, then they are more likely to win the political and economic support that they need to carry on. And how can the settlers guarantee that this is the view that most people share? By provoking outrage and violence on the part of the Arabs. In other words, actively to encourage Palestinian terrorism and violence.

And the settlers have been doing just that. In the words of Israeli Reserve General Matti Peled the settlers have 'openly declared war against the peace process. Not only are they allowed to carry out with impunity pogroms against Palestinian cities and villages, they are also given free time on the state-owned media.'

With powerful supporters inside the Israeli government and military, even the most extreme settlers are assured of a degree of support, although at times this support may be covert.

The signing of the Oslo Peace Accord between Israeli Prime Minister Yitzhak Rabin and Palestinian leader Yasser Arafat was a blow to the settlers and other right-wing forces within Israel. From the moment that the hope of peace became a possibility these ultra-nationalist and religious extremists vowed to destroy the Accord. It would, in time, lead to the assassination of Rabin by Yigal Amir, who had also organised student tours of the Kiryat Arba settlement.

Before that, however, other attempts were made to derail the peace agreement before the full details of it had even been fully worked out. None of these attempts were as dramatic or as viciously premeditated as Baruch Goldstein's outburst of violence. On Friday, 25 February 1994, Goldstein joined the ranks of the most notorious spree killers in the world.

The date was significant. Not only is Friday the regular weekly Islamic holy day, this particular date also fell during Ramadan, the most holy month in the Islamic calendar. It also coincided with the Jewish religious festival of Purim, which marks the anniversary of the assassination of a Persian minister by Jews in order to stop a planned massacre.

Goldstein spent time with his four children that morning, holding them lovingly, tenderly. He visited the synagogue and found time to write a note to fellow workers at the clinic where he worked as a doctor.

In Hebron the al-Ibrahimi mosque, which houses the Tombs of the Patriarchs, was packed tight with worshippers.

Just after dawn there were around seven hundred men, women and children gathered at the mosque, down on their hands and knees, facing Mecca and praying to Allah. While they were inside praying, Goldstein, dressed in the olive-green army uniform of the Israeli army reserve, arrived. He was armed with an assault rifle, though it is disputed whether he was carrying a Galil semi-automatic or an M16. It would have been no surprise for the Arabs to see him armed: many Jewish settlers routinely carry such military firearms. In the words of one American anti-Zionist Jew, 'They swagger through the town, pointing their weapons at passers-by, and laugh as their targets scurry out of their way.'

Goldstein approached the guard at the mosque, Mohammad Suleiman Abu Sarah, and demanded, in Arabic, to be allowed to enter. The guard refused, pointing out that it was forbidden for non-worshippers to enter during prayer time. Goldstein responded by swinging his rifle butt at the Arab guard, knocking him down and then pushing his way into the mosque.

Silently, Goldstein took up position at the back of the mosque, raised his weapon and started firing at the prostrate and defenceless people at prayer. Abu Sarah described the scenes of carnage: 'I saw seven people die immediately. They were hit in the head, and their brains spilled out. It was total chaos. Everyone was running here and there to try and hide. The mosque was full of blood and wounded people, dead people.'

Another eyewitness recalled: 'People started screaming and running away. Others who were hit were calling for help. People were swimming in blood. It was difficult to distinguish between the dead and the living, because everyone was covered in blood.'

The shooting continued for about ten minutes, with clip after clip of ammunition being emptied on the panicked, screaming people trapped inside the mosque. Some people who managed to escape came under fire from members of the Israeli army stationed outside the mosque. Although what happened is still subject to controversy and disagreement, there is little doubt that the Israeli soldiers did open fire. What is disputed is the number of dead and injured caused by the action of the soldiers, and their motivation for shooting at these unarmed people. There are Palestinians who claim that the soldiers were in cahoots with Goldstein and that they killed at least six Arabs. The official Israeli line is that the soldiers did not fire and had no knowledge of Goldstein's actions. This story is at odds with the statements of the soldiers themselves: they claimed that they opened fire because they felt they were under threat from the enraged crowd.

Eventually Goldstein was overpowered, smashed over the head with a fire extinguisher. Not surprisingly, he was then beaten to death by the angry, bloodied crowd.

The death toll is also a matter of dispute. Initially the Israeli Defence Force put the toll at 39 dead. This was later scaled down to 29. The Palestinians claimed that up to seventy people had been murdered by Goldstein and the soldiers together. The controversy was not to end there. Witnesses claimed to have seen a second gunman helping Goldstein. They point out that the Israeli soldiers on duty at the mosque saw Goldstein arrive carrying an M16, yet the shootings were carried out with a Galil. The official line was, and remains, that Goldstein was a lone fanatic, working on his own, driven by personal hatred and rage to carry out his awful crimes.

What are not in dispute are the consequences of his horrific act of spree killing. Riots broke out all over the West Bank as angry Palestinians reacted with violence to the horror of the attack. The militant Hamas movement, one of the prime movers in the Intifada in the occupied territories, began to view all settlers as justifiable targets whereas before they had limited themselves to attacking military targets and those Palestinians collaborating with the occupying forces. The peace talks stalled and restarting the agenda became more difficult as the Palestinian negotiators were forced by an outraged population to adopt a more intransigent tone.

Goldstein's act of terrorism made the prospect of peace seem remote once more. In this respect he had succeeded in his aim. Driven by a set of fanatical beliefs, a paranoid hatred of Arabs and a distrust of the Israeli government, his calculated aim was to destroy the peace process. He almost succeeded.

Unlike the other spree killers we have looked at, Goldstein was not universally viewed as a monster. To his militant brothers and sisters on the Zionist far right, he was a martyr. Rather than feeling disgust at what he had done, many applauded his act. Not a monster, a martyr. On the evening of the massacre there was dancing in the streets on Kiryat Arba. One female settler was widely quoted as saying, 'We should kill five hundred, not fifty!'

Patrick Cockburn described the settlement of Kiryat Arba in June 1998. 'Just past the electrically operated sliding steel gates at its entrance a triumphal causeway leads off to the right. It ends in an octagon-shaped plaza, surfaced in cut stone at the centre of which, illuminated at night by ornamental lights, is the massive gravestone of Baruch Goldstein . . . Goldstein's victims are not mentioned on his gravestone. It calls him a saint. The incised letters read: "Having given his life on behalf of the Jewish people, its Torah and its ancestral homeland, he was an innocent, pure-hearted individual." '

A saint. And a saint's tomb always draws the faithful. Goldstein's tomb draws extremists from all over Israel – and beyond. It is a shrine to the forces of hatred, and will remain so as long as it still stands.

In September 1998 Goldstein's widow attempted to gain compensation for her husband's death from the Israeli government. She claimed that Goldstein had been killed by a 'lynch mob' because he was Jewish. Her claim was rejected. When a law was passed banning memorial sites at the graves of terrorists, Baruch's father tried unsuccessfully to block the decision to remove the memorial at his son's grave. Baruch's father claimed that removing it would 'insult the memory' of his son. Although this claim was rejected by the Israeli Supreme Court on 14 November 1999, the site still remains.

The similarities between Goldstein and neo-Nazis such as Benjamin Nathaniel Smith and Buford Furrow do not have to be laboured. They are as obvious as they are striking. One can only speculate on what the reaction would have been if 29 Jews had been gunned down by a lone neo-Nazi.

* * *

The day after Larry Gene Ashbrook mouthed anti-religious obscenities and shot at teenagers attending a church rally in Fort Worth, a spree killer went on the rampage in South Africa. Although this murderous spree generated fewer column inches in the world's press than Ashbrook's attack on the church, it is still nevertheless a case worth looking at. Despite the political and cultural differences between post-apartheid South Africa and Fort Worth, Texas, the two attacks have a number of factors in common.

Sibusiso Madubela, aged 28, had been a member of the Pan-Africanist Congress during the fight against apartheid. Smaller and more militant than the African National Congress, the PAC engaged in many forms of struggle against the racist regime, including armed struggle by its guerrilla wing, the Azanian Peoples' Liberation Army (APLA). Madubela had been a fighter with the APLA, holding the rank of captain. With the fall of apartheid, the APLA, along with other guerrilla groups, was supposed to be absorbed into the regular South African army, renamed the South African National Defence Force (SANDF).

Predictably, this joining together of former enemies did not proceed smoothly. Resentments and tensions continue to exist. This is hardly surprising since the army's structure consists largely of white officers commanding black foot soldiers. It is also a sad fact that many of these officers remain supporters of apartheid, and that a core of them are active right-wingers. But it must also be admitted that the stricter discipline of a regular standing army has not been easily accepted by former guerrillas used to less formality and less military rigour.

Many of these tensions are evident at the Tempe army base in Bloemfontein, one of the first bases to integrate the members of the national liberation movements and the regular army. The base has been plagued with problems, including arms thefts by racist opponents of the new government, far-right activism and a number of command decisions that have been widely interpreted as being racially motivated. There have also been a number of instances of violence by white officers against black subordinates, including a case in which Madubela, stationed at the base, and two other black officers were tear-gassed. The British Army, called in by members of the post-apartheid government to monitor the process of integration, warned in 1998 that the base was a potential 'powder keg' waiting to explode.

Aside from such treatment, Madubela, like some of his colleagues from the national liberation units, had other reasons to feel aggrieved. An important cause for complaint was that because of the integration with the SANDF he was demoted from captain to lieutenant. This demotion rankled and it was clear that Madubela deeply resented what had been done to him.

When Madubela's father died at the end of August 1999, Madubela was granted five days' compassionate leave to attend the funeral and come to terms with his loss. Due to return on 30 August, Madubela did not return to the base until 9 September. He had been declared 'absent without leave' (AWOL) after the third day of his extended absence. A week later, when he was paid he saw that his wages had been cut: he had not been paid for the time that he was AWOL.

On Thursday, 16 September, Madubela asked to see the commanding officer at the base to discuss the pay cut. He was told that the commander was away and would not be back on base until the following Monday. Madubela declined to discuss the problem with another officer.

A short while later Madubela got hold of a Vektor R4 semi-automatic rifle, a locally produced variant of the Israeli Galil that Baruch Goldstein had used in the Hebron massacre. At around 9.00 a.m. Madubela entered the battalion head-quarters and started shooting. He moved from office to office, seeking targets on whom to vent his rage. Within minutes he had gunned down several officers, all of them white. Six officers – Jacques Coetzer, Reg Sieberhagen, Johan Lombard, Doughie Douglas, Willie Nell and Tertius Lombard – were all killed and a number of others injured. Still firing, Madubela moved to the Personnel section where he continued his murderous spree. A civilian office worker, Marita Hamilton, aged 57, was hit and killed.

Madubela was not shooting at random. He pushed aside black officers who tried to stop him and, although all his victims were white, there were also a number of whites who came into his sights and whom he chose not to shoot. By this time other soldiers had arrived at the scene and, seeing that Madubela was not going to stop, they shot and killed him. In the words of a police spokesman, 'He had to be shot because he would have killed more people.'

In a few terrible minutes Madubela had killed seven people and injured another five, some of them seriously, before losing his own life.

The immediate public reaction focused entirely on the race angle. Madubela was black, all his victims were white. It was, therefore, a 'racially motivated' massacre. However, the fact that he had not fired at every white person suggests that race was not in itself the whole story. Madubela had pointed his gun at his secretary, who was white, and had turned away without firing. This is at odds with the behaviour of those spree killers such as Benjamin Smith, Buford Furrow and Baruch Goldstein who are motivated exclusively by race. This is not to deny the racial element entirely, because it clearly exists as an important factor in this crime.

Within South Africa reactions were polarised. There were those within the ANC government and in the upper echelons of the SANDF who tried to downplay the racial motive. They counselled caution, and were unwilling to pre-empt the police investigation into the murders. Within the PAC, of which Madubela was still a supporter, there was nothing but sympathy for him. Convinced that he had not been motivated by racist feelings, they explained the outburst of murderous rage as a consequence of *white* racism within the SANDF. They also demanded that Madubela should be buried with full military honours. 'Sibusiso Madubela was a member of the SANDF and he deserves a funeral with full honour for his stature as an employee of the SANDF and as a dedicated soldier to his country,' said Ngila Muendane, Secretary-General of the PAC. This request was turned down by the SANDF.

On the right the reaction was predictable. They saw Madubela's outburst as an example of black racist violence. It was proof, in their eyes, that the different races should not and cannot mix.

There were few people willing to look beyond race to see what else could have contributed to Madubela's violence. Defence Minister Mosiuoa Lekota was one of the few to attempt to do this. He pointed out that the killings were not premeditated and added: 'We want to go inside and look at this young man. He recently lost his father. What was the impact of the loss? Nobody has psychoanalysed what the relationship was between him and his father.' Although there is an obvious political advantage in shifting attention away from racial tensions in the SANDF to Madubela's own life, Lekota was correct to point to Madubela's recent bereavement as a key area for investigation.

Madubela, like Larry Gene Ashbrook, Michael Ryan and Martin Bryant, had lost his father and had suffered badly because of it. In reviewing all of these cases the relationship with the father emerges as the single most important one, far outweighing those with siblings or with the mother. Without the restraining or calming influence of the father, these men seem to go to pieces very quickly. It is surely not coincidence that both Ashbrook and Madubela exploded into extreme violence very soon after their bereavement.

Where strong father–son relationships exist, the sudden breaks may mean that the bereaved sons are left feeling stranded. They are rooted in the world through their fathers, and when they die the sons are left rootless and unsure of themselves. This is even the case where the relationship is not necessarily a happy one. Ashbrook had a stormy relationship with his father, yet when his father died the son went off the rails within a matter of weeks.

Another point of similarity between Madubela and many of the other spree killers we have looked at is a strong sense of grievance. This grievance may be real, as in Madubela's case, or imagined, and it drives a feeling of resentment that is extremely powerful. This resentment becomes a driving force that shapes the person's actions and personality. In constantly brooding on this sense of grievance it becomes a central, obsessive theme that feeds on itself. Small incidents are blown out of proportion and used as 'evidence' to support the grievance. In Madubela's case his grievances were real enough, and the final straw was the cutting of his wages. If it had happened at any other time the chances are that nothing would have come of it, but the conjunction of his father's death and one more incident to add to his overwhelming sense of injustice was too much. The result proved to be deadly for his seven victims and himself.

There are other areas of commonality that we can draw out from these cases but these will be reserved for a later chapter. For now we can turn to the final case that we will examine, that of Howard Unruh.

Whereas all the cases we have looked at so far in this book have taken place in the very recent past, it would be a mistake to imagine that spree killing is a phenomenon exclusive to the final two decades of the twentieth century. Obviously examples exist before this period, but Howard Unruh's case is interesting both because it is one of the first 'modern' cases of spree killing and because it parallels many of the more recent cases reviewed in this book.

Born in Camden, New Jersey in January 1921, Howard Unruh was a quiet, introspective boy who did reasonably well at school though he was by no means an outstanding pupil. Slightly shy and nervous, he seemed to spend more time on his own reading the Bible than playing with his fellow school students. His parents divorced when he was around nine years old, and he and his brother stayed with their mother, Freda.

As Unruh grew into adolescence, his attachment to his mother became more pronounced, as did his introversion. He did not socialise well with his peers, and preferred to spend time on his own. Much of this time was devoted to reading the Bible (still), building up his stamp collection and playing with his train sets – all largely solitary activities. They were also extremely orderly hobbies, with little room for spontaneity, creativity or exploration. This rigidity in outlook was also reflected in Unruh's approach to learning: he relied on collecting and sorting facts rather than linking things together to form an understanding of things. Instead of learning in the usual way he took to memorising lists, and indeed he went to great lengths to train his memory so that his powers of recall were markedly higher than average.

It was likely that this form of mental exercise was a semi-deliberate bid to impose some control over his own mind. As Unruh moved into adolescence he suffered a great deal of confusion about his sexuality, a confusion that was exacerbated both by his intense religiosity and by his social isolation. It later transpired that he felt no desire for young women of his own age. According to one doctor, Unruh suffered 'vague, half-conscious feelings . . . of fear, anxiety and disgust in his dealings with girls his own age.'

In contrast to this feeling of disgust for girls of his own age, Unruh felt a strong desire for his mother. His emotional bond to her was far more powerful than normal. He was a quintessential 'mummy's boy' and this feeling of attachment further estranged him from his peers. It also led to Unruh experiencing fantasies of having sex with his mother, which induced considerable feelings of guilt. Not only did these fantasies make him feel guilty because they broke all social taboos, but they also directly contradicted the ardent Christianity that he believed in. Another component of this confused sexuality was also emerging at around the same time: an attraction to young men. There is evidence that Unruh had made sexual advances to his younger brother, though these approaches had been firmly rebuffed.

This confusion and inner struggle was hardly evident to anybody else. Any hint of it was fiercely repressed. Unruh attended church, was a keen Bible student and, after graduating from high school in 1939, got himself a job and a girlfriend. The relationship did not last long. Emotionally cold and unwilling to even kiss her, it ended shortly after it began. He had gone along with it because that was what was expected of him.

The outbreak of the Second World War proved to be a godsend for Unruh. Not only did it complement his long-standing interest in war, it also meant that he could avoid facing up to the realities of who he was. There was no need to resolve the thorny problem of sex and sexuality when he could join up and get away from it all. Unruh followed the war correspondents avidly, keeping a scrapbook and committing to memory the reports that he collected.

In 1942 Unruh enlisted and, during basic training, turned out to be an excellent shot. As a rifleman, he achieved the rating of sharpshooter, one of the highest grades possible. In his own obsessive style, target practice and stripping down and cleaning his rifle became all-consuming activities that rivalled Bible-reading in importance.

When Unruh was shipped to Europe to fight in the war his world suddenly changed for the better. From being something of a nonentity, his skill with a gun gave him a power and a position that he had never dreamed of. He started to keep a diary, methodically recording the details of his kills. He noted the times, dates and places, as well as the positions of the bodies as he killed for his country in Italy, France, Belgium and, finally, Germany itself.

At the end of the war Unruh returned home and, like many veterans, he found domestic peacetime life something of a letdown. He moved back home with his mother and became once more a reclusive and lonely young man. On the outside it appeared that nothing had changed. He was still the same quiet young man, hard to notice, easy to ignore. Without a uniform and a gun, the status that he had earned on the battlefield disappeared as suddenly as it had appeared.

The experience of the war does seem to have made one obvious change to Unruh, however. He had finally admitted to himself that he was gay. Admitting it to himself did not mean admitting it to anyone else, but given the climate of the era that is hardly surprising. As with many homosexual men of that time, he had to keep up a front to a certain extent. Despite this and his continued devotion to the Church and to Bible classes, Unruh had become quite promiscuous. He claimed that his first gay experience was in Philadelphia, at a cinema where he was masturbated by a complete stranger. From then on he often met with strangers for sexual encounters. Eventually he even contracted gonorrhoea and had to be treated for it.

As with everything else in Unruh's life, all his encounters were logged in his diary. Times, dates, names and places were carefully recorded – as were the slights that he felt he had suffered from his neighbours. Every misplaced word, disrespectful intonation, sharp look or other imagined insult was itemised in the same diary.

Having fought in the war and seen the kind of respect that he could command, Unruh was now keenly aware of how little respect he actually had in the small community of East Camden where he had grown up. He was a loner, a young man of 24 with no job, no friends and no apparent interest in mixing socially with those around him. Furthermore, the natural paranoia induced by his secret gay lifestyle added to his injured pride. He became convinced that people were talking about him, whispering behind his back. No matter how discreet Unruh tried to be about his sexual activities, he was sure that people knew about him.

Unruh's paranoia became more pronounced as time went on. As with many of the other cases we have reviewed, a suspicious nature combined with a sense of grievance began to develop gradually into an awareness of conspiracies that had him as the target. Unruh felt that people were plotting to get him. Sooner or later, he realised, he would have to take action.

In his diaries Unruh began to annotate entries with cryptic comments. According to published sources, he used the word 'retaliate' over two hundred times in his diary. Beside some of the names of local people he would add 'Ret. W.T.S.' or 'D.N.D.R' – 'retaliate when time suitable' and 'do not delay retaliating'.

And what were these actions that demanded Unruh's retaliation? Petty arguments over change in a grocery store, someone calling 'Hey, you' rather than addressing him by name, someone else spreading imagined rumours about him. In other words, there was nothing out of the ordinary: the simple frictions of everyday life were magnified and assigned an importance that they did not warrant. But such are the consequences of rampant paranoia, as we have seen again and again.

Unable – or unwilling – to get a job, Unruh took himself off to evening classes and then enrolled in a pharmacology course at Temple University in Philadelphia. He stuck it out for a few months, but he found the subject boring and was unable to concentrate. He quit and returned to the security of home. Surrounded by his train sets, his stamp collection and a growing collection of military memorabilia that he had smuggled back from Europe and that he had supplemented with local purchases, he was left to brood.

Unruh built himself a shooting range in the basement of his mother's house and began to spend more and more time there, honing the shooting skills that had stood him in such good stead during the war. There in the dim light he could fire away at will, fantasising about the retribution that his neighbours so richly deserved. Hadn't he fought so valiantly during the war? Hadn't he proved himself worthy of respect and attention? He added to his collection of guns, buying himself a German Luger 9mm pistol sometime in 1947. With this reawakened interest in weaponry Unruh started to drop out of Bible classes and stopped going to church, reducing still further the little social contact he had with other people in the community.

On the evening of 5 September 1949, Unruh went to a cinema in Philadelphia, staying there very late, possibly because he was hoping to meet somebody for sex. On his return home he saw that somebody had tampered with the gate to the house. He interpreted this as a hostile act, another in the long string of acts that he was sure were directed exclusively at him. It was too much to take. Before going to bed he left a note for his mother, asking her to wake him at eight o'clock the next morning.

Freda Unruh did as asked, and then cooked her son's breakfast. Unruh showered, shaved and dressed in his best clothes before going down to eat. Having enjoyed his breakfast he then disappeared down into the cellar where his shooting range was. Around half an hour later he came back upstairs to the sitting room. When his mother came into the room shortly afterwards he spun round on his heel and raised his arm high, ready to bring down a heavy monkey-wrench on her. Freda cried out and backed away, alarmed both by the action and by the strange look in her son's eyes. Frightened, she turned and fled to a neighbour's house.

As his mother escaped to safety, Unruh calmly put down the monkeywrench and walked out of the house. His first stop was a cobbler's nearby. There John Pilarchik, also a war veteran, was busy working in his shop. Unruh walked to the door, raised his arm and fired once with his Luger 9mm. Pilarchik took the shot full in the face and died instantly.

Next stop was the barber's shop, two doors away. There Clark Hoover was busy cutting six-year-old Orris Smith's hair. The boy's mother was sitting a few feet away, watching. Unruh walked into the shop, muttered, 'I've got something for you, Clarkie,' and fired again. He killed Hoover and then fired at the child, shooting him in the head in front of his screaming mother. As the boy toppled over, Unruh calmly walked back outside.

The tailor's was next. Thomas Zegrino was out but his young wife, Helga, was working in the back of the shop. She would have to do as a target. She tried to plead with the tall young man in front of her but Unruh was in no mood to show mercy. He fired several shots, making Helga his fourth murder victim.

The Cohens ran the pharmacy down the road. Unruh hated them with a vengeance, and had long waited for his chance to wreak revenge on them. He claimed that the pharmacist, Maurice Cohen, had short-changed him on a number of occasions, and that his wife, Rose, was always spreading rumours about him. In his statement to the police, Unruh claimed that Rose 'was always talking about me and very belligerent towards me and seemed to take pleasure in bawling me out in front of people.'

The Cohens had been alerted by the other shootings and were trying to get away from their house when Unruh arrived. Maurice was attempting to escape from an upstairs window. He was shot and killed, his body plummeting to the street below. Rose took refuge in a cupboard. Unruh fired several shots into the cupboard, then yanked the door open and shot Rose in the head. Maurice's elderly mother was trying to phone the police when she was shot in the head at point-blank range. The only member of the family to escape Unruh's murderous killing spree was Charles Cohen, the family's twelve-year-old son who had hidden in a cupboard while those he loved were massacred as Unruh moved from room to room.

Having finished with the Cohen household, Unruh then moved on to the pharmacy itself. There he found James Hutton, an insurance agent who had long dealt with Unruh's family. Unruh claimed that he said 'Excuse me, sir,' to Hutton and that when the insurance man didn't respond quickly enough Unruh shot and killed him.

Moving on, Unruh spotted a two-year-old child, Thomas Hamilton, looking out from a window of a house on River Avenue. Unruh's skills in marksmanship ensured that the little boy died instantly, killed by a shot between the eyes.

Next to die was Alvin Day, a TV repair technician unlucky enough to be in the wrong place at the wrong time. Whereas all the other victims so far had been known to Unruh, even if only by sight, Day was a complete stranger. It did him no good: Unruh was in no mood to differentiate between those he reckoned had done him wrong and anybody else who crossed his path.

Like Day, Helen Wilson, her son John and her mother Emma Matlock were also strangers. They were stopped at a red light in their car when Unruh casually sidled up to the vehicle. He fired at all three occupants of the car. Helen Wilson and her mother died there and then. The child, only nine years old, was hit in the head but managed to cling to life. Transported to hospital, he died of his injuries the next day.

An unnamed van driver became a target, but escaped unscathed as the bullet went wide. A teenager crossing the street took a shot in the leg but survived.

Still taking out his resentment against those who had 'wronged' him, Unruh next tried for a bar on River Avenue. By this time the shooting had been going on long enough for people to be finally moving into action. Frank Engel bolted the door of his bar and shepherded his customers to the back only a few moments before Unruh tried to gain entry. Finding the way barred, Unruh responded with a volley of shots but then gave up. Engel meanwhile had retrieved his own weapon, a .38 pistol. Taking aim from a window in the apartment above the bar, he fired once at the crazed gunman.

Unruh was hit but seemed not even to notice. Instead he continued on to a restaurant where he again tried unsuccessfully to gain entry. The grocery store was also locked, and though Unruh fired several shots into it he did not manage to hit the people cowering inside.

Finding that the remaining shops were barricaded, and able to hear the approaching sirens of the police cars, Unruh walked back towards his home. On the way he stopped off at the home of Madeline Harrie, whose house backed onto Unruh's. In the kitchen he found Mrs Harrie and her teenage son, Armand. Unruh fired three times at his neighbour and hit her once. Her son rushed to defend her and was shot twice. Amazingly, neither was killed. Unruh then pistol-whipped the boy before leaving.

With the police almost upon him Unruh retreated home. He went up to his room just as the first police cars and motorcycles roared into River Avenue. The impression that the police had just entered a war zone, with dead bodies in the street and blood everywhere, was completed when they too came under fire. The police shot back immediately, but the gunman simply took cover for a moment, then resumed hostilities. In the ensuing exchange of bullets Unruh managed to avoid getting hit despite the vastly superior firepower arrayed against him. In the middle of it all a local reporter actually phoned him and Unruh took the call. A bizarre conversation ensued in which a polite but understandably preoccupied Unruh answered, 'I don't know. I can't answer that yet – I'm too busy' when asked why he was shooting people.

Unable to stop Unruh with bullets the police tried tear gas. As the choking fumes seeped through the house Unruh called out that he was giving up. He threw out his gun and then staggered into the street where over fifty police officers were waiting for him. A large crowd had gathered and they rushed forward to get the man who had killed thirteen people in the space of as many minutes. It is highly likely that, had the police not intervened at that moment, Unruh would have been beaten to death or lynched.

'What's the matter with you?' one of the arresting officers demanded indignantly. 'You a psycho?'

In a reply that became as famous as his rampage, Unruh is quoted as saying 'I'm no psycho. I have a good mind.'

A psychiatrist disagreed. Unruh was diagnosed as suffering from paranoid schizophrenia and declared unfit to plead. A commitment hearing was held at which he was declared insane and a 'danger to himself or others'. He was ordered to be transferred to the secure unit of Trenton State Psychiatric Hospital where he remains to this day.

Now in his late seventies, Unruh remains in the same secure unit. Every year a new commitment hearing is held and he has been declared insane at every one of them. His doctors now describe him as a model patient who has never shown any inclination to violence. A spindly, white-haired old man, he is now in greater danger of becoming a victim of the violence of younger, more dangerous patients than of instigating any trouble himself. Yet in spite of Unruh's good behaviour and his advanced years, requests to have him moved to a safer unit elsewhere have been turned down by the courts.

At the hearing in 1996, Unruh's psychiatrist Chung Lyou-Kim repeated that Unruh was suffering from paranoid schizophrenia but added that he shows '. . . no active symptoms. He accepts the fact that he needs hospitalisation and medication. When you talk to him, he is very bright and pleasant, but he doesn't initiate conversation.' Judge I. DiMartino, who had been involved with the case for many years, was unmoved. Afraid that Unruh would somehow escape from a less secure unit than the one at Trenton, he turned down the transfer request.

A year later Judge Linda G. Rosenzweig again refused the transfer request. James Klein, Unruh's publicly appointed attorney for 22 years, stated that 'He shows his age. I don't see him capable of running away from anyone.' Psychiatrists described how Unruh sits by himself in a corner, afraid of the other criminally insane patients. Judge Rosenzweig responded by saying that 'I cannot and will not ignore history.'

The refusals to transfer the elderly mass murderer were applauded by Charles Cohen, who had survived the slaughter of his family by hiding in a cupboard. The apparent change in Unruh does not impress him. 'He was quiet and reserved before he killed my family. He's quiet and reserved now,' he said. 'The only reason he hasn't killed again is because he has been locked up in maximum security.'

Although Howard Unruh committed his crimes over fifty years ago, he followed a pattern that we have seen repeated throughout this book. In that sense he is very much the 'father of modern mass murder', as he has been described many times. His personality, his behaviour and his crimes link him directly to killers such as Michael Ryan, Thomas Hamilton, Martin Bryant and the others.

One aspect of Unruh's case worth examining in greater detail is his habit of keeping a detailed journal. This was a habit that he started as a young man when he would record long lists of facts to memorise. This rote-learning of lists suggests a possible link to Asperger's Syndrome, sometimes called Asperger's Disorder, named after Hans Asperger, an Austrian doctor who first described the condition in 1944. Generally considered as a mild form of autism, sufferers of Asperger's Syndrome usually appear to be intelligent, coherent and in many respects functionally 'normal'. However, they also display problems relating to others, especially to their peer group, and have obsessive interests in things like train timetables, car numberplates and other such bits of trivial information. They will also appear to be emotionally cold or socially unresponsive. It is also a fact that male sufferers outnumber females by an appreciable margin.

Unruh, like many of the other spree killers we have examined, had a fanatical interest in firearms. While in the army he would spend hours taking apart and putting together his rifle. He carefully recorded in his diary the kills he scored during the war. He built himself a shooting range in the basement of his mother's house. He collected guns and military memorabilia. This behaviour was little different from that of Michael Ryan, Thomas Hamilton or Martin Bryant, for example. We are not seeing here a casual interest in guns: this is more like a full-blown obsession with the minutiae of firearms, ammunition and shooting.

Sufferers from Asperger's Syndrome frequently display well-developed language skills and are generally of average or slightly above average intelligence. Very often their verbal skills are matched by equally good writing skills. Unruh's diaries are by no means unique among the activities of spree killers. We know that Larry Gene Ashbrook and Benjamin Nathaniel Smith, to quote two recent cases, also kept journals.

In the next two chapters we shall return to this and the other factors common to spree killers that we have discussed and shall attempt to draw some preliminary conclusions. Before we do so, however, it should be noted that we have by no means exhausted the list of spree killing cases since the Second World War. There are numerous cases that have not even been mentioned and to list each one in detail would require a much longer work than this. Needless to say, these other cases include a number of racist spree killers, including black killers who expressly went out to murder white victims, religious and political bigots and more 'crazy loners', as well as a number of military and police officers who used their weapons to go on murder sprees.

In every case that we have looked at, however, the killers were male. One of the few cases that might be considered spree killing by a female is that of Brenda Spencer, the sixteen-year-old girl who gunned down two victims and injured nine more after opening fire at a school in San Carlos in 1979. The incident inspired the Boomtown Rats song 'I Don't Like Mondays' that was a hit both in the United States and the UK.

While Spencer's case has many similarities with other instances of spree killing, including the random nature of the attack and the fact that Spencer fired from her bedroom window and did not attempt to escape, there are also a number of important differences. Chief among them is the fact that she was out of her head on drugs and drink when she carried out the attack. At an unsuccessful parole hearing in 1993, Spencer revealed for the first time that she had been taking the powerful hallucinogenic drug PCP (also called 'Angel Dust') and alcohol during her attack. This is at odds with the other cases of spree killing we have looked at, where alcohol and drug-taking were not factors. In fact, the only other case where drugs may have been involved is that of Mark Barton, who was taking the antidepressant Prozac. The Spencer shootings, therefore, are not a clear-cut example of spree killing but rather of drug-induced psychosis.

Apart from Spencer's case, which is anyway an uncertain instance of the crime concerned, during extensive research into spree killing I could not find a single unequivocal example of spree killing by a female. It might be argued that this is because females do not have the same access to firearms as do males, but in a society such as the United States there are many women who have access to guns, either their own or those belonging to their partners or to other members of their families. Lack of access to weapons cannot be the reason why no female spree killers exist. Which of course raises the question – why is it only men who commit this type of mass murder?

TIMOTHY MCVEIGH

Timothy McVeigh was not a spree killer. Though his crime claimed more lives by far than any perpetrated by the mass murderers featured in this book, he clearly does not fit the profile described in the next chapter. However, it is also clear that McVeigh shares some common characteristics with many of the men who are spree killers, and it is this point of contact which makes him worthy of consideration as a Lone Wolf killer.

To fully understand both the enormity of his crime and the motives which drove him to commit it, we need to understand a little of his story. His crime – the bombing of the Alfred P. Murrah Building in Oklahoma City on 19 April 1995, claiming 168 lives and causing hundreds of injuries – was, until the 11 September 2001 World Trade Center massacre, the single worst terrorist outrage ever committed on American soil. The initial reaction was to blame foreign terrorists, particularly Islamic fundamentalists who had caused such mayhem in the Lebanon, in Africa and in other parts of the world. The idea that it could be an American seemed too appalling and beyond belief. Only a monster would rain down such violence and destruction on his fellow citizens.

Timothy James McVeigh was born on 22 April 1968 in Lockport, New York, not far from the Canadian border at Niagara. His father, Bill McVeigh, had been born and brought up in the surrounding area and was employed at the Harrison Radiator factory, where car radiators were made for General Motors. Tim's mother, Mildred (or Mickey as she was known), had grander ambitions than Bill, whom she'd married in 1965. She had planned on becoming an airline stewardess but surprised everyone by accepting Bill's marriage proposal in 1964.

In many respects Tim's early life, at least as described by Lou Michel and Dan Herbeck in *American Terrorist* (probably the closest we'll ever get to an authorised biography), seems idyllic. Life at home was easy-going: his father worked hard; his mother doted on him. If this book is to be believed then McVeigh's life is straight out of TV's *The Waltons* – complete with wise old grandpa in the background to whom the young boy and his two sisters could turn whenever they needed to.

The fundamental differences in temperament and outlook between Bill and Mickey McVeigh could not be reconciled easily. Bill, solidly working class and Catholic, was happy to work hard to provide for his family – it was what all good men had to do. However, this traditional vision of the family was not in tune with Mickey's own view. She wanted much more from life. By this point she had found work as a travel agent, and the prospect of travel, excitement and the chance to get away from home was simply too good to miss. The couple split in 1979. The two girls decided to stay with their mother; Tim, on the other hand, opted to stay at home with his father.

This first separation did not last long. Six weeks after moving to Florida, Mickey and her two daughters were back in Lockport. Tim had been taken ill; Bill had called his wife and she had returned to nurse her son almost immediately. The couple decided to make another go of the marriage but it was, ultimately, a futile exercise. The marriage existed on paper only. Mickey, often away from home working as a travel guide, was already having affairs with other men. Bill worked long hours at Harrison, and was the sort of taciturn, impassive individual who seemed, to his children, distant and unapproachable.

If there was a source of emotional support and succour for Tim it came from his paternal grandfather, Ed McVeigh. The older man always had the time and the patience for his grandson, and when things were rough at home Tim would always be assured of a welcome at his grandfather's house. It was here that Tim first learned about guns, awakening the interest in weapons that was to shape his life to such a great extent.

Despite the marital problems at home, there is no reliable evidence that Tim McVeigh was anything more than just another neighbourhood kid. His academic record was good and his behaviour in the classroom exemplary. He had no shortage of friends, nor was he one of those boys who seem to spend all their time on their own or locked in the solitude of their bedroom. While he was not especially close to his parents, there does not appear to have been much outright generational conflict. Indeed, when his parents' marriage finally collapsed for good in 1984, he showed little outward reaction. The marriage had existed in name only for some time, and the final separation proved to be almost a non-event that he felt able to brush aside. As previously, he chose to stay with his father rather than move away with his mother and sisters.

At this point it is worth contrasting McVeigh's life as a child and adolescent with the pattern of behaviour common to some of the spree killers profiled in this book. First and foremost McVeigh's relationship with his father was very different from that of many other spree killers. Rather than being an overwhelming and overpowering influence, Bill McVeigh was a somewhat diffident character, a man not prone to outward signs of emotion nor excessive meddling in the lives of his children. Providing a good home was central to his conception of what it is to be a good father; it did not mean that he intended to try to run his children's lives for them.

In the absence of a dominant father, the only other candidate capable of fulfilling that role was Ed McVeigh. But while their relationship was warmer than that of Tim's with his father, there is no evidence to suggest that Tim was in any way dominated by his grandfather.

Social isolation is another key characteristic that is noticeable by its absence. McVeigh, apparently, did not suffer from a lack of social skills. He had a wide circle of friends and acquaintances, though perhaps few very deep friendships. There is no record of anyone ever calling Tim McVeigh a loner. These friendships included girlfriends, and there is no record of him having any kind of deep-seated sexual problems or dysfunction. Neither did he seem to have trouble holding down a job. Even as a teenager he was ready, willing and able to work, in marked contrast to the likes of Michael Ryan, Larry Gene Ashbrook, Martin Bryant and others.

Violent fantasies and a high level of paranoia are also missing from the picture painted of the young Tim McVeigh. In their book, Michel and Herbeck report on McVeigh's high level of interest in science fiction, superheroes and comics, but there seems to have been nothing untoward about this, and certainly no suggestion that the material he was collecting was especially violent or deviant. Again the contrast between McVeigh and some of the other men featured in this book is very apparent. In fact it is only when we come to guns that we find a crossover between McVeigh and the spree-killer profile mentioned later in this book. Much of the relationship between Tim and his grandfather revolved around guns: target practice, gun lore, hunting. The two of them shared a love of weapons, relishing the enjoyment of hitting the target, of handling a gun, of shooting at the pests that attacked the vegetables in Ed's garden. To quote from *American Terrorist*: 'For Tim, the gun was nourishment for his self-esteem.'

Is this significant? Certainly guns were to remain a central feature of McVeigh's life, and the politics of gun ownership was one of his main concerns, but there is no evidence that his interest became obsessive or escalated to a dangerous degree. Unlike many of the spree killers, he did not use guns as a substitute for a social life; guns did not endow McVeigh with imagined prowess or power. To all intents and purposes, the adolescent Timothy McVeigh was an 'all-American boy' – the kid next door, no different from thousands of other suburban kids across the States.

It is, therefore, undeniable that McVeigh does not fit the profile of mass murderers such as Martin Bryant, Thomas Hamilton, Michael Ryan and others. In that case the question is: how closely did he match people like Benjamin Nathaniel Smith, Buford Furrow and Baruch Goldstein? In all of these cases ideology was a key driver of their actions, and so we must begin to assess McVeigh's life as an adult in order to glean some understanding of his world view.

After graduating from high school, McVeigh won a scholarship to attend a business college in nearby Pendleton. He had intended to study computing, a hobby and a subject close to his heart in which he'd achieved excellent grades at school. He had a good aptitude and scored the highest in the class when it came to the maths test (99 per cent). In spite of this excellent start, McVeigh did not take well to student life. He found the lectures boring, and there was not enough time spent playing with computers and programming – the compulsory courses in English, maths and the humanities he saw as a waste of his time.

He dropped out of college and headed back to the kind of work he'd been doing while at school: flipping burgers. This was not to say that he had completely given up on education. The time he had on his hands was spent reading voraciously on any and every subject that he could find. In particular he read widely around the vexed issue of guns and gun ownership. It wasn't just the technical aspects that interested him, but the wider social context. The debates about gun control were as contentious as ever, and there was (and remains) a degree of paranoia on the part of the gun lobby regarding the motives of the Federal Government and other proponents of stricter gun control. While gun ownership is guaranteed under the Constitution, there is a belief among many that the Federal Government is plotting to take away the citizen's right to bear arms.

While some of the books and magazines that he read were relatively straightforward exhortations to resist the erosion of gun rights, or simple philosophising on the virtues of individualism and self-reliance, there was also a darker strain of material. Chief among this was *The Turner Diaries*, possibly the most widely read racist tract in contemporary America. Cast as a novel, the book, by neo-Nazi William L. Pierce (writing as Andrew Macdonald), tells the story of Earl Turner, an upstanding white American engaged in a race war against the Federal Government – a war triggered in part by the imposition of tighter controls on weapons ownership.

The book is virulently racist, casting Jews and blacks as the sworn enemies of the Aryan race. There can be no peace, no co-existence, between Aryans and non-Aryans; it is a fight to the death. Racial enemies, including white 'race traitors', are shown no mercy. In one scene Earl Turner describes seeing thousands of bodies hanging from trees and lamp-posts, including the corpses of hundreds of women: 'They are the white women who were married to or living with blacks, with Jews, or with other non-white males.' In another scene a stolen truck is laden with ammonium nitrate fertiliser and heating oil, driven into Washington DC and parked outside a government building. When the bomb is detonated it destroys the building, killing 700 people in the process. The parallels with Oklahoma are obvious and helped to establish, in the eyes of many, McVeigh's guilt and William Pierce's culpability.

To say that McVeigh merely liked the book is something of an understatement. He regarded it as a pivotal document. In it he saw something other than paranoid racial fantasy: it was a wake-up call to Americans. Not only did he read and reread the book avidly, he also recommended it to numerous friends, acquaintances and colleagues. Of all the books and magazines that he read during this period of his life, it is this one that had the most lasting, and many would say the most damaging, impact on his life.

Another key influence at this time was survivalism, a practice and philosophy that clearly managed to fuse notions of independence and self-reliance – traditional virtues which many considered under attack – with a degree of political and racial paranoia. Again this chimed in with worries about gun control. A central tenet of survivalism was the idea that society was close to collapse – a collapse that could be attributed to racial problems in the inner cities, the increasing powers of Federal Government, problems caused by Arab oil producers or any other convenient conspiracy theory. And as society collapsed into lawlessness and chaos, guns would become even more important. The idea was that not only were guns necessary to defend home and family, but also that they would become an ersatz currency when the dollar was a worthless piece of paper. In McVeigh's words, a survivalist was defined as: '. . . someone who is prepared to overcome any obstacle that may be thrown at them that is not part of daily life, including stockpiling foods for disasters such as economic, natural or man-made. It would also include defence build-up of armaments, including guns, ammunition, and barter items such as toilet paper, food and bullets that you put aside in case the dollar broke down and was worth nothing.'

McVeigh was not alone with these ideas, they were becoming common currency among gun enthusiasts, and some of the themes were seeping into mainstream culture. Books, magazines and videos served an audience convinced that their country was going downhill fast. In his case this interest extended beyond the theoretical. He planned on storing food and supplies, building up a supply of guns and ammunition, preparing himself for the day when they'd be needed. While working at the local Burger King was fine for giving him room to read and ponder the state of the nation, it was not a good source of funds. He applied for a pistol permit and, having gained one, applied for a job as a security guard. But having a gun was no good if you didn't know how to use it. To this end he used sandbags and logs to build himself a shooting range in the back yard of his father's house.

It was in 1987, at the age of nineteen, that McVeigh became an armed security guard for the Burke Armoured Car company in Buffalo. His home town was largely white, but working in Buffalo, especially in the run-down inner-city districts, he first came into contact with Afro-Americans and other minorities. He was often employed on the cheque-runs, delivering money to the cheque-cashing shops which existed on the East Side of the city, where large numbers of the population were on welfare.

There have been numerous reports that, like many of the other security guards working that run, McVeigh commonly referred to the black inhabitants as 'porch monkeys' and other racial epithets. Up until this period he had had minimal contact with minorities: for example, he claimed not to have come across a single black person during his entire school career. Was he a racist? This is a point of dispute among various commentators and other people who had contact with McVeigh. In *American Terrorist* Michel and Herbeck certainly play down the suggestion that McVeigh was a white supremacist, though this is contradicted by other evidence, including his brief membership of the Ku Klux Klan.

In any case he took well to his new career. His enthusiasm, hard work and shooting skills soon paid off. He was given better assignments; he saved enough money to buy himself a better car, better guns and even a patch of land that he and a friend bought together. However, all this was to change when he decided, in May 1988, to join the Army. The decision seemed to take everybody – friends, family and colleagues – by surprise. But once the decision had been made there was no turning back.

Passing his aptitude tests with flying colours meant that he had the choice of services to join: Army, Navy, Air Force and Marines, who were all interested in the young man with a near perfect score. There was little hesitation it seems on his part – he signed up for the Army. He arrived at Fort Benning, Georgia, on 30 May 1988 for his three months' basic training. At that stage his sights were set on joining the Army elite in the Special Forces or the Army Rangers.

Training was hard, with new recruits pushed to their limits and then some. Despite the harsh environment, or perhaps because of it, McVeigh found himself at home. He fitted the army and the army fitted him. The hard work, the discipline, the routine, all made perfect sense to him. It was at Fort Benning where he first met Terry Lynn Nichols who, ultimately, was charged with McVeigh for the bombing at Oklahoma. Nichols, then aged 33, was the oldest recruit in the company. Promoted squad leader in the same platoon as McVeigh, he soon struck up a lasting friendship with the younger man.

Although they had very different backgrounds and experiences, they shared many interests, including politics. They also shared a deep mistrust of central government, as well as an interest in guns, gun rights and the Second Amendment. 'Two days into training, Tim and Terry were like brothers,' says one witness, quoted in *American Terrorist*. 'They were drawn to each other. It was almost like Tim idolised Terry.'

After Fort Benning – and achieving a perfect score for an infantry recruit – McVeigh and the others in his platoon (including Nichols) were shipped out to Fort Riley in Kansas for more specialised training. Here the men were trained on tanks, armoured troop carriers and other armoured vehicles. For McVeigh, being trained as a light-infantry gunner was ideal. His love of weaponry was well satisfied as he learned to use the M249 Squad Automatic Weapon. This light-machine gun, with a maximum effective range of around a kilometre, is able to fire at a rate of around 750 rounds per minute. For a man whose interest in guns showed no signs of diminishing, it was an ideal choice.

It wasn't just his interest in guns which was growing. His political interests were becoming more and more focused. In discussions with Nichols and others at Fort Riley, the paranoia about the Federal Government was becoming more intense. The conspiracy theorists on the far right were starting to target the United Nations as the seat of a world conspiracy. They felt that the UN, together with the US Federal Government, was working to create a 'one-world government', which would abolish the sovereignty of individual nations, and do away with any form of resistance to it worldwide. Some saw the hands of the Jews behind this world conspiracy; others saw it as some form of Satanic movement; a few saw it as both. McVeigh, Nichols and others seemed drawn to this paranoid world view, but the contradiction between this and their own membership of the US armed forces does not appear to have caused them too many problems.

McVeigh's proficiency with weapons was rewarded in 1989 when he was made a gunner on an armoured troop carrier. Here he had the use of three types of weapons: guided anti-tank missiles; a 25 mm cannon that fired both anti-aircraft and anti-armour shells; and a 7.62 mm machine gun that was capable of firing up to a thousand rounds a minute. As with his other jobs in the army, McVeigh's positive attitude to the job ensured that he was one of the best.

It was no surprise to anyone that McVeigh re-enlisted for another four years in September 1990. His proficiency did not go unnoticed and he was given permission to try out for the Special Forces in November 1990.

His dream of becoming a Green Beret was within sight when the Iraqi invasion of Kuwait signalled the start of the

Gulf War and Operation Desert Storm. The Green Berets would have to wait. McVeigh and his unit were being shipped off to Saudi Arabia. He and his platoon arrived in January 1991, and they spent seven or eight very tense weeks preparing to go into battle. Ironically, back home in the States, there were many on the far right who saw the Gulf War as part of the UN world conspiracy. To them, Saddam Hussein was doing the right thing standing up to Israel, the US and its allies. However, for McVeigh there were more immediate things to worry about.

The ground war started on 21 February, after five days of solid air attacks on Baghdad and other targets across the country. As the allied forces rolled forward they confronted not the highly organised, fanatical forces they had been told to expect, but a weary, bedraggled army that surrendered by the thousand rather than fight for Saddam Hussein. Many of these surrendering troops were crushed to death by the armour that sped deep into Iraq towards the capital. People like McVeigh were as much at risk from 'friendly fire' as they were from the Iraqi army.

McVeigh's moment of glory arrived when his unit came under fire from a dug-in position. All of his skills as a gunner came into play – a single round of the 25 mm cannon 'vaporised' two Iraqi soldiers and lined up the shots that destroyed an enemy gun emplacement. He was later to receive the Army Commendation Medal and a number of other medals for his service in the Gulf War.

After the fighting was over, McVeigh remained with his unit until late March, when he was called back to the States to try out for the Green Berets. The time he spent in Iraq meant that he saw for himself the poverty of the country that had been all but bombed back into the Stone Age. It also gave him a chance to see for himself the disparity between events on the ground and the sanitised messages carried by the news media. It was a contrast that merely added to his overwhelming sense of unease and distrust. And, despite his part in it, he felt discomfort in being a member of a United Nations force fighting another country.

Back home he received a hero's welcome. America was on a high, and McVeigh arrived back in the midst of this patriotic euphoria. He was feted by family, friends and complete strangers alike. In this emotional maelstrom he finally got to try out for the Special Forces. It was not a good move. The emotional turmoil of three months in the Gulf had taken their toll. McVeigh tried hard, but physically he could not cope with the demands placed on him. Reluctantly he pulled out; there was nothing else he could do.

After spending some time with his family (with whom he put on a brave face and did his best to hide the depths of his disappointment), McVeigh returned to Fort Riley to join his unit. However, his interest in extreme right-wing politics continued to flourish. For a while he had been distributing copies of *The Turner Diaries* and other books, and this was to become increasingly important. He also joined the Ku Klux Klan, though he later claimed that he knew little of what the group stood for, a statement that invites disbelief. There is also the first direct evidence at this time of racist behaviour, and in fact he was reported to his superiors for this.

From then on McVeigh's army career took a downward slide. His scores as a gunner were still extremely high, but there lurked a discontent below the surface that would not go away. If an outlet existed at all, he found it in his continued involvement with guns. He had started travelling to gun shows and selling books and literature there. It was an activity that was to be of prime importance for him once he resigned from the Army towards the end of 1991. For a soldier whose career had seemed so promising, and for one who had seen action in the Gulf, the end was sudden. But, given his beliefs and feelings, it was also inevitable.

The Army was followed by a long period of aimlessness during which McVeigh's views on the government, gun control and the state of society hardened still more. He worked for a while as a security guard, including a stint at a high-tech company involving secret work for the military. But even at work he had other things on his mind, and it was not uncommon for him to hand out far-right literature to co-workers. He also met up again with Terry Nichols and some of his other ex-army buddies.

On 28 February 1993 federal agents of the Bureau of Alcohol, Tobacco and Firearms (ATF) raided the compound of a religious sect known as the Branch Davidians, led by its charismatic head, David Koresh. The raid, looking for a stockpile of illegally held weapons, went badly wrong. In the ensuing shoot-out casualties fell on both sides: four agents and six followers of Koresh were killed; Koresh himself was among the wounded. The ATF agents retreated while Koresh and his followers barricaded themselves inside. What should have been a routine search for weapons had turned into a bloody siege that grabbed the attention of the entire nation.

The Waco siege lasted for several weeks during which McVeigh travelled down to see for himself what was going on. He took the opportunity to sell the kind of anti-government literature that he had been peddling at gun shows and to friends and acquaintances. While at the siege he was even interviewed and photographed for an article in a college newspaper. He left shortly after, travelling across the country to visit another ex-army buddy, Mike Fortier, stopping off to visit gun shows and hanging out with some of the dealers at the shows before finally heading back to hook up with Terry Nichols and his brother James.

It was while he was with the Nichols brothers, preparing to drive down to Waco again, that the siege came to a fiery climax. On 19 April 1993 the Waco compound went up in flames, with the occupants still inside. The ATF used exploding gas canisters and armoured vehicles to attack the wooden structure. In the fire, which burned out of control, over 80 people were killed, including David Koresh.

Like many other people, McVeigh interpreted the events that were relayed live on national TV as a massacre by the Federal authorities. It was the New World Order (NWO) in action, killing those who opposed it, murdering those who would not give up their rights as American citizens. Above all it was a fight about guns. It was the clearest example that the NWO would attempt to disarm the population. For McVeigh it was a turning point. After Waco life could never be the same again. The time for words was over.

For the next two years McVeigh toured around the States selling weapons, literature and weapon-related paraphernalia at gun shows. It was a rootless existence, but he was fired up with rage and, over time, this gave rise to a feeling that he had to do something and do it big. During this period he came into contact with numerous individuals and fringe groups, some more extreme than others. Rumours abound about whom he had contact with and the nature of those contacts. There are as many conspiracy theories as there are conspiracy theorists, but some names crop up again and again. Neo-Nazis such as Dennis Mahon and Andreas Strassmeier are frequently mentioned, as is a far-right community called Elohim City. In *American Terrorist* Michel and Herbeck considerably down-play these connections, as they do other aspects of McVeigh's more extreme views and behaviour.

At some point a plan was formed to bomb the Alfred P. Murrah Building in Oklahoma City. Previously the building had been a target for far-right activists. A group called the Covenant, the Sword and the Arm of the Lord (CSAL) had intended to blow the building up with a missile but the weapon had exploded while being assembled. Some of the members of the CSAL later wound up at Elohim City. The Murrah Building housed numerous offices, including the local branch of the ATF, some of whose agents were suspected of having been involved in the Waco siege.

McVeigh was not acting alone; he was aided in many of his activities by Nichols, Fortier and, possibly, others unknown. He was not an explosives expert by any means, but there were books, manuals and the know-how of others on the extreme right. Once the decision had been taken to create a truck bomb, just like the one that he had read about years earlier in *The Turner Diaries*, he started to assiduously acquire the key ingredients. What they couldn't buy they stole and stored in rented garages and sheds. When money started to run low, McVeigh decided to turn on a former friend on the gun-show scene, a dealer called Roger Moore. McVeigh had stayed at Moore's ranch on a number of occasions before the two had fallen out. Now that he needed the money he felt no compunction in organising a robbery, which Nichols actually carried out. The enterprise netted them around $60,000 worth of guns, gold, jewellery and cash.

In October 1994, McVeigh's grandfather, Ed, died. Tim travelled back up country for the funeral, but in many ways the death of his grandfather meant that there was even less holding him back than before. While back home, McVeigh spoke to his sister, Jennifer, about what he was planning, though there is considerable controversy about how much detail he went into. He also composed a letter to the ATF on her computer which included the line: 'all you tyrannical motherfuckers will swing in the wind one day for your treasonous actions against the Constitution of the United States.'

In December McVeigh and Fortier finally cased the Murrah Building. They drove around the building a few times but didn't stop. There was a daycare centre on the second floor, but it was behind black glass and McVeigh claimed that he saw no sign of it. The fine details of the plan were worked out: where the getaway car would be parked; where the truck would be left; the route of the drive to the Murrah Building and the route out of the city.

On 18 April 1995 McVeigh drove a Ryder Rental truck (loaded with one hundred and eight 50-pound bags of fertiliser, three 55-gallon barrels of liquid nitro-methane fuel and the rest of the bomb-making ingredients), to Geary Lake. Here, early in the morning, he intended to meet up with Terry Nichols so that they could finally put the truck bomb together. McVeigh later insisted that he had done most of the work himself, and that Nichols had arrived later to help him finish off. Many people have disputed this version of events, and there are witnesses who claim that there were three vehicles and a team of men involved rather than just McVeigh and Nichols and their vehicles. Once the bomb was ready the two split up, with McVeigh heading into Oklahoma.

On Wednesday 19 April, the second anniversary of the Waco raid and the 220th anniversary of the Battle of Lexington, McVeigh awoke early. He had spent the night in the truck, and now he drove carefully towards his target. He pulled over at one point and lit one of the fuses with a lighter. He stopped again at a traffic light and lit a second fuse. At 8.57 a.m. the Ryder truck was captured on a CCTV camera as it cruised towards the Murrah Building. He pulled in at a drop-off point, just below the daycare centre, and stopped the engine, calmly got out and locked the door. He took one last look at the truck, at the fuses burning ever shorter, at the acrid grey smoke inside the cab, and then walked away.

He crossed the street and headed towards the alley where he had left his getaway car. He was almost there when the monumental blast shook the street. It demolished the front part of the building and severely damaged dozens of other buildings in the surrounding district. Pieces of the truck showered the area, as did glass and concrete – deadly shrapnel that injured hundreds. Dazed and confused by the blast, many started to run towards the building, towards the epicentre of the explosion that had erupted so violently and unexpectedly. But not McVeigh. He removed the DO NOT TOW notice from the windscreen of his car and then headed away from the maelstrom he had created.

The bombing claimed 168 lives, including those of 19 young children. In the initial aftermath, while the bodies were still being pulled from the rubble, suspicion fell on Middle Eastern terrorists. It was inconceivable to many that an American could commit such an atrocity on his fellow citizens.

McVeigh was apprehended on a minor traffic charge a little less than two hours after the detonation. He was kept locked up for two days before the FBI finally tracked him down. Once he was caught, and his picture splashed all over the media, Tim McVeigh became the most hated man in America.

McVeigh is dead now. Finally executed on 12 June 2001, his death was witnessed by over 250 people, some watching the event via a live video link. He remained silent as the lethal injection was applied, staring straight ahead, refusing to say a word as he became the 169th victim of the Oklahoma bombing. And, though he is dead, the story of the bombing is very much alive and kicking.

For the vast majority, McVeigh and his two accomplices Nichols and Fortier are the lowest of the low. Lunatics and fanatics, driven by ideologies that make no sense, they were prepared to slaughter the innocent to drive home a point.

However, there are others who have a very different view of Timothy McVeigh.

There are some on the far right, those who largely share McVeigh's views on politics, who view him as a martyr. Some refused to accept that he was guilty; instead they either proclaimed his innocence completely, or else suggested that he was the Lee Harvey Oswald of the 1990s. Those who proclaimed him innocent were therefore in for a shock when he admitted his guilt. Those who saw him as a 'patsy' claim that he had been set up by the true conspirators in this case. The identity of these conspirators varies, as one would expect, but there are many who are convinced that the Oklahoma City bombing was the work of the Federal Government. The bombing, they contend, was organised with the sole intention of bringing in legislation to curtail civil liberties, particularly with respect to gun ownership. This has echoes, one notes, with similar sentiments expressed by Australian conspiracy theorists with regard to the Martin Bryant case. The most lunatic of the McVeigh conspiracy theories suggests, quite seriously, that he has not been executed and that this was a staged affair. McVeigh, it would appear to these people, has been rewarded by the US government with a new identity and a handsome pay-off; reward for his part in the plot to disarm America.

On the other hand there are those who view McVeigh as guilty but who also believe that there were many others involved. Some of these commentators suggest that there has been a cover-up, and that little effort has been made to catch 'persons unknown' because it would reveal a degree of government complicity or, at best, incompetence. There is good evidence that there was more to the bombing than merely the involvement of McVeigh and the two army buddies he claimed to have coerced into helping him. We know of his links to neo-Nazis; we know that there are credible witnesses who saw other people building the bomb; and we know there are witnesses who saw two people in the Ryder truck moments before it exploded.

It is extremely unlikely that we have heard the last of this case. Even with McVeigh out of the way there are too many questions still to be answered. Was there a conspiracy? The answer is probably yes, though to what extent remains to be seen. If we accept that McVeigh did it, and most credible observers are now agreed that he did, one must ask, what was it that drove him?

McVeigh was evidently not a spree killer, but there are clear points of intersection between this profile and his life. His entire set of ideological beliefs revolved around guns and gun ownership. Add to this a paranoid world view and a degree of racism and you have an explosive mixture. It is worth pointing out that although he did not appear to be sexually dysfunctional, there remained a clear lack of a steady sexual or emotional relationship to his life. All these elements are common to people like Benjamin Nathaniel Smith and Buford Furrow.

However, one must be wary of trying to reduce complex issues to a superficial set of psychological causes. There is a tendency among some observers to impose a facile kind of Freudian explanation on these kinds of cases. Some people have posited that McVeigh was motivated by anger directed at his mother for leaving him. As evidence they point to statements he made about the place of women and working mothers. From this they attempt to draw wider conclusions. This is the same kind of thinking which refuses to accept that people can act in horrible ways based on sane reasoning. It is this kind of thinking or, rather, lack of thinking, which views all attacks on the status quo as being ultimately driven by some kind of infantile revolt against mother or father. The truth is that such Freudian psychobabble has been thoroughly discredited in the scientific world, yet it is still used to castigate those who fight the system and fight for change.

The fact is that Tim McVeigh was a soldier. He had been trained to fight and kill, and he did so, in Iraq, at the behest of his government. He used those same skills, that same callous disregard for human life, when he turned against that government. When he describes the death of innocent children in the Oklahoma City bombing as 'collateral damage', he is merely echoing the chilling sentiments of those who taught him to kill.

At the end of his trial, in which he had refused to speak, he made a single, final statement: 'I wish to use the words of Justice Brandeis, dissenting in Olmstead, to speak for me. He wrote, "Our government is the potent, the omnipresent teacher. For good or ill, it teaches the whole people by its example."'

Perhaps the hardest lesson to be learned by society is also the simplest: 'As ye sow, so shall ye reap.'

Postscript

Terry Nichols, like McVeigh, was charged with conspiracy to use a weapon of mass destruction (including the planning and execution of the robbery against Roger Moore), use of a weapon of mass destruction, destruction by explosions and eight counts of first-degree murder. The main conspiracy charge included the deaths of the other 160 people not listed in the first-degree murder counts. Unlike McVeigh, for the first-degree murder counts Nichols was found guilty of the lesser charge of involuntary manslaughter, though guilty on the other counts. For this he was sentenced to life imprisonment. However, State (as opposed to Federal) prosecutors are now seeking to indict him for 160 counts of first-degree murder, and if he is found guilty they plan on seeking the death penalty that he escaped the first time around.

The only other conspirator that was charged, Michael Fortier, plea-bargained. In return for being the main witness for the prosecution, he was charged with transporting stolen firearms, conspiracy to transport the firearms, lying to federal officials and knowing about the crime and failing to report it. For this he was sentenced to twelve years in prison and ordered to pay a $200,000 fine.

To date, McVeigh, Nichols and Fortier have been the only people convicted with crimes associated with the Oklahoma City bombing.

PROFILE OF A SPREE KILLER

Having reviewed a number of cases of spree killing in detail, we are now in a position to begin to draw conclusions. It should be clear by now that there are elements that are common to many of these cases. By drawing these features out we can make an attempt to flesh out a generic 'profile' of a spree killer. Obviously caution needs to be exercised here. Each of the cases that we have examined is unique, and as such contains features and elements that do not recur elsewhere. By the same token, it should not need to be stressed that each of the spree killers is a unique individual, and that in attempting to generalise about aspects of their personalities the aim is not to diminish their individuality.

Before we begin, it would perhaps be instructive to define more fully what it is we mean by spree killing. As a specific form of crime it is characterised by more than just a high body count. Spree killing is, in fact, characterised by the following:

- *Random or semi-random selection of victims.* While the victims of a spree killer may include close friends and family, they will also include people selected at random from a particular neighbourhood, workplace, etc. Even if a spree killer sets out to target specific racial or religious groups, individual victims from within the target group are selected at random. This clearly differentiates spree killings from those tragic incidents where a father or other male relative may kill a number of members of his family. While such incidents may be marked by a large number of victims, the tensions that caused the crime are usually located entirely within the family unit. Although such murders may be the most tragic and extreme form of domestic violence, they are clearly not the same type of crime as those committed by mass murderers like Thomas Hamilton et al. Although some spree killings – such as the

Mark Barton case – include an element of such crimes, and many spree killers have slain members of their families during their rampage, the focus of the violence clearly extends beyond the family unit and is directed at society at large.

- *The killings take place during a compressed timescale*. Many of the rampages that we have examined lasted only for a few terrible minutes. This compressed timescale means that the violence is extreme, bloody and murderous. While there may be some criminals who kill more than one victim, they do not usually do so in one short burst of violence. Serial killers and contract hit men, for example, may use extreme violence and may kill many victims but their crimes are spread over a period of many months or even years. With spree killers, although the initial outburst of violence may then lead to a stand-off with police – as was the case with Michael Ryan, Martin Bryant and Howard Unruh, for example – it is almost always after the level of violence has considerably diminished.

- *The intention is to kill as many people as possible*. The violence is intended to maximise the number of victims in the short time available before capture or the arrival of the police. The spree killer does not appear to have a set list of victims – he does not set out specifically to kill three or four or five – he simply sets out to kill. To achieve this high kill-ratio, the spree killer will usually select an automatic or semi-automatic weapon, often more than one, and will be armed with a large number of rounds. In shooting at his victims, the spree killer will be aiming for the chest or the head, seeking to guarantee the kill rather than merely to injure.

- *There is little attempt by spree killers at escape*. Indeed, it is true to state that many spree killers commence their crimes knowing full well that they will not survive. Most other violent criminals will obviously attempt to evade capture. In contrast, spree killers will either take their own lives or encourage the police to kill them. Mark Barton was only voicing the wish that many of his fellow spree killers have shared when he wrote to the police that they 'should kill me if you can'. In America the phrase 'suicide by cop' has been coined to characterise the incidents where a suicidal person goes haywire with a gun, clearly intending to be killed by police fire. Many spree killers are clearly suicidal, and if the police do not oblige by killing them they will kill themselves rather than risk capture and incarceration.

- *During the violence the spree killer will display a high degree of control.* Most spree killers appear to be lucid, rational and firmly aware of what they are doing. They do not fire randomly at anything that moves. They do not spray the walls with bullets. They do not laugh uncontrollably or otherwise appear hysterical or hyped up. This calm, almost rational behaviour extends to the selection of victims. Targets are carefully selected from the available pool of victims. They are lined up, aimed at, executed. This is in marked contrast to the behaviour that one might initially expect. The popular view is that the spree killer is a psychotic who shoots at anything that moves, but if this were the case then few such killers would murder so many people in such short periods of time.

- *During his rampage, the spree killer will show little or no mercy.* Many of the cases we have reviewed here make harrowing reading, but the murder of innocent young victims is the hardest to understand. The extreme brutality displayed by spree killers means that children make just as good targets as adults. For some, such as Thomas Hamilton and Buford Furrow, children will even be primary targets. But even where children are not the primary target, spree killers will often show no compunction about massacring them. The cases of Martin Bryant, Mark Barton, Larry Ashbrook, Howard Unruh and others prove this. When victims appeal for mercy they are shown none. It is a frightening fact that the only way to escape is to hide.

- *Finally, the sprees of murder and mayhem appear to be carefully planned rather than spontaneous eruptions of violence*. Although the 'trigger' for the spree may be a spontaneous act, it has often been preceded by a good deal of planning and/or fantasising on the part of the mass murderer. In some cases this planning is little more than a series of violent daydreams and macho fantasies. In other cases it is extremely detailed and extends to such things as choice of targets, weapons preparation and so on. This premeditation is in marked contrast to the public perception of spree killings as random, spontaneous events. It is more likely that mass murders within the family are such spontaneous outbursts of murderous rage: this is yet another means of differentiating these 'domestic murders' from spree killing.

Clearly all of the cases that we have looked at conform to this pattern of violence. Furthermore, having formulated a clear definition of what constitutes a case of spree killing, we can now look at those factors that contribute to this specific pattern of behaviour.

The most obvious feature that unites all of the spree killing cases we have examined (and, indeed, those that we have not covered) is that each of the perpetrators is male. This simple biological fact is no mere accident. Crimes of violence are predominantly carried out by men, but we also know that in almost every category of violent crime, from robbery to murder to child abuse, there are also a minority of women offenders. Even with such extreme crimes as serial killing there are women offenders such as Myra Hindley, Rose West and Eileen Wuornos. As mentioned in the previous chapter, there are no recorded cases of female spree killers – Brenda Spencer is the only possible candidate and her case simply does not conform to the definition of spree killing given above. Therefore we must look at those aspects of society and of specifically male psychology that contribute to this phenomenon.

One thing that is apparent in most of the cases we have reviewed here is that the relationship between the spree killer and his father is primary. Although other relationships may exist, including that with the mother, it is the father–son link that is by far the most important. Indeed, in some cases – Martin Bryant's, for instance – the mother hardly figures at all. Michael Ryan, Martin Bryant, Mark Barton, Larry Gene Ashbrook and Sibusiso Madubela all had very strong attachments to their fathers. In Michael Ryan's case his attachment to his mother was such that he shot and killed her during his rampage. Professor Mullen's psychological assessment of Martin Bryant includes the observation: 'Mr Bryant was not able to give a description of his mother other than as someone who washed his clothes and cooked him food.'

It is also clear that in most of these cases this relationship with the father is far stronger than is considered healthy. Although we must beware of using such socially and psychologically loaded terms as 'healthy' and 'unhealthy' – as though there are two distinct and mutually exclusive states – we can characterise a good father–son relationship as one in which the father figure both provides a useful male role model and creates the space for the son to grow to independence. Most research to date has concentrated on the growing child's primary attachment – almost always to the mother – but it is becoming increasingly clear that for boys the relationship with the father, or a father figure, assumes great importance as he is growing up. We know that an absent father figure means that some boys grow up without an adequate role model, and that this may lead to behavioural difficulties with some children. By the same token boys who have a father who is authoritarian or violent may also suffer behavioural problems. Dr Anthony Storr observed that boys without a father figure or whose father is authoritarian and/or violent 'have less chance of developing into a confident male than a boy whose father lives at home and is actively concerned with him.'

In the cases we have reviewed the father may not have been necessarily authoritarian or violent, but clearly he was a figure who loomed large. Dominant, overprotective and central to the lives of their sons, they seemed to leave little room for their children to develop. They provided more than just a role model: their own masculinity was such that the emerging masculinity of their sons was submerged and stunted. In part it is likely that these men were motivated by nothing more than a desire to protect their children, especially where these boys may have already displayed problems. In seeking to protect their sons they did them a greater injury.

Furthermore, this type of father represents a very strong masculine role model: powerful, competent, knowledgeable and authoritarian. Not surprisingly, the growing child wishes to emulate his father. However, because the father is so strong, so overwhelming, there is little room for the child to achieve. The presence of this strong role model means that the growing child knows what it is he aspires to, and yet there is little chance that he can actively develop his own masculinity. His failure to become his father is all the more keenly felt because of the closeness of the relationship and because of the strength of the father's image.

This dominant role, overshadowing the development of the son, will almost certainly have created a strong underlying sense of frustration. While the boy may have adored or idolised his father and thought the world of him, he would also have felt suffocated by and afraid of him. This frustration would have been exacerbated by the feelings of dependence that the father engendered. In the case of Larry Gene Ashbrook, for example, it was clearly a love-hate relationship that moved towards violence as his dependence on his father increased and as his father became less able to cope because of old age.

The children of such overprotective and dominant fathers will often grow up with low self-esteem, low self-confidence and little sign of independence. All of these are attributes that we can apply to many of the men we have looked at. This dominant father may also unwittingly intensify problems that the growing child has in forming relationships with his peers. Any problems in socialisation that the child has may become considerably worse because of the father's presence. Learning to cope with rejection is a necessary social skill that all children must acquire. If the child is overprotected and is thus shielded from the pain of being rebuffed, then rejection does not become the learning experience that it should be. Alternatively, if the father is so strong a figure that he overwhelms a child with his presence, then an already nervous child may feel little inclination to attempt to make new relationships.

Such a child may move into adulthood without having undergone the maturation process necessary to equip him for independence. Most importantly, he will not have formed any strong relationships with his peers. He will have been viewed by them as a loner, as someone strange or weird. It is likely that this introversion will have meant that at school he either underperformed academically or that he remained socially isolated. Again, these attributes of social isolation are common to many spree killers. 'He was a loner.' 'He always kept himself to himself.' 'We knew that he wasn't right' – these remarks apply to many of the cases, indeed they could be direct quotes from any number of news reports.

If the father is such a dominant figure, why do they let their sons go on the rampage? The answer, of course, is that they don't. It is surely no coincidence that many of these explosions of violence occurred after the death of the father. Michael Ryan, Martin Bryant, Mark Barton, Larry Gene Ashbrook and Sibusiso Madubela all went to pieces after the death of their fathers. In the case of Ashbrook this happened only weeks after the death of his father. In Madubela's case the elapsed time between his father's death and his own rampage was even shorter.

Not all of the spree killers that we have looked at follow this pattern, of course. It is notable that Benjamin Nathaniel Smith and Buford Furrow, both racist killers, did not have this degree of dependence on the father. While Furrow seems to have had a strong relationship with his parents, we do not have enough information on Smith's family background other than the fact that it does not appear to have been overtly dysfunctional. What we do know is that in a relatively short time Smith had developed an extremely strong relationship with Matt Hale, the Pontifus Maximus or Supreme Leader of the World Church of the Creator. The closeness of this relationship only became apparent after Smith's rampage. We know that fascism depends for its appeal in part on the 'leadership principle', and that absolute devotion to the leader (Führer, Duce or a Micky Mouse 'Pontifus Maximus') is something that dedicated fascists will cling to. It does not seem too far-fetched to suggest that Matt Hale represented the dominating and authoritarian father figure that Smith was looking for. Whether Smith's real father was such a dominating figure remains to be seen, but there is little evidence to suggest it.

The other racist spree killer we have looked at is Baruch Goldstein, and again we do not have sufficient data to draw conclusions about his relationship with his parents. But there are certainly no indications that his father was overly dominating. Finally, Thomas Hamilton had no relationship with his real father, though it appears he had a strong relationship with his grandfather who, we must remember, was his adoptive father. The strange circumstances of Hamilton's early life, when he was told that his mother was his sister, clearly affected him deeply.

Of the men who do follow this pattern of being dominated by their father, we know that in many ways they are still children. They have not matured into fully adult males, and like children they find it difficult to cope with the world on their own. When the father figure is removed, so is their coping mechanism. The father who sorted things out, who made sense of the confusion and who got things done is no longer there. Suddenly the son has to call on reserves of self-reliance that he does not have. Faced with a hostile world the strain is considerable, and the immature male does not know how to cope.

Inevitably this leads to frustration, anger and rage. However, it is likely that many young men grow up with equally strong bonds to their fathers. Why is it that there are not many more spree killers? What other contributing factors are there?

Another common thread that runs through all of these stories is that these men are not in stable sexual or emotional relationships with a partner. In some cases there appears to have been a degree of sexual dysfunction, with Thomas Hamilton's fixation on very young boys the most extreme example. Of all the cases we have looked at only Baruch Goldstein was in a stable relationship, but we already know that he was motivated by religious and political hatreds that put him apart from most other spree killers. Mark Barton had been married twice and both wives were to die violent deaths. As we have seen, he was a main suspect in the first murder as well as the self-confessed perpetrator of the second. We should also recall the allegations that he sexually abused his daughter. Buford Furrow's stormy relationship with Debra Mathews had collapsed. Benjamin Smith was already known to police because of his violence towards his ex-girlfriend and was a suspected Peeping Tom. Michael Ryan was sexually frustrated, had not been involved in a sexual or emotional relationship for a number of years and probably started the Hungerford Massacre with a botched rape attempt. Martin Bryant had formed a number of relationships but he was, by his own account, deeply scarred by the failure of a previous one. Howard Unruh harboured an incestuous desire for his mother and felt deeply guilty because of his homosexuality. Although we know little about Madubela, we do know for certain that he was not married and that he lived alone on the army base where he vented his rage. Finally, Larry Gene Ashbrook was also a loner who had not been in a relationship for a number of years.

Clearly the fact that none of these men was involved in a stable relationship was a primary contributing factor. In such a situation without anyone else to turn to the day-to-day frustrations of life are internalised, building up rather than diminishing. This unhealthy state of affairs is compounded when there is no outlet for pent-up sexual energy. Freud put forward a theory of sublimation that suggests that one mechanism for coping with this pent-up sexual energy is to channel it in a different direction. Such frustration can be released, Freud suggested, in activities such as sport. One need not be a Freudian to see that many of the spree killers we have looked at channelled their feelings of frustration in one particular direction: a fascination with guns.

Unable to form lasting relationships (sexual or otherwise) with other adults they formed instead substitute relationships with guns. Michael Ryan, Thomas Hamilton, Martin Bryant, Buford Furrow, Larry Ashbrook and Howard Unruh all had a fascination with firearms that bordered on the obsessive. The phallic symbolism of guns should not be overlooked, nor should we be blind to the feelings of power and control that they afforded to these men. Feelings of inferiority and inadequacy could be banished instantly, the gun providing stark evidence of power and superiority. With a gun to hand none of these men were lonely or inadequate. Each was transformed into a powerfully masculine figure. Where their own masculinity had been overshadowed by that of the strong father figure, with a gun in their grip the image of their own maleness was enhanced and accentuated.

It is no surprise that this fascination with guns ran so strong and so deep through these damaged lives. The emotional energy that they had never had a chance to lavish on another human being was lavished instead on the cold metal of handguns and rifles. Guns could not reject advances: always available, always on hand, the gun became crucial to these men. Thomas Hamilton talked about his guns as though they were his children. Martin Bryant displayed detailed knowledge of guns, even if his shooting skills were said to have been poor. Michael Ryan spent most days at a gun club. Howard Unruh even built a shooting range in the basement of his mother's house, unaware of the psychological symbolism of such an action.

We should not confuse the feelings some of these men had for their guns with those of other people with a normal, maybe sporting interest in weapons. The devotion displayed here bordered on the obsessive. In some ways this devotion to guns matches that of sufferers of Asperger's Syndrome, who display an obsessive interest in one particular subject, be that train-spotting, collecting telephone numbers or learning about a single aspect of car engines. The way these spree killers spent hours of the day taking their guns apart, cleaning them and putting them back together again served as a substitute for more social activity and as a rigid, ritualistic form of behaviour that is reminiscent of the automatic behaviour that gives autism its name.

It is instructive to remember that as Thomas Hamilton became more and more despondent he retreated to his guns to a greater and greater extent. He was not the only one to turn to his guns in times of stress and difficulty. In the way that most people seek solace in the arms of a loved one, Thomas Hamilton and those like him sought refuge in the explosive noise and violence of the gun.

In addition to being fascinated by guns, many of the killers we have surveyed here shared a strong attraction to violent and authoritarian belief systems. In the case of the racially motivated spree killers the reason for this commitment to violent ideology is glaringly self-evident. Gun ownership and a belief in violence is central to Christian Identity politics, to the pagan neo-Nazism of the World Church of the Creator – and to the religious extremism of Zionist settlers in Palestine. However, these are not the only ideologies of violence that we have come across. Michael Ryan and Martin Bryant were both known to have strong interests in 'survivalism'.

Originating largely in the United States, survivalism is rooted in the grey area where neo-Nazism, patriotic militias and gun-ownership advocacy coexist. Survivalism as a distinct subculture was championed by people such as Kurt Saxon and many of those who would take part in the militia movement that came later. A central tenet of survivalism is that society will undergo some form of collapse, either through war, revolution or natural disaster. When central authority implodes, survivalists believe that only those who are armed and ready will make it through the subsequent years of chaos and violence that are inevitable. Many survivalists actually give the impression that they cannot wait for the collapse to come – indeed, they look forward to it with glee. Armed to the teeth and stocked up with guns, food and supplies, some American survivalists have retreated to the wilderness already. The Aryan Nations camp in Idaho, for example, is built on survivalist lines.

Predicated on a philosophy of 'survival of the fittest', survivalism tapped into a vein of racial paranoia prevalent in suburban America. For many of the philosophy's adherents the collapse of society will either be brought on by, or will lead to, an all-out race war. The movement of blacks and other ethnic minorities from the inner cities into the suburbs, following the 'white flight' from the city centres that happened a decade or two earlier, only exacerbated these underlying tensions. Another central concern of survivalism, naturally, is gun ownership. Without weapons the survivalist cannot fight off the hordes who will attack him and his nearest and dearest after the collapse. Any hints of restriction on gun ownership are vociferously attacked by survivalists, usually in conspiracy-theory terms, as an attack by central government on the rights of the 'free man' to bear arms.

In more popular terms survivalist fantasies were on display in films such as *Rambo – First Blood*, a film in which an American Vietnam War veteran, played by Sylvester Stallone, takes on the armed might of the federal government. This one-man-against-the-world/lone-wolf scenario feeds in directly to spree-killing fantasies and, regrettably, to spree-killing reality. It is no surprise that a number of the killers featured in this study were drawn to such films and to the numerous books, magazines and videos that cater for these violent interests.

Typically these films – and, indeed, the entire survivalist credo – appeal to those men who have a very traditional view of what it is to be a man. This view of masculinity is again rooted in the concept of the strong father figure, but it takes on a more defined and ideological flavour when rationalisation is sought for it. A belief in 'ultra-machismo' goes hand in hand with a set of philosophies that seek to legitimise this outdated view of gender roles. If we accept that survivalism, neo-Nazism and Zionist fundamentalism share this macho view of the world, then it becomes significant that a large majority of the spree killers included in this study embraced the survivalist world-view.

Our small sample of mass murderers is by no means unique: a large number of the spree killers not included in this book also shared one or more of these authoritarian philosophies. Even Thomas Hamilton's views of the Scout movement and the type of exercises that he inflicted on the young boys in his charge had distinctly militaristic and authoritarian overtones.

That said, it does appear that those murderers driven mainly by an ideological or religious motivation differ in many respects from those for whom ideology is less well defined or explicit. For one thing, ideological spree killers are more specific in their targets: they clearly set out to kill members of a group that they see as enemies. In doing so they see themselves as part of a community that is defined in relation to the 'Other' that they attack. Buford Furrow and Benjamin Smith defined themselves as 'Aryans', members of the 'white race' locked in struggle with Jews, blacks and other non-Aryans. In a limited sense, then, they see themselves as 'included' in a community, whereas the non-ideological spree killers appear to regard themselves as total outsiders.

All of the spree killers covered in this book share one other notable characteristic: a strong sense of grievance. In some cases the grievances, real or imagined, are rooted clearly in the individual's self-centred concerns. Thomas Hamilton, Martin Bryant, Mark Barton, Larry Gene Ashbrook, Howard Unruh, Sibusiso Madubela and, to a degree, Michael Ryan all harboured deep-seated grievances about their particular situations. Sometimes these grievances seemed well founded. Thomas Hamilton was rightly convinced that people were spreading rumours about his activities and motives. Sibusiso Madubela *had* been demoted when his guerrilla group had been merged with the South African National Defence Force and he had lost pay after going AWOL. But sometimes, however, the grievances looked less plausible. Martin Bryant, Howard Unruh and Larry Ashbrook all suffered a degree of personality disorder that made it genuinely difficult for people to offer them employment and show them the respect they thought they deserved. Regardless of this, all of these men felt that they were victims of injustice, and the hurt that this caused them ran so deep that they could not distance themselves from it.

Again we find that the racists and the ideologues differ from the other spree killers. They too felt grievances, but these were rooted firmly within the preoccupations of the society in which they lived. We can say that these men felt *external* grievances as distinct from the *internal* grievances that the non-ideologues suffered. These external grievances were based on notions of race and religion that define the world in terms of group conflicts. Despite the fact that Furrow and Smith came from different strands of the extreme right, they both felt that they, as white men, were under attack by alien forces. They felt that the racial group with which they identified was being destroyed by the forces of the federal government, which itself was in the hands of the Jews and which aims in every way to destroy the 'white race'. Baruch Goldstein, a member of the very group that Furrow and Smith saw as their ultimate enemy, shared this same way of thinking. In his eyes it was the Jewish people who were under attack, this time by Palestinians who were occupying land that was historically part of Judea.

Although these men's grievances were externally focused, that does not mean that they suffered only an 'intellectual' sense of injustice. On the contrary, these men were emotionally involved to a high degree. When Smith came into contact with the police because of his racist activities, for example, he saw himself as suffering an injustice. His grievances were intensely personal, and no less strongly felt than those of people like Larry Ashbrook. This difference in focus, between internal and external grievances, is another point of differentiation between racist or ideological spree killers and others, and it is worth noting at this point.

Whatever their individual grievances may have been it is also a fact that all of these men jealously nursed them and wove them into the fabric of their lives. There could be no moving on, no forgetting nor any sense of progression. The killers saw themselves as victims, and that sense of victimisation could only grow rather than diminish. Every act, every encounter and incident had to be interpreted in terms of this all-encompassing sense of victimisation. Like a wound that becomes steadily worse as it is picked at, there could be no psychological healing, only a steady deterioration.

We see the world through a set of filters that make up our particular mindset. Every act of perception is a creative act in which we actively interpret the input from our senses in order to understand it. Perception as such is not a passive act at all. Dutch sociologist Jan Huizinga realised that we apply a set of 'game rules' in this process. These rules, which may be unconscious, mean that we fit what we see and hear into our view of reality according to our preconceived ideas of the world. Robert Anton Wilson, in his book *Quantum Psychology*, quotes an example of a policeman hitting a man in the street. One observer will see this as a valid exercise in law and order. Another observer will note that the policeman is white and the man is black and will view the act as a racist attack. Still another observer will have seen the black man pull a gun and will interpret the scene as an act of self-defence by the policeman, while yet another observer may have heard the policeman saying 'Stay away from my wife' and will draw different conclusions. What this example shows is that – for all of us – perception is not about the passive reading of signals.

Psychologists have constructed experiments in which a violent crime scene is staged. Witnesses have then been questioned as to what they saw and in most cases what they saw depended to a large extent on their own particular prejudices. One result showed that white people with an antagonism to ethnic minorities saw that the victim of the crime was white and the perpetrator black, whereas the scene had actually been devised with a black victim and a white criminal.

In the cases of the men we are studying this filtering of perceptions meant that they constantly 'saw' incidents that confirmed their individual grievances and downplayed, mis-interpreted or otherwise ignored those events that conflicted with their world-view. This meant that their worst fears were constantly being confirmed. Feeling forever victimised, and seeing evidence for this persecution all around them, any paranoid tendencies latent in their psychological make-up were naturally brought to the fore.

It is difficult to separate the feelings of grievance from the paranoia that these feelings engendered, but it is clear that all of these spree killers suffered to a greater or lesser extent from a strong sense of persecution. It is no great surprise to discover that paranoia is another element that is common to the ideologies that these men were attracted to. Neo-Nazism and survivalism both view the world in conspiracy-theory terms. Zionist fundamentalism, founded on religious dogma and hundreds of years of real persecution, also has a strain of paranoia running through it. In the cases where there is no clear ideological complexion, such as those of Mark Barton and Larry Ashbrook, there is clear evidence that a strongly delusional world-view with a conspiracy-theory bias had developed. Mark Barton blamed others for his trading losses, and in the notes that he left with his slaughtered family he pointed the finger at those who 'greedily sought my destruction'. Larry Ashbrook, as we have seen, was convinced that he was the victim of a vast conspiracy that included the police and the CIA.

This type of persecution complex has one very important bearing on these cases. By positing a conspiracy, by wallowing in these feelings of victimisation and persecution, these spree killers absolved themselves of any responsibility for their condition. Michael Ryan was unemployed and friendless because of other people, not because of his own antisocial personality. Thomas Hamilton was the target of rumours and attempts to curtail his activities with boys' clubs because he was a victim of smears by the Scout movement, not because of his own dubious behaviour. Buford Furrow had difficulty holding down a job because of his politics, not because of his unstable personality and bad temper. None of these men were able to accept responsibility for their actions. It should be no surprise that their behaviour strikes us as immature; they clearly missed out on important stages of growing up.

This wallowing by spree killers in feelings of victimisation is accompanied and reinforced by fantasies of revenge and retribution. These fantasies will often be developed over a long period of time, and may be extremely vivid and realistic. Frequently videos, magazines and other media will be used to enhance and develop such fantasies. Michael Ryan, for example, was said to be an avid fan of violent action videos such as *Rambo*, *The Terminator* and so on. Howard Unruh collected military memorabilia and guns. Thomas Hamilton even wanted to lend his copies of *Alien* and *The Terminator* to some of the boys who attended his clubs. Martin Bryant collected gun-related publications and was rumoured to watch violent videos. These violent fantasies may occasionally even be expressed in public and, as in the cases of Howard Unruh and Benjamin Smith, may even be written down in diaries and journals.

These fantasies may serve initially as an outlet for anger and frustration. In that sense there is nothing intrinsically unhealthy about them. In the cases we are reviewing, on the other hand, they were not a simple exercise in daydreaming or a momentary escape from reality: they were a replacement for reality. In these fantasies the men concerned were transformed from socially inadequate loners to extremely powerful and respected figures. In fantasy at least, these men could achieve the warped masculine image to which they aspired. In fantasy they could use their guns to gain power and respect. They could, of course, act out again and again the violence that they would eventually unleash for real on an unsuspecting world.

In a number of the cases we have looked at there has also been evidence of real violence occurring before the actual killing spree. As we have seen, Larry Ashbrook attacked his father; Benjamin Smith attacked a girlfriend and was reported to the police for domestic violence; Michael Ryan was said to have attacked his mother. Buford Furrow was said to have been involved in violent arguments with Debra Mathews. In the most dramatic such case Mark Barton was accused of murdering his first wife and her mother. In all of these cases the violence was not directed at random victims – it was aimed directly at people within the immediate family unit or at a partner. This domestic violence was relatively self-contained and therefore 'safe'. It carried little risk of interference from outside authorities, and rarely led to long-lasting repercussions.

The fact that this violence did not lead to severe 'punishment' may have served both to bolster the perpetrator's ego and to reinforce an image of violent masculinity. In many ways this equation of men and violence coincided both with the killers' belief/interest in extreme ideologies and with supposed social norms that they saw expressed in videos and magazines.

These incidents of violence may have occurred in the home but there was little expression of hostility to outsiders. In fact, in a few of these cases the men concerned projected very different pictures of themselves. Thomas Hamilton, for example, was always scrupulously polite when being verbally abused by parents who opposed him. Buford Furrow was considered a bit weird but friendly. Mark Barton always had a ready smile for his neighbours. Benjamin Smith was always calm, polite and coherent when confronted about his racism. Larry Ashbrook was presentable and polite when he turned up at the newspaper office to state his case. These outwardly calm and polite exteriors were façades to cover up feelings of intense anger and hostility. Such repressive behaviour, this bottling up of anger, represents not a victory of the conscience but a frustrating buckling down and an unhappy acceptance of social norms. It is not the sort of behaviour that one can engage in for years on end without suffering for it.

It should be obvious that feelings of victimisation, persecution, sexual frustration and a strong sense of paranoia, combined with a love of weapons and an attraction to violent ideas and imagery, do not make a healthy combination. Given this explosive mixture it is little surprise that many of these men displayed symptoms of severe personality disorders even before they finally cracked. Nearly all of these spree killers had come into contact with mental health officials or with law enforcement agencies at one time or another before their eventual rampages. In none of these cases, however, had this contact with state agencies resulted in any amelioration of their condition. For this reason we can say that these outbreaks of horrific violence represent failures by society to recognise the dangerous mental space that these men occupied.

These factors developed over long periods of time, but at some point they came to a head and the results, as we have seen, were explosions of murderous rage that consumed many lives before they were finally extinguished. Here too we must ask ourselves whether there are common features that immediately preceded the killing sprees. We have touched on one such factor already, namely the loss of the strong father figure. But are there others?

In the case of the loss of the father figure, the potential spree killer is left suddenly to cope with a world from which he has been protected to some extent. Social inadequacies that have been obscured by the presence of a protecting and competent father are vividly exposed. A strong sense of routine and direction disappear, leaving the son floundering with too much time on his hands and no idea what to do next. Inevitably, underlying frustrations are compounded and new ones arise. Part of the grieving process often involves strong feelings of anger and abandonment directed at the departed person, but in these cases these natural feelings are extremely strong and may assume a violent character.

Another common element seems to be financial. This may be connected to the loss of the father, as in the case of Larry Ashbrook, but it is not always so. Mark Barton, for example, was suffering huge financial losses thanks to his Internet day trading. Buford Furrow was also having financial problems because of his difficulties holding down a job. Thomas Hamilton was heavily in debt and was facing financial ruin because he had been devoting himself to running his boys' clubs rather than to working. The little revenue that these clubs generated was threatened when so many parents started preventing their children from attending his events.

On other occasions the trigger mechanism may simply be an unexpected situation that exposes once and for all the complete inability of the spree killer to cope. Michael Ryan was unable to cope with his botched attack on Susan Godfrey. Faced with a situation he was unable to handle, he responded by killing her and then, having embarked on such a course, he simply could not think of any way out other than to carry on killing. Martin Bryant, having started out by killing the people he blamed for his father's suicide, then compounded the problem by going on his killing spree. Sibusiso Madubela was enraged by the loss of pay after going AWOL and, unable to deal with the situation sanely, turned to his gun to solve it for him.

In the case of the racist spree killers, we find a different set of trigger mechanisms. Aware of the political implications of their violent acts, these men select dates, places or targets that have a particular social resonance. Benjamin Smith decided to go on a killing spree during the 4 July weekend. Baruch Goldstein selected a date that had religious significance. It indicates, one has to admit, yet another difference between 'ideological' and 'non-ideological' spree killers.

To conclude, then, can we draw up a profile of a typical spree killer? It should be clear that although there is a super-set of characteristics that are common to all of the cases we have reviewed, not every case will share every characteristic. Therefore in defining this super-set we should not imagine that we have described every feature of the cases under discussion. Nor should we think that we have defined a 'diagnostic' symptomology that can be applied without further thought to future cases of spree killing. Real life rarely allows such simple procedures to work, and any attempt to generalise from a small sample set is inherently risky.

One must also point out again that there are numerous differences between the cases of racist spree killers and the other cases we have reviewed. It could well be that the racist spree killers are a distinct sub-group and as such need to be reviewed separately. While there are numerous overlaps between both types of spree killer, the motives of the ideologues may well prove to be both much simpler and more complex. Simpler because the violence is contextualised by a detailed political ideology, providing a framework that can explain the legitimacy or otherwise of such acts of mass violence. More complex because the interactions between this ideology and an individual's psychological make-up are more difficult to analyse.

With those caveats firmly in mind we can make a first attempt at generalising from the cases which we have reviewed:

- *The spree killer is invariably male.* Although there is nothing to say that future female spree killers will not appear, based on the experience of the last fifty years spree killers will tend to be male.

- *The spree killer will have had a father who is overly authoritarian and/or dominant.* In a case where the father has been absent, or where he is not unduly dominant, another father figure may well substitute.

- *The spree killer has problems with social interaction.* He will usually be considered a loner and will have few friends. Problems with socialisation may be traced back to his childhood. He is unlikely to be in regular or stable employment and may have a long history of employment difficulties.

- *The spree killer will exhibit paranoid tendencies.* He will possess a strong sense of grievance and persecution. In extreme cases he will see the world filtered through detailed conspiracies that revolve around him or the peer group with which he identifies.

- *There may be a degree of sexual confusion or dysfunction.* The spree killer will not be involved in a stable sexual or emotional relationship with another adult.

- *The spree killer will be involved with or attracted to extreme ideologies or religious beliefs.* These beliefs will feature fixed gender roles, and may be considered as generic 'macho' ideologies with a propensity to violence and/or a conspiracy-theory world-view.

- *Violent tendencies will be expressed through violent fantasies, rhetoric or abusive behaviour directed 'safely' within the family unit or against partners.* This violence will often precipitate the end of any emotional relationship the spree killer may have formed.

- *The spree killer will have a strong fascination with guns, weapons and/or other militaria.* He will have access to guns and may belong to a gun club, shooting range, etc. This interest in guns may be stronger than customary and may exhibit signs of being obsessive.

SPREE KILLERS AND SOCIETY

In this, our final chapter, we shall direct our attention away from the spree killers for a moment and consider the wider context of their actions. Specifically, we shall look at how society has responded to spree killings to date and, more pertinently, discuss if there is anything that we can do to prevent further cases occurring in the future.

As we have already mentioned, spree killings of the type that we are looking at occur in all types of societies, from advanced Western countries such as the United States to African countries such as Uganda and South Africa and to Asian countries such as South Korea. It is one of these Asian countries – Malaysia – that gave us the word 'amok' which so aptly describes this type of frenzied violence. As the following passage from van Wulfften Palthe, written in 1936, makes clear, 'running amok' is a behaviour that is familiar to Malay communities throughout South East Asia:

Suddenly, without warning, without those around him being in any way prepared for it, a native springs up, seizes the first weapon he can lay hands on, usually a sword or knife, and rushes like one possessed through his house and garden into the street. Like a mad dog, he attacks every living thing that gets in his way, and succeeds with marvellous skill in dealing deadly stabs and blows: his mental eye may, indeed, be clouded (the natives call the condition 'meat gelap', clouded eyes), but his primary motor and sensory functions have in no way shared in the clouding, and it is not seldom that an amoker will in a moment or two leave five or six dead or desperately wounded persons on the ground in his wake! His mad lust for attack is not restricted to human beings, he will chop into carabaos (draft cattle) posts, and, in short, anything and everything that he meets.

With wild cries of 'Amok! Amok!' everyone in his neighbourhood seeks safety in flight. When there is nothing left for him to kill, he turns his spirit of destructiveness against himself, so that if he is not previously 'knocked out', the most terrible self-inflicted wounds may be the result; he is finally overpowered, when he has become exhausted, with his throat cut or with his belly laid open, and often, too, with horribly mutilated genital organs. The true amoker does not become satiated, he does not stop of his own accord. Those in the neighbourhood know that fact all to well, and will, if they get the chance and are plucky enough to attempt it, do everything in their power to make an end of the amoker (if this is done by the police or military, who usually shoot him down, the news-papers will report it as 'neerleggen', or 'knock out'). For this reason, it is very seldom that an amoker is overpowered while still living and not too seriously injured to come to examination.

The weapon of choice may be dissimilar and the social context is certainly very different, but in many respects the description that van Wulfften Palthe gives us is very apt and clearly accords with the cases that we have previously described in detail. Although such outbreaks of violence are rare, they are a feature of Malay society and as such are dealt with quickly by the local population or the police. In contrast to our own society, such violence is not the cause of concerned hand-wringing and earnest questions. It is accepted as a form of madness that people can fall victim to.

In many of the cases we have covered, the outbreaks of violence were followed by shocked headlines, traumatic news footage, political statements and anguished questions. Sensationalised news reports might have continued for many days or weeks after such violence as people struggled to come to terms with the scale of the violence and attempted to find motivation in the seemingly motiveless attacks. People want to understand why: they seek clear-cut reasons that allow them to make sense of something that is beyond their understanding. Inevitably there are those who will provide reasons, and with their reasons they will provide suggestions as to how society can respond to and prevent further cases of spree killings. Typically, commentators and members of the public alike are apt to demand that 'something be done', as though it is possible to legislate for each individual's mental state.

Many of the things that populist politicians and newspaper columnists put forward as contributing factors – or, indeed, as the sole causes – of spree killings are suspiciously similar to those that are proposed as causes of other forms of violent crime or other social problems. The primary candidates are generally violent videos, pornography, the breakdown of the nuclear family, permissiveness in general and, increasingly, the Internet. That this ragtag collection of 'causes' is used to explain everything from school truancy to violent crime to teenage pregnancies does not mean that we should not take them seriously. Many people are willing to be swayed by simplistic explanations and, in the case of something as horrific as the Dunblane Massacre or Larry Ashbrook's killing spree inside a church, such simple interpretations become even more attractive in that they offer a simple key to understanding, and, just as importantly, they offer the promise of simple solutions.

Violent videos have been suggested as important contributory factors in a number of key cases including those of Michael Ryan and Martin Bryant. While it is certainly true that both of these men liked to watch violent 'action' videos of the kind that Hollywood regularly churns out, there is little to suggest that they actively set out to emulate the violence portrayed by the likes of Arnold Schwarzenegger, Sylvester Stallone et al. If it is true that these films fuelled a violent fantasy life, it must also be said that such fantasies can feed from the unlikeliest of sources. If one wishes to seek out corrupting influences, it is likely that the Bible, the Torah and the Koran have between them influenced more fanatics, psychopaths and killers than anything else. The people who propose banning violent videos are generally motivated by the Bible, the Torah and the Koran, so one would not imagine that they would suggest for one moment banning these religious works.

Despite the paucity of evidence linking spree killers and video violence, the question has cropped up so often that we have to ask it ourselves: do violent videos generate violence in the viewer?

This question has been hotly debated in the last two decades, although that debate is far from reaching a conclusion. There have been many studies carried out that look at this thorny issue, many of them focused on the effects of media violence on children. Although many of these studies are inconclusive, or can be criticised for methodological reasons, it is currently reckoned that there is, on balance, some correlation between the amount of violence a child watches and his or her behaviour. This does not mean that a causal link has been proven – it merely suggests that television and film violence can be a factor in some children's behaviour. This media portrayal of violence is said to have three harmful effects: firstly, children learn aggressive behaviour and adopt aggressive attitudes; secondly, children become desensitised to real-world violence; and finally, children develop a neurotic fear of becoming victims of violence themselves.

Although we are primarily interested here in the effects of filmed violence on adults, it is worth making a few remarks before moving on. Television and video are just two of the sources that children learn from and these media do not exist in social isolation. If television portrays violent behaviour as both effective and socially acceptable then clearly there is a problem. However, we find that violent behaviour is endemic to society and is not solely the creation of the media. Many of these studies have focused on poor, socially disadvantaged children who offend disproportionately and watch higher than average amounts of television. If such children are more likely to engage in violent behaviour is it because they live in communities where crime and violence are rife or because of what they have seen on television?

Secondly, one of the primary criticisms one can make of Hollywood violence is that it is extremely unrealistic. The very real effects of violence are not shown or are glossed over. Gunfights take place and nobody seems to get hit. The heroes of these films appear to be virtually indestructible: if he (or, increasingly, she) gets hit then the wound is superficial and seems to be painless. If a villain is shot he keels over and dies with barely a whimper. Where is the blood, the pain, the suffering? Perhaps if the portrayal of television and video violence was more realistic then it would both cease to be attractive and lead to greater empathy with the victims of real violence. If children become desensitised to violence it is surely because they have never been shown its horrific reality.

Finally, it is sadly true that many people, not just children, develop a fear of crime and violence out of all proportion to the real risks. However, this is just as likely to be caused by police officers, politicians and media pundits focusing so much attention on the 'fight against crime' as it is to be caused by children watching *Power Rangers* or *Xena, Warrior Princess*.

Do these studies yield useful information about the kind of crimes we are examining? The answer is that they do not. In the cases we have looked at there is no evidence to suggest that any of the spree killers on our list were inspired to commit their crimes because of the films they watched. A propensity to violence was present in all of them and, as we have discussed previously, this was an important facet of their personality. They were already drawn to violent ideologies and imagery, and this was as likely to come from magazines and books as anywhere else. Howard Unruh, for example, was very obviously influenced by what he read in the Bible, which, with its Old Testament emphasis on revenge and retribution, has inspired many other criminals past and present. Can we say that Michael Ryan and Martin Bryant would not have killed if they had not watched violent videos? The answer has to be an emphatic no. With maladjusted individuals there is no way we can know where they will draw inspiration or gather materials for their fantasies. Trying to censor what the majority of the population can or cannot see on this basis is both unfair and unworkable.

It is also worth reiterating once more that spree killings occur in many cultures, even in those where television and video are largely absent. If such rampages were directly influenced by exposure to fictional portrayals of violence then we would expect to see proportionately more cases of spree killing in those countries with a preponderance of violent TV. That correlation does not exist, and in the case of primitive tribes in South-East Asia who have not had any exposure to television or video and yet who are as familiar with 'running amok' as the Malays there can be no doubt that media violence does not have any influence.

If the evidence that violent videos are partially to blame for spree killing is unclear, then we can say that there is even less evidence relating to pornographic or sexually explicit videos. Obviously we are not dealing with sexual crimes here, although sexual dysfunction or frustration is an underlying factor that contributes to the unstable personalities of those who commit spree killings. In fact, the evidence clearly suggests that even with sex crimes, there is little connection between exposure to pornography and actual sexual offences. Despite cases like that of Ted Bundy, where he claimed that pornography turned him into a serial rapist and murderer, the evidence points the other way. In the cases we are looking at here, pornography has been directly linked to the case of Howard Unruh and Martin Bryant – and, of course, Thomas Hamilton was accused of making semi-pornographic videos featuring the boys in his care.

In Howard Unruh's case sexual confusion contributed to his instability, but these problems predated any interest he had in pornography. Although we do not know what kind of magazines he was said to have had, the chances are that they would have been not very explicit 'beefcake' magazines featuring muscular male models. Nobody can seriously suggest that the sight of a few muscle-bound men wearing skimpy briefs is likely to turn anyone into a mass murderer. In Martin Bryant's case he was said to have purchased pornographic videos during his trip to Amsterdam, and it was claimed that at least one of these films featured bestiality. Again, having looked at the details of Martin Bryant's life and the mental problems that he suffered as a result of his low IQ, there is nothing to suggest that he was inspired by anything more than a high degree of frustration and anger at what he saw as society's rejection of him. In Thomas Hamilton's case the police did not find any pornographic videos or any type of paedophile-magazine pornography. The videos that he did take were viewed by the police: although what they showed was clearly disturbing, there was nothing overtly sexual or indecently explicit about them. Some of his films are said not to have been recovered, but as no child ever came forward to make a complaint of actual sexual abuse against him, we must assume that Hamilton was satisfied with the films and pictures of boys dressed in nothing but the shorts he supplied. Was he driven to mass murder by pornography? Clearly not.

Increasingly the Internet is taking the place of video as the primary media scapegoat. It is blamed for social calamities by alarmist politicians, police officers and religious leaders. As a medium the Internet has yet to be policed, certificated and censored to the degree that television, cinema and video have been. It is still relatively early days yet, and many governments and international authorities are working towards measures to impose a higher degree of control on a technology with which they are still uncomfortable. Ultimately it is going to be a combination of government and market forces that will impose the controls which are still largely lacking at the moment. In the meantime, accusing the Internet of being a subversive or permissive medium is guaranteed to win column inches and television sound-bites, and the sheer volume of these denunciations will add impetus to the moves to impose controls on it. So far the only two cases of spree killing in which the Internet has been cited as a contributory agent are those of Mark Barton and Benjamin Smith.

In the Barton case the Internet was very clearly a major factor in the financial mess that he had created for himself. His disastrous activities as an Internet day trader meant that he was losing thousands of dollars a day and was sinking ever deeper into debt. Immediately after the massacre, attention was focused on the Internet day-trading companies and their methods of doing business. Many were quick to point the finger at the Internet, as though somehow anybody could thereby be drawn innocently into a venture that could lead to financial disaster. The fact is that undertaking risky financial investments is an activity that requires nothing more than a bank account and a willingness to gamble. Although day trading may be more exciting and, possibly, more addictive, more people lose money by playing the market through banks, insurance companies and stockbrokers than as day traders. This, of course, does not make for good headlines. In fact, access to financial information via the Internet gives many investors the chance to monitor the performance of the investments their financial advisors recommend.

The fact that Mark Barton lost a fortune on the Internet rather than through a bank, racetrack or casino is an accident of circumstance. Paranoid, potentially violent, prone to depression and with a marriage that was fast breaking apart, Barton was a time-bomb waiting to explode. To blame the Internet is an easy option that completely misses the point. Even if day trading were more closely controlled, the chances are that sooner or later Barton was going to flip. He had probably already killed two people; that he killed again was no surprise to those officers who believe he should have been nailed the first time.

In the case of Benjamin Nathaniel Smith, the Internet was only tenuously linked to him, yet that did not stop it becoming a major talking point in the aftermath of his racist killing spree. Attention was focused not on his personality nor on what he had done but on trying to find out what had turned a middle-class college kid into a dogmatic, violent fascist. Like many racist and neo-Nazi groups, the World Church of the Creator uses the Internet extensively to spread its vile creed and many commentators seized on this as a likely factor. Logging on to one of the many websites that form the WCOTC presence on the Internet, one is usually presented with a message box that proclaims that the site is for 'Whites Only!' This sets the tone for the rest of the site content, which is unashamedly racist, violent and offensive. Looking at these sites one can read Matt Hale's paranoid rants, download sections of books, link to other neo-Nazi sites and generally bathe in the extremist ambience that the WCOTC generates.

That neo-Nazis use the Internet to spread their message is seen as condemnation enough of the entire Internet in some quarters. 'The messages of violence and hate are now accessible to all: how can we protect our children from this poison?' This kind of thinking inevitably leads to calls for 'action' by government or by the Internet service providers who host these websites. In other words, it leads to an argument for censorship, and we find ourselves once more in the same kind of debate as that about violent videos and pornography. What is one of the main assumptions that underlies these calls for censorship? It is that some people do not have the intellectual ability or moral understanding to make up their own minds about something, be it racist rhetoric, on-screen violence or explicit sexuality.

Banning racist websites will not make racism go away. Racist organisations and political groups existed long before the Internet, and will probably exist long after the Internet has been superseded. Many Internet users jealously guard the relative freedom that it offers; attempts to ban sites have inevitably failed. By its nature the Internet is international, and websites banned in one country are 'mirrored' in other countries almost immediately, as has been shown on numerous occasions in the last few years.

If the only response to racist websites is to ban them, what does that say for the strength of the anti-racist argument? Banning something almost always creates sympathy for it, and banning racist websites is sure to engender a degree of sympathy for them that they would not normally receive. Focusing attention on racist sites also serves to ignore the very strong anti-racist presence on the Internet. It is not just neo-Nazis who are politically active on the web, their opponents are both more numerous and just as well organised. Finally, one cannot help but to point out that censorship very often backfires on those who propose it. Andrea Dworkin and many other feminist activists fought long and hard to pass anti-porn censorship laws in several states of America and in Canada – only to find that some of the first victims of these very censorship laws were magazines and books by lesbian feminists, safe-sex campaigners and, ironically, some of Dworkin's own novels.

Finally, to return to Benjamin Smith's case, there is little evidence that he became a neo-Nazi because of what he saw on the Internet. One must ask the same type of question we have asked about some of the other cases: would Benjamin Smith have gone on the rampage if he had not had access to the Internet? The answer is almost certainly that the Internet made no difference. In fact, had the racist websites been censored or removed it would have added to his racial paranoia, convincing him even more that he was at war and making his violence more likely.

Although it may seem that the issue of censorship is a digression, it is in fact extremely germane. In this respect at least, spree killing does not differ from other forms of criminal behaviour. Where readily identifiable causes do not exist, then there are sections of the media that will invent them. When appealing to the lowest common denominator, an absence of evidence can be no impediment to a good headline. Besides, there is nothing that certain pro-censorship lobbies like more than a fresh public outrage to create a moral panic to further their cause.

If video violence, pornography and the Internet are not major factors in these cases, then we know for sure that one other factor is absolutely fundamental: access to guns. It is probably true to say that in nearly every case reviewed in this study the debate about gun control has flared up in the aftermath of the violence. But, as experience in Malaysia and other parts of South-East Asia has shown, people can go on a killing spree without access to guns. A machete, a sword or other weapon can be used by a spree killer to kill and maim, but such cases, in the West at least, rarely result in multiple deaths and certainly do not cause such public outrage as the gun-related cases we have covered earlier.

In the case of the two British spree killers listed here, Michael Ryan and Thomas Hamilton, public outrage was such that the already stringent British rules governing gun ownership were tightened up both times. When Michael Ryan left a trail of dead and injured in Hungerford, many people were shocked to discover that he had been able to obtain such dangerous weapons. Why would any civilian need to possess a Kalashnikov AK47 and an M1 carbine? What possible legal use could such lethal weapons have in a civilised country? For many people it was a shock to discover that such military weapons could be acquired by members of the public. Britain does not have a gun culture in the same way that the United States has, and for the most part the gun subculture that revolves around British shooting clubs and sporting competitions keeps a low profile. Many British people go their entire lives without ever coming into contact with guns, and so the discovery that individuals in the heart of the community could get hold of such murderous weapons became a major cause for concern following the numbing shock in the wake of Ryan's crimes.

In the aftermath of the Hungerford Massacre the police declared an amnesty on illegally held weapons, and people were encouraged to hand in their guns without fear of prosecution. Over forty thousand weapons were handed in to police during the amnesty. Of more lasting effect was the change in the law concerning the possession of weapons. The Firearms (Amendment) Act of 1988, drafted in direct response to Hungerford and riding a wave of anti-gun feeling, outlawed semi-automatic and pump-action rifles and carbines and military weapons such as rocket launchers, and generally tightened up the regulations regarding shotguns.

It was hoped that another massacre like Hungerford could not take place, that the more stringent rules would somehow stop deadly weapons getting into the wrong hands. Thomas Hamilton proved at Dunblane what a vain hope this was. Predictably there was then another firearms amnesty, which netted over 22,000 weapons, and another change in the law. The Firearms (Amendment) Act 1997 banned handguns, apart from .22 pistols kept at licensed clubs, and changed some of the regulations concerning ammunition.

These changes in the law have, it must be admitted, accorded largely with public opinion in the UK. Colin Smith, the Chief Constable of the Thames Valley Police, who was commissioned to write the official report on the Hungerford Massacre, concluded in his report: 'Little that occurred during these events or contributed to their cause indicates the need for any specific change in the legislation or procedures relating to firearms. However, the public are not only amenable to, but will demand, that this tragic event is used as a catalyst for changes in both the law and administrative procedures which have long been thought desirable and well overdue.'

Inflamed public opinion, particularly when it has been subjected to a shocking tragedy such as Hungerford – and further excited by the wave of sensationalist and misleading reports from the tabloid press that followed it – is hardly amenable to reasoned argument and clear, unprejudiced thinking. There are a number of questions that need to be asked about these changes in the law and the thinking that underlies them. Firstly, can we say that these types of restriction make any difference to the incidence of spree killing? Would these killings have occurred if the new laws had been in place? Finally, is it right to pass such legislation because of the actions of people like Michael Ryan and Thomas Hamilton?

In response to the first question we have already seen that spree killing – running amok – occurs in all societies, from the most primitive to the most advanced. It is first and foremost caused by the conjunction of a number of different factors, including a number of psychological elements that are beyond the reach of any law. The fact that we have chosen to focus on the most violent and deadly of the spree killers should not obscure the fact that people can and do go on the rampage armed with nothing more than kitchen knives. For example, following the Dunblane Massacre Horrett Cambell went on the rampage at St Luke's Primary School in Wolverhampton. Armed with a machete, he attacked a number of adults, including teacher Lisa Potts, in an attempt to get at the children. Although he was subdued before he could kill anybody, it illustrates that even in the West spree killers do not always go for guns.

Would the killings at Hungerford and Dunblane not have occurred if the newer, more stringent gun control laws had been in place at the time? Clearly, any answer has to be speculative. But we do know that Michael Ryan and Thomas

Hamilton were both members of gun clubs. Even with the strictest rules enforced, they would still have had access to weapons. Unless *all* access to firearms had been deemed illegal, the chances were that these obsessive men would still have managed to get their hands on guns. Thomas Hamilton was not afraid of bureaucracy and form-filling and he was not cowed by officialdom. It is clear that he and Michael Ryan would have methodically worked through every legal obstacle in order to gain access to firearms. Where such obstructions put off many of the rest of the population, they do nothing to stop the true obsessive.

Which brings us neatly to the final question. Are these changes in the law fair? Just as it would be unfair to censor material because it might adversely effect a few unstable individuals, it seems equally unfair to impose restrictions on gun ownership because of what a few maladjusted individuals might or might not do. A society that polices itself according to the standards of its most unstable or most disturbed citizens is heading for a quagmire of legal restrictions and prohibitive laws that would remove many of our most fundamental freedoms. Such a society risks handing over all power, authority and responsibility to the state, leaving little room for the individual to make up his or her own mind about things.

At the time of these changes to the law many gun enthusiasts were joined by civil libertarians in protesting against what were essentially illiberal and ill-thought-out laws. Who would obey the law? This was one of the most pertinent questions asked by the opponents of the changes in the rules. Criminals who already possessed firearms illegally were obviously going to hold on to their guns regardless of the law. They were not going to hand them over because they had suddenly become even more illegal. Similarly, those people who illegally trade in firearms would continue to disregard the law. The only people who would abide by the new rules would be those who already upheld the law, and they would generally be those least likely to commit crimes with their weapons.

Police figures show that the majority of weapons used in violent crime are acquired illegally. Paradoxically, the more restrictions that have been placed on firearms ownership the more the criminal use of weapons has grown. The black market in weapons has mushroomed, and the use of guns has become an almost accepted part of many criminal subcultures. The supply of illegal weapons has continued to rise even after the changes to the law in the wake of Dunblane. If the intention of these laws was to remove weapons from the community then they have manifestly failed. Instead, the law has succeeded in penalising those gun owners who have stuck to the rules and has done nothing to stem the trade in illegal weapons.

The gun debate in Britain pales into insignificance compared to the debate in the United States. In fact, the National Rifle Association (NRA), one of the most successful and powerful lobby groups in the United States, has used the British experience of gun control as a warning of what might happen when gun control laws go haywire. In an hour-long infomercial shown on US cable channels, British gun enthusiasts, including a former police officer, are shown bemoaning their fate and explaining how their hobby has been criminalised and almost legislated out of existence. The warning to their American counterparts is clear: don't let this happen to you.

Given the much higher gun-crime figures in the US, the long history of gun ownership enshrined in the Constitution and controversy over the limits of federal power, the American debate about guns is as explosive as it is acrimonious. After each of the cases we have looked at in this book, the debate about guns has flared up once more.

The American gun-control debate is complex and deeply rooted in the political landscape of the United States. To discuss it adequately would take too much time and would add little that is pertinent to our main subject. Suffice it to say that the arguments for and against gun control are rehearsed again and again in the American press and other media, and that every new outrage reignites this debate. Along with race, gun control is one of the most polarising issues in American society and there seems to be little hope that the opposing sides will see sense and move to compromise.

As far as the spree killers we have looked at are concerned, none of them had difficulties gaining access to weapons. Benjamin Nathaniel Smith, denied a weapons permit because of his domestic violence, found little difficulty buying a weapon illegally. Larry Gene Ashbrook, paranoid and mentally disturbed, had had a gun since his days in the Navy. Buford Furrow, violently racist and anti-Semitic, came from a political subculture that turned gun ownership into a fetish. Restricting gun ownership will do nothing to stop these kinds of men so long as obtaining firearms through illegal means is relatively easy. The proponents of gun control must face up to the truth that taking the gun out of American society will require a fundamental cultural change. Changing the law will be the easy part. Enforcing the change and cracking down on illegal weapons will be much harder and will not be accomplished without a great deal of struggle.

The final word on this matter belongs to Joe Vandiver, Leigh Ann Barton's father: 'I just don't want my daughter's death to come down to gun control. He didn't kill my daughter with a firearm. He killed my daughter with a hammer . . . I know Mark's problems were not guns . . . [Even with the strictest gun control laws in place] there was no legal reason why he couldn't buy a firearm.'

Finally, there is one other issue that has frequently arisen in connection with society's response to spree killings: the matter of mental health. It is probably safe to say that every one of the spree killers we have looked at has exhibited some symptoms of psychiatric illness. In the cases of Larry Gene Ashbrook, Buford Furrow, Mark Barton and Martin Bryant there is little doubt that they were suffering personality disorders that brought them into contact with mental-health authorities. In some of the other cases, such as Thomas Hamilton and Benjamin Nathaniel Smith, there was repeated contact with the police and other public authorities. Why were none of these men stopped before they went into action? This is the question that surviving victims, grieving relatives and concerned members of the general public have asked repeatedly.

It is not an easy question to answer. With hindsight it is easy to spot those factors and trends that pointed the way to the eventual explosions of violence. At the time, however, the paths that the killers would take did not seem so clear-cut. Let us be clear about one thing: these men were not monsters. They were human beings – damaged, dangerous, but human nevertheless. In many cases, especially in those of Martin Bryant, Michael Ryan, Thomas Hamilton, Howard Unruh and Larry Gene Ashbrook, the tabloid media have gone all out to present accounts of them that are barely recognisable. By turning these men into monsters, demonising them as much as possible, the media creates a gap between them and the public. 'These men are monsters. They are beyond under-standing and beyond sympathy': that is the message that comes from the tabloid press and television.

In examining these disparate cases many common elements have been identified, and with these common factors come questions about society, gender roles, the nuclear family and so on. They are difficult questions with no simple answers. Yet simple answers are what many people want. They want certainty, and some sections of the media will pander to this need. You want a simple answer? All right: Thomas Hamilton was sick, he was a child-abuser, he was a psycho, he was an Act of God, he was evil incarnate. And what can you do about people like him? You stop him watching videos, you stop him getting guns, you lock him up, you put him away. And how do you know who the next Thomas Hamilton is going to be? He's the local weirdo, the loner, the mental case, he is not like us. In turning spree killers into monsters we are confirming our own 'normality'.

The obverse of this tendency to demonise is to regard any sign of antisocial behaviour as inherently sick and therefore in need of treatment. In the wake of the Benjamin Nathaniel Smith and Buford Furrow cases, it was seriously suggested that extreme racism was a form of mental illness. This tendency was nowhere better illustrated than by Dr Alvin Poussaint who, in the *New York Times* on 26 August 1999, asked: 'They Hate. They Kill. Are They Insane?' In this article, which triggered a flurry of comment in newspapers and magazines across the world, he stated that racist fanatics '. . . meet all the criteria for a major psychiatric illness' and that

'. . . like all others who experience delusions, extreme racists do not think rationally.' These extremists, he contended, had '. . . racist feelings which were tied to fixed belief systems impervious to reality checks, [and] were symptoms of serious mental dysfunction.'

The article was written in the wake of Buford Furrow's attack on the North Valley Jewish Community Centre, and in his case there is clearly evidence that he was suffering severe personality problems. However, the article referred not just to Furrow but to extreme racists in general. Therefore, ignoring Furrow's case for the moment, we must ask ourselves whether this characterisation of extreme racism as mental illness is valid. As has been mentioned in previous chapters, a number of extreme philosophies, including Christian Identity and other forms of neo-Nazism, support a conspiracy-theory world-view. Neo-Nazis see themselves as taking part in a struggle for the future of the 'Aryan race', and they see the world through a lens that depicts their opponents as Jews or the pawns of Jews. This can induce a state of paranoia and we know that people like Benjamin Nathaniel Smith exhibited very paranoid behaviour.

There is a big step, however, between pointing out this tendency to paranoia and attempting to pathologise it. The logical conclusion of this point of view is to attempt to class all nonconformist philosophies, from neo-Nazism to Marxism to Anarchism to Christian evangelism, as symptoms of mental instability. Religious belief itself is often a 'fixed belief system impervious to reality checks' and therefore, according to Dr Poussaint's logic, symptomatic of 'serious mental dysfunction'. In the end, according to this point of view, only those belief systems that accord with the established consensus can be viewed as non-symptomatic of mental dysfunction.

While Dr Poussaint may have the best of motives, the authoritarian conclusions of his train of thought do little to explain the roots of extreme racism and even less do they help to stem the spread of such beliefs. While there may be a number of traits in common between neo-Nazism and some symptoms of mental illness, they are different and distinct. In the cases we have looked at it is not just extremist belief systems that have caused these men to spawn such violence: there are a host of other factors at play. Not all neo-Nazis turn into spree killers, just as not all spree killers are neo-Nazis. Neo-Nazism is a political problem and, as such, it needs to be opposed using political means. It should be pointed out that many anti-racist groups dismissed Dr Poussaint's views swiftly and categorically, correctly pointing out the faulty logic at work and the authoritarian conclusions it leads to.

This tendency to cast all spree killers as monsters or extreme racists as mentally ill helps to obscure the facts. Many spree killers clearly exhibit symptoms of psychiatric disease, particularly those who are driven by internal grievances rather than specific ideological concerns. These men are the products of their upbringings and are very often the victims of isolation and rejection. They are not monsters and to treat them as such serves only to obscure the roots of the problem and in no way helps us move to an understanding of what really drives them. We also know that some spree killers, while driven by extremist philosophies also have a number of personality traits that they share with 'non-ideological' spree killers. To dismiss these men as merely mentally unstable is to focus on just one side of a complex equation and to ignore the dangerous power that some political philosophies carry with them.

Spree killers are here to stay. They are part of the human psychological landscape, a feature of our social environment. Perhaps, as we grow to understand the phenomenon more deeply, we can begin to act on the danger signs and attempt to counsel and treat those individuals who might one day explode with such deadly violence. Perhaps, with time, we might be able to reduce the incidence of spree killing. For now, however, spree killing is on the rise – and shows no signs of abating.

POSTSCRIPT

Since early 1999, when *Lone Wolf* was first published, there has been no let-up in the number of new cases of spree killing across Europe and the United States. While there is little to be gained from going through each of these new cases in detail, it is nevertheless worth mentioning those that bear some relevance to the other cases we have examined in greater detail.

On 1 November 1999, in Bad Reichenhall, Germany, a sixteen-year-old boy, named by police only as Martin P., opened fire from an upstairs window of his house, killing two neighbours instantly and injuring four others, one of whom was later to die of his wounds. The boy then turned the gun on his eighteen-year-old sister, shooting her five times. Then, as police and commandos assembled outside, he put a gun in his mouth and blew his head off.

Police later revealed that the boy, described as shy and retiring and devoted to his father, was a keen fan of violent videos and computer games. He was also revealed to be obsessively interested in Nazism: his room was decorated with pictures of Hitler, swastika flags and Second World War memorabilia. The police denied reports that the boy was linked to any neo-Nazi political parties or activist groups. A gun enthusiast, like his father, the boy gained access to the guns he'd used by breaking into a cabinet while his parents were away. There was no obvious motive for the spree.

With so few details of the case available, there is little that can be added to this bare-bones account other than to point out the conjunction of factors that are significant: the boy was both something of a loner and also very close to his father; he was interested in guns, war and the violent imagery of video and computer games; he was keenly interested in neo-Nazism.

On 2 November 1999, in Honolulu, Hawaii, at around 8.00 a.m., Byran Uyesugi, aged forty, walked into the Xerox building where he worked. He went up to the second floor and entered a conference room where some of his colleagues were meeting. He pulled out a 9mm handgun and started shooting. Within minutes five people lay dead. He then moved to another room and gunned down two more co-workers. One of the dead was Martin Lee, Uyesugi's manager. As people started to flee the scene, Uyesugi calmly left the building, climbed into a company van and drove off.

Half an hour later the police raided Uyesugi's home but he was not there. Police recovered a huge stockpile of weapons and ammunition, including eleven handguns, five rifles and two shotguns. At the same time police began to evacuate other Xerox buildings, afraid that the armed and dangerous killer, still on the loose, had yet to finish with his fellow workers.

A passer-by spotted Uyesugi in the parked Xerox van, calmly reading a magazine. Police surrounded the vehicle and began negotiating with him. Five hours later, at around 2.50 p.m., he surrendered to the police without further incident.

The incident is Hawaii's worst ever case of mass murder, and the relatively crime-free island society was left reeling by the unprecedented level of violence.

The picture of Uyesugi that emerged was one of an introverted single man, deeply involved with his hobbies that included guns and shooting. Although he had no criminal record, it was reported that it had been recommended he go on a 'stress and anger management' course after an incident at work in 1993. Neighbours also reported that he seemed aloof and that his behaviour was sometimes very odd: for example, he used to smash his fists on the dashboard of his car. Co-workers described him as 'mild-mannered and re-clusive'. Although he had a licence for the eighteen weapons that the police recovered, he was denied a permit for more because of his problems at work.

Despite intense speculation about Uyesugi's job status and work-related problems, no direct motive for this spree killing has emerged so far. Whatever it was that triggered his violence, Uyesugi has yet to reveal it to the police or to his family.

From our perspective this report seems very familiar. Many of the factors that feature in the other cases were also present here. Although much of the press comment around the case focused on workplace violence, there were also calls to tighten Hawaii's gun-control laws – already among the most stringent in the United States. Very few commentators seemed willing to draw detailed analogies between Uyesugi's case and those of other recent US spree killers such as Mark Barton, Nathaniel Smith, Buford Furrow and Larry Ashbrook.

On 3 November 1999, a lone gunman, wearing army fatigues and dark glasses, walked into Northlake Shipyard in Seattle and opened fire. Armed with a 9mm handgun, he fired between seven and nine shots before fleeing the scene. In his wake he left shipyard employee Peter Giles, aged 27, dead, and three others injured. One of these, Robert Brisendine, aged 43, died in hospital a few hours after the shooting. The gunman disappeared from the scene, and although a police sketch elicited hundreds of calls the police have so far failed to apprehend him. Police have refused to speculate on the motive for the attack.

While this case bears a superficial resemblance to many of the others we have looked at, there are also some major differences. The first of these is simply that the killer got away. As we have previously pointed out, escape is not a priority for most spree killers. Even in the first two new cases listed here neither of the perpetrators made any serious attempt at escape. Secondly, the Seattle killer was obviously disguised. Again, this is not a characteristic of any of the other spree killers we have looked at. It suggests, for the moment, that this crime was not in fact an act of spree killing but rather an execution of some kind. If the murderer is finally apprehended then we may learn more, but in my opinion it is highly likely that a different motive for these killings will emerge.

On the morning of Sunday, 28 November 1999, the south London suburb of Thornton Heath was turned upside down when Eden Strang, aged 26, marched naked into the Roman Catholic church of St Andrews and attacked worshippers with a samurai sword. In the time it took for shocked parishioners to subdue him, Strang had viciously slashed at eleven victims. The most severely wounded was Paul Chilton, aged fifty, who almost died. The senior surgeon dealing with the case,

Stephen Ebbs, described the incident to the *Croydon Advertiser*:

> The blade used was extremely sharp and used with great strength and force. It was a clean cut. Almost unbelievably the blade passed through teeth. I have never seen anything like it . . . This is the most severe injury I have seen inflicted on one human being by another.

In addition to his facial injuries, Paul Chilton's index finger and thumb were severed from his right hand. Over forty pints of blood and plasma were used in the operations to save Chilton's life.

Eden Strang was described by friends and neighbours as a 'polite young man' with no previous record of violence or mental problems. A graduate with a degree in computing, Strang had been unemployed for a lengthy period and had, in the three weeks prior to the attack, been working as a pizza-delivery man.

Strang was ordered to be detained indefinitely in a secure psychiatric hospital after he was found not guilty by reason of insanity at his trial in June 2000. 'It is necessary in order to protect the public from serious harm from you,' Strang was told by Judge Michael Hyarn.

The case highlights once more many of the unifying elements that we have previously discussed. It also brings into sharp relief the debate about gun control. It shows once again that no law can be used to legislate against such acts of random, terrible violence. It is true that the toll of injuries would have been far higher if Strang had had access to guns, but it is also true that in the absence of such weapons he grabbed whatever else he could. His need to vent his murderous rage was such that any weapon would have sufficed in the circumstances.

In the absence of guns, and realising that a call to ban swords was unlikely to catch the public imagination, many of the tabloid commentators sought scapegoats elsewhere. The *Daily Star*, basing their story mainly on Strang's degree subject, sought to pin the blame on the Internet. He had, the tabloid newspaper insisted, spent hours every day surfing the Internet looking for details of martial arts weapons and training. As a newspaper the *Daily Star* is aimed at those sections of the population least likely to have access to a computer and the Internet. Blaming the Internet was therefore an easy option and one likely to coincide with their readers' perceptions of the web as a haven for child pornographers, neo-Nazis and dangerous anarchists.

From our point of view it highlights the fact that the censorship issue is not peripheral to the subject of social responses to spree killing. It is an integral feature of the public response and one that is likely to become more of an issue as gun controls become tighter, making the availability of firearms less easy to blame for the violence.

Yet another case – that of Friedrich Leibacher – indicates yet again that no society is free of incidences of spree killing. On 27 September 2001, Leibacher, aged 57, donned police uniform, entered the regional parliament building in Zug, near Zurich, and opened fire on the 80 local politicians, civil servants and journalists gathered for the morning session. Armed with an assault rifle, machine gun, pistol and grenades Leibacher massacred fourteen people and injured many others before turning the gun on himself.

Described as a 'querulous troublemaker', Leibacher had a long history of instability, including a conviction from 1970 for child sex offences. It is impossible not to draw parallels with the Thomas Hamilton case. Like Hamilton, Leibacher was a person who had made numerous complaints against those in authority, and who was increasingly prone to paranoia. His attack on the government building was the termination of a two-year campaign started after a petty argument with a bus driver.

As in the Hamilton case, the murderous attack led to stunned headlines across the world, in addition to those of his normally placid homeland.

As we head into the next century the incidence of spree killing is clearly rising. Unless society attempts to understand the phenomenon there is little prospect that any adequate response to it can be formulated.

Look out for other compelling True Crime titles
from Virgin Books

KILLERS ON THE LOOSE – UNSOLVED CASES OF SERIAL MURDER
by Antonio Mendoza
Revised and updated edition

According to a recent FBI study of serial murder, it has climbed to an 'almost epidemic proportion'. It is believed that there are currently up to 6000 people a year dying at the hands of serial killers. The FBI and other law enforcement agencies estimate that there are between 35 and 50 serial killers on the loose at any given time. Other estimates put the number of killers closer to 500. In either case, officials expect these numbers to continue their dramatic rise. This is an up-to-date edition of an original in-depth study of serial killers at large, written by one of the world's foremost authorities.

£6.99 ISBN: 0 7535 0681 5

JACK THE RIPPER, THE FINAL CHAPTER
by Paul H Feldman

A haunting journal that came to light in 1991 and was published in 1993 as *The Diary of Jack the Ripper* was believed to be a hoax. Yet no one was able to explain how it was forged, or by whom. The reason, as Paul Feldman explains, is because the journal is genuine. In this, the most exhaustively researched and extensive Ripper investigation ever undertaken, Paul Feldman cuts through the cover-ups and wild theories surrounding the Ripper mystery to prove undoubtedly that James Maybrick was Jack the Ripper. As well as uncovering crucial new evidence about the murders, Feldman presents sensational revelations from the Ripper's living descendants.

'. . . my own feeling was that Feldman has taken game, set and match.'

Colin Wilson

£6.99 ISBN: 0 7535 0637 8

I'LL BE WATCHING YOU – TRUE STORIES OF STALKERS AND THEIR VICTIMS
by Richard Gallagher

Stalking is on the increase – and it isn't only celebrities who become the targets of irrational individuals. Men and women with everyday jobs who lead ordinary lives can just as easily become someone else's obsession. Each year, hundreds of people fall victim to terrifying harassment by people they may never have even met. Richard Gallagher has exhaustively researched this disturbing phenomenon to provide a serious investigation into this unsettling but fascinating crime. Featuring interviews with victims, police, psychologists – and those who 'stalk the stalkers' – he has unearthed remarkable accounts of obsession and delusion. It's a book whose time has definitely come.

'A carefully researched collection of case histories of stalking . . . a compelling picture of a disturbing trend.'

Books Magazine

£6.99 ISBN: 0 7535 0696 3

UNSOLVED MURDERS – WHEN KILLERS ESCAPE JUSTICE
by Russell Gould

The Black Dahlia. JonBenét Ramsey. PC Keith Blakelock. Rachel Nickell. Their killers have never been brought to justice. These, and several other compelling cases, make up this study of the most puzzling murders of the late twentieth century. Could six-year-old beauty queen JonBenét Ramsey have been killed by a member of her own family? Were British government agencies responsible for the murder of activist Hilda Murrell? How could the so-called Zodiac killer's reign of terror continue unchecked for so long? Russell Gould draws upon all of the evidence – and all of the theories – to bring together the definitive, uncensored account of these unsolved crimes.
£6.99 ISBN: 0 7535 0632 7

All new titles!

MY BLOODY VALENTINE – COUPLES WHOSE SICK CRIMES SHOCKED THE WORLD
Edited by Patrick Blackden

Good-looking Canadian couple Paul Bernardo and Karla Homolka looked the epitome of young, wholesome success. No one could have guessed that they drugged, raped and murdered young women to satisfy Bernardo's deviant lusts. Nothing inspires more horror and fascination than couples possessed of a single impulse – to kill for thrills. Obsessed by and sucked into their own sick and private madness, their attraction is always fatal, their actions always desperate. The book covers a variety of notorious killer couples: from desperados Starkweather and Fugate, on whom the film *Natural Born Killers* was based, right through to Fred and Rose West, who committed unspeakable horrors in their semi-detached house in Gloucester, England. With contributions from a variety of leading true crime journalists, *My Bloody Valentine* covers both the world-famous cases and also lesser-known but equally horrifying crimes.
£7.99 ISBN: 0 7535 0647 5

August 2002

DEATH CULTS – MIND CONTROL, MAYHEM AND MURDER
Edited by Jack Sargeant

The deadly belief systems of cults worldwide hold an immense fascination for those gullible enough to look for 'ultimate truths'. Throughout history, the irrational has been a close companion of reason, and thousands of people have joined cults and even committed acts of atrocity in the belief they would attain power and everlasting life. From Charles Manson's 'family' of the late 1960s to the horrific Ten Commandments of God killings in Uganda in March 2000, deluded and brainwashed followers and leaders of cults have been responsible for history's most shocking and bizarre killings.
£7.99 ISBN: 0 7535 0644 0

DANGER DOWN UNDER
Patrick Blackden

Australia is one of the most popular long-haul tourist destinations, but its image of a carefree, 'no worries' BarBQ beach and beers culture set in a landscape of stunning natural beauty tells only one side of the story. _Danger Down Under_ lets you know what the tourist board won't – the dark side of the Australian dream. The mysterious vanishing of Briton Peter Falconio in summer 2001 is just one of many puzzling unsolved cases of tourist disappearances. With a landscape that can be extremely hostile to those unfamiliar with its size and extremes and an undying macho culture – not to mention the occasional psychotic who murders backpackers, or crazed gangs of bikers and cultists – there is much to be cautious of when venturing down under.

£7.99 ISBN: 0 7535 0649 1